BALLAD
OF AN AMERICAN

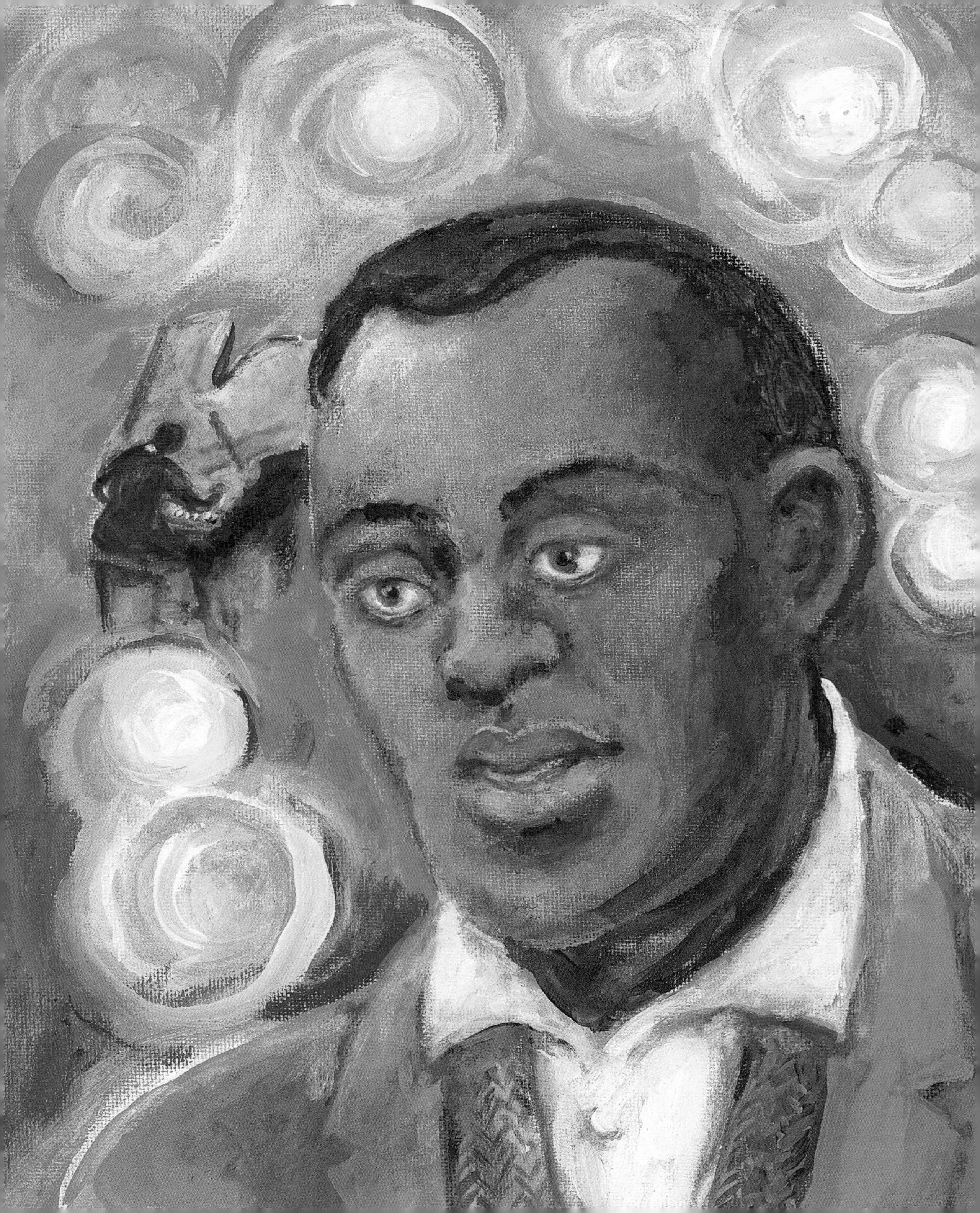

BALLAD
OF AN AMERICAN
A GRAPHIC BIOGRAPHY OF
PAUL ROBESON

ART AND TEXT BY
SHARON RUDAHL

EDITED BY
**PAUL BUHLE AND
LAWRENCE WARE**

R

RUTGERS UNIVERSITY PRESS
NEW BRUNSWICK, CAMDEN, AND NEWARK, NEW JERSEY, AND LONDON

ROBESON

SCHOLAR
ATHLETE
ACTOR
SINGER
GLOBAL ACTIVIST

CLASS OF 1919
CENTENNIAL

LIBRARY OF CONGRESS CATALOGING-IN-PUBLICATION DATA

Names: Rudahl, Sharon, illustrator. | Buhle, Paul, 1944– editor. | Ware, Lawrence, editor.
Title: Ballad of an American : a graphic biography of Paul Robeson / Sharon Rudahl, Paul Buhle, Lawrence Ware.
Description: [1.] | New Brunswick : Rutgers University Press, 2020. | Summary: "The first-ever graphic biography of Paul Robeson, Ballad of an American, charts Robeson's career as a singer, actor, scholar, athlete, and activist who achieved global fame. Through his films, concerts, and records, he became a potent symbol representing the promise of a multicultural, multiracial American democracy at a time when, despite his stardom, he was denied personal access to his many audiences. Robeson was a major figure in the rise of anti-colonialism in Africa and elsewhere, and a tireless campaigner for internationalism, peace, and human rights. Later in life, he embraced the civil rights and antiwar movements with the hope that new generations would attain his ideals of a peaceful and abundant world. Ballad of an American features beautifully drawn chapters by artist Sharon Rudahl, a compelling narrative about his life, and an afterword on the lasting impact of Robeson's work in both the arts and politics. This graphic biography will enable all kinds of readers-especially newer generations who may be unfamiliar with him-to understand his life's story and everlasting global significance. Ballad of an American: A Graphic Biography of Paul Robeson is published in conjunction with Rutgers University's centennial commemoration of Robeson's 1919 graduation from the university"—Provided by publisher.
Identifiers: LCCN 2020012078 | ISBN 9781978802070 (paperback) | ISBN 9781978802087 (hardcover) | ISBN 9781978802094 (epub) | ISBN 9781978802100 (mobi) | ISBN 9781978802117 (pdf)
Subjects: LCSH: Robeson, Paul, 1898–1976—Comic books, strips, etc. | African American singers—Biography—Comic books, strips, etc. | Singers—United States—Biography—Comic books, strips, etc. | African American actors—Biography—Comic books, strips, etc. | Political activists—United States—Biography—Comic books, strips, etc. | African American civil rights workers—Biography—Comic books, strips, etc. | LCGFT: Biographical comics.
Classification: LCC ML420.R73 B3 2020 | DDC 781.5/42092 [B]—dc23
LC record available at https://lccn.loc.gov/2020012078

CONTENTS

BALLAD
OF AN AMERICAN

CHAPTER I

SON of a SLAVE ~ STAR of RUTGERS

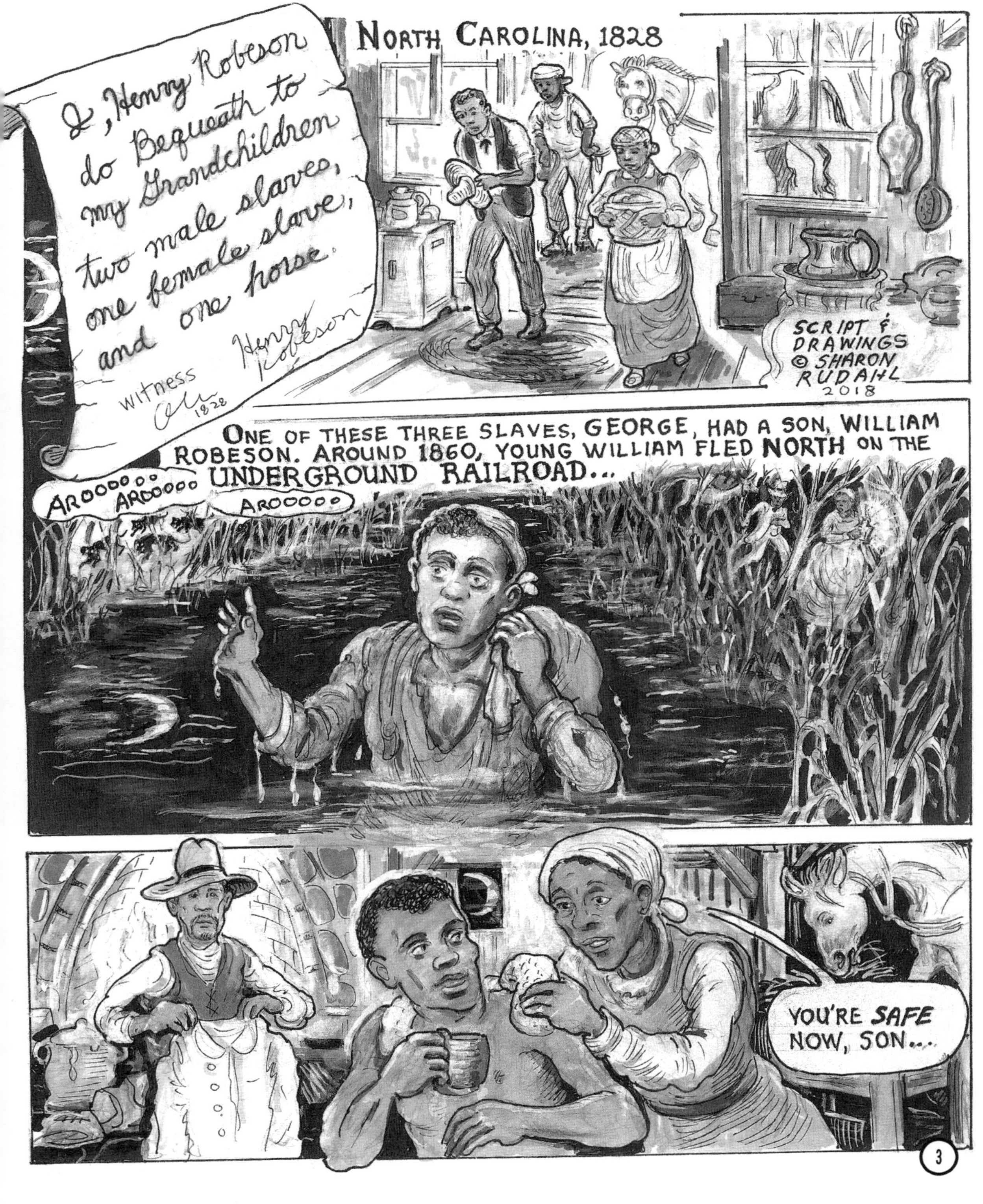

I, Henry Robeson do Bequeath to my Grandchildren two male slaves, one female slave, and one horse.
Henry Robeson
witness
1828
NORTH CAROLINA, 1828
SCRIPT & DRAWINGS © SHARON RUDAHL 2018
ONE OF THESE THREE SLAVES, GEORGE, HAD A SON, WILLIAM ROBESON. AROUND 1860, YOUNG WILLIAM FLED NORTH ON THE UNDERGROUND RAILROAD...
AROOOOOOO
AROOOOOO
AROOOOOO
YOU'RE SAFE NOW, SON...

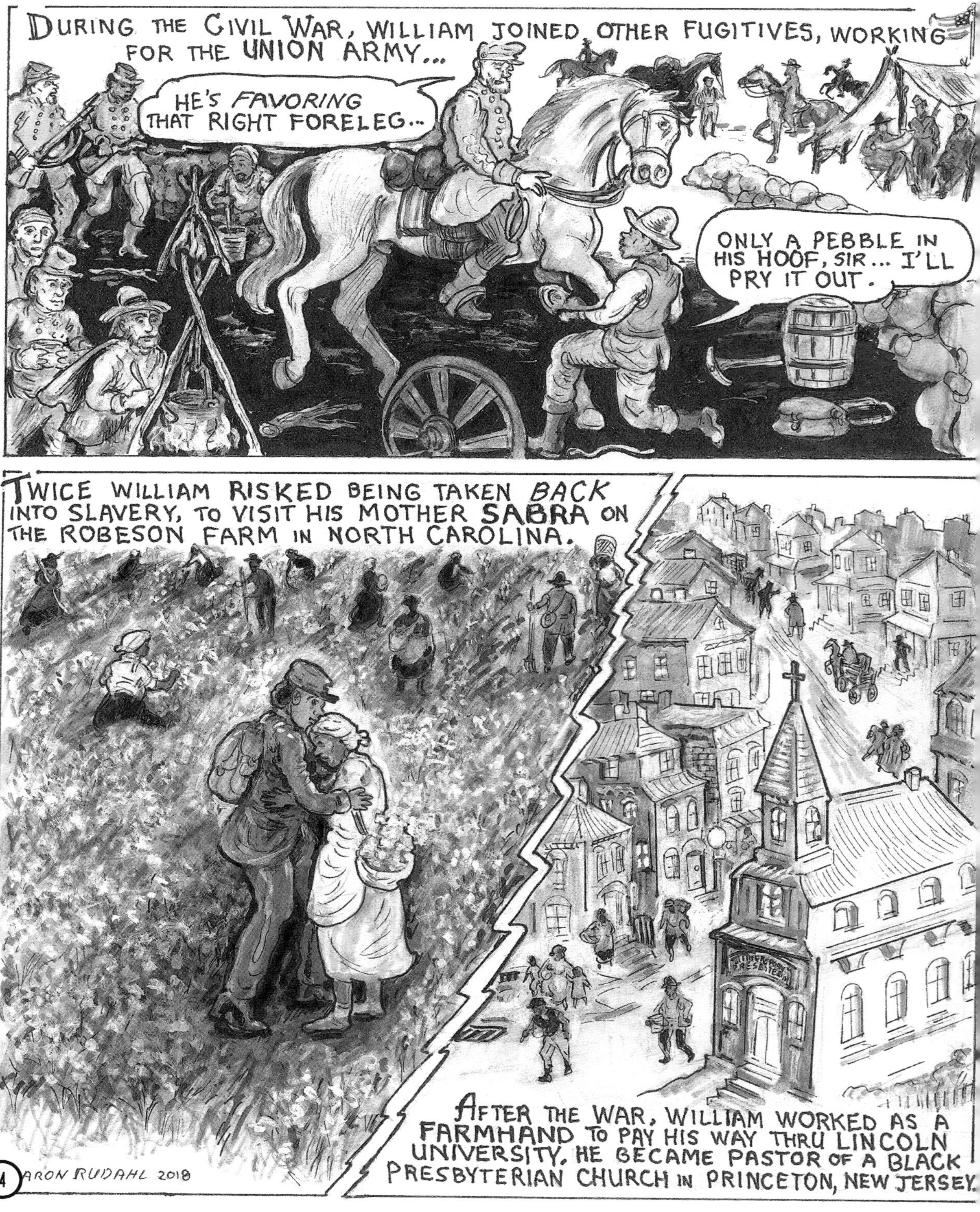
DURING THE CIVIL WAR, WILLIAM JOINED OTHER FUGITIVES, WORKING FOR THE UNION ARMY...
HE'S *FAVORING* THAT RIGHT FORELEG...
ONLY A PEBBLE IN HIS HOOF, SIR... I'LL PRY IT OUT.
TWICE WILLIAM RISKED BEING TAKEN *BACK* INTO SLAVERY, TO VISIT HIS MOTHER SABRA ON THE ROBESON FARM IN NORTH CAROLINA.
AFTER THE WAR, WILLIAM WORKED AS A FARMHAND TO PAY HIS WAY THRU LINCOLN UNIVERSITY. HE BECAME PASTOR OF A BLACK PRESBYTERIAN CHURCH IN PRINCETON, NEW JERSEY.
ARON RUDAHL 2018

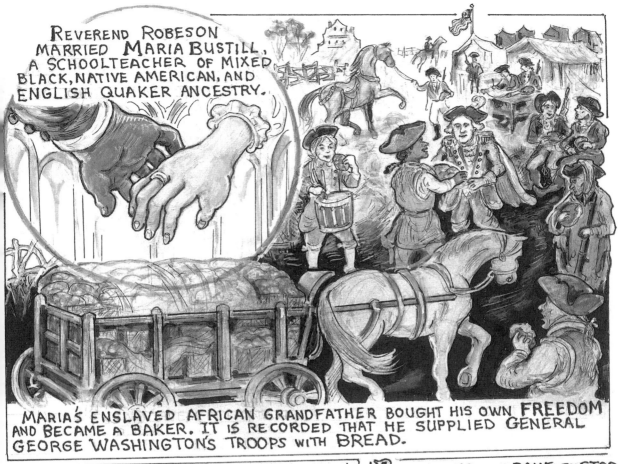

REVEREND ROBESON MARRIED MARIA BUSTILL, A SCHOOLTEACHER OF MIXED BLACK, NATIVE AMERICAN, AND ENGLISH QUAKER ANCESTRY.

MARIA'S ENSLAVED AFRICAN GRANDFATHER BOUGHT HIS OWN FREEDOM AND BECAME A BAKER. IT IS RECORDED THAT HE SUPPLIED GENERAL GEORGE WASHINGTON'S TROOPS WITH BREAD.

IN 1898, THE YEAR THE LAST OF WILLIAM & MARIA'S FIVE CHILDREN WAS BORN, PIONEER BLACK JOURNALIST IDA WELLS APPEALED TO PRESIDENT MCKINLEY.

"NOWHERE IN THE CIVILIZED WORLD SAVE THE U.S. CAN MEN HUNT DOWN, SHOOT, HANG OR BURN TO DEATH AN UNARMED, ABSOLUTELY POWERLESS INDIVIDUAL..."

THANK YOU, MISS WELLS— NEXT!

BUT NOTHING WAS DONE TO STOP THE WAVE OF BIGOTRY AND VIOLENCE ENGULFING THE SOUTH.

SHARON RUDAHL

20

5

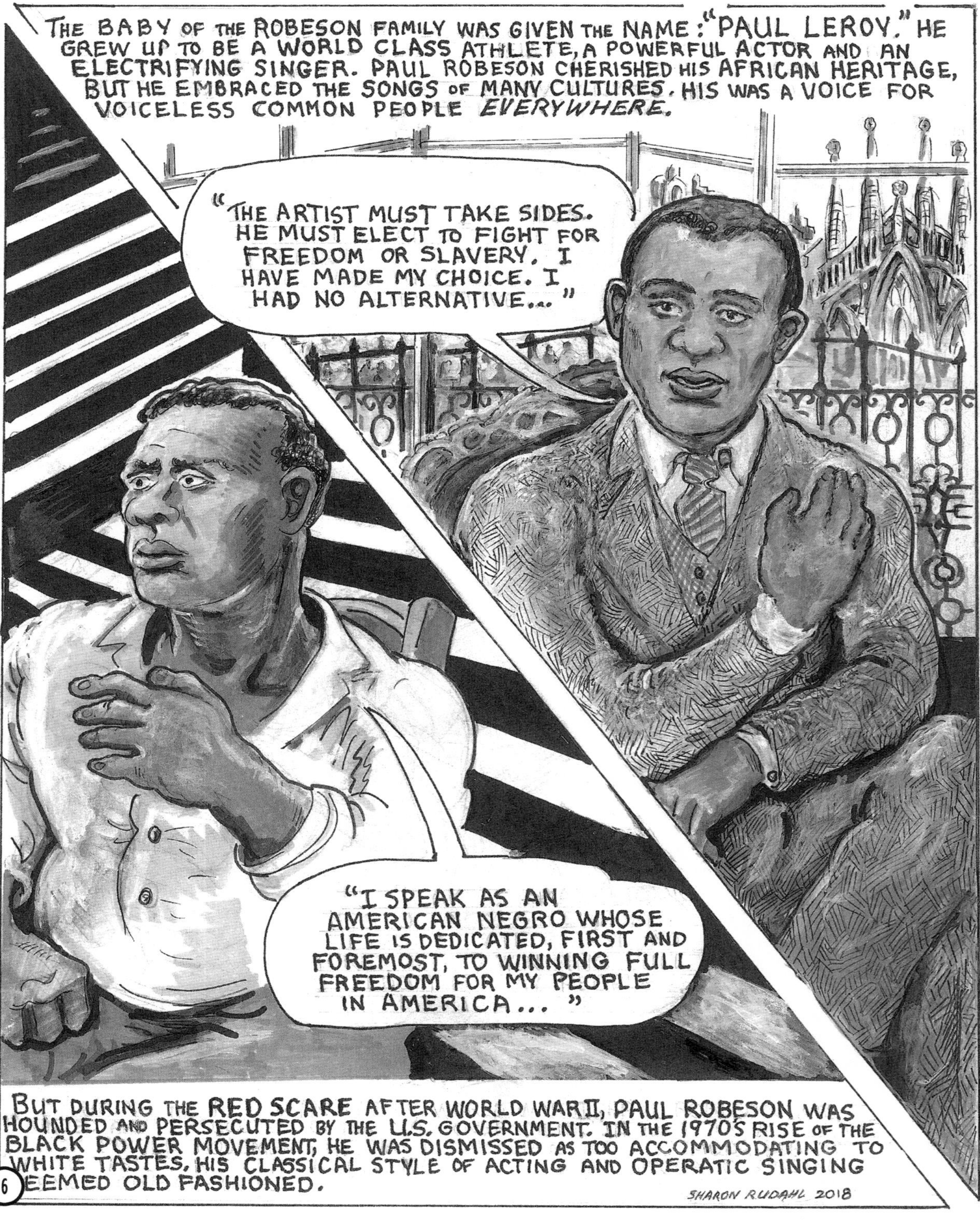
THE BABY OF THE ROBESON FAMILY WAS GIVEN THE NAME: "PAUL LEROY." HE GREW UP TO BE A WORLD CLASS ATHLETE, A POWERFUL ACTOR AND AN ELECTRIFYING SINGER. PAUL ROBESON CHERISHED HIS AFRICAN HERITAGE, BUT HE EMBRACED THE SONGS OF MANY CULTURES. HIS WAS A VOICE FOR VOICELESS COMMON PEOPLE *EVERYWHERE.*
"THE ARTIST MUST TAKE SIDES. HE MUST ELECT TO FIGHT FOR FREEDOM OR SLAVERY. I HAVE MADE MY CHOICE. I HAD NO ALTERNATIVE..."
"I SPEAK AS AN AMERICAN NEGRO WHOSE LIFE IS DEDICATED, FIRST AND FOREMOST, TO WINNING FULL FREEDOM FOR MY PEOPLE IN AMERICA..."
BUT DURING THE RED SCARE AFTER WORLD WAR II, PAUL ROBESON WAS HOUNDED AND PERSECUTED BY THE U.S. GOVERNMENT. IN THE 1970'S RISE OF THE BLACK POWER MOVEMENT, HE WAS DISMISSED AS TOO ACCOMMODATING TO WHITE TASTES. HIS CLASSICAL STYLE OF ACTING AND OPERATIC SINGING EEMED OLD FASHIONED.
SHARON RUDAHL 2018

THE BALLAD OF PAUL ROBESON BEGINS IN THE HARDSCRABBLE BLACK COMMUNITY OF PRINCETON, NEW JERSEY. CHURCH EVENTS, ORGANIZATIONS, AND CHARITY WERE ITS LIFEBLOOD, THE REVEREND WILLIAM ROBESON AND HIS WIFE MARIA LOUISA ITS BEATING *HEART.*

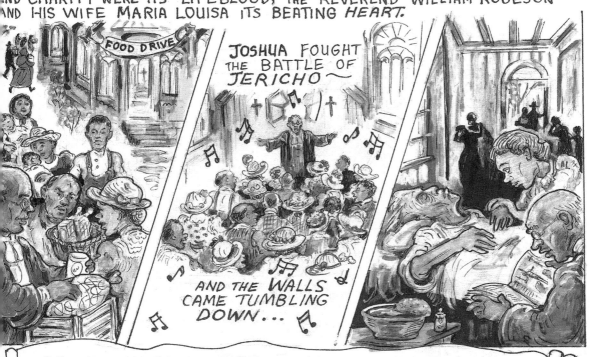

FOOD DRIVE

JOSHUA FOUGHT THE BATTLE OF *JERICHO* ~

AND THE *WALLS* CAME TUMBLING DOWN...

WHEN PAUL WAS BORN, HIS PARENTS WERE ALREADY MIDDLE-AGED. WHILE HE WAS STILL A SMALL CHILD, MARIA BECAME AN *INVALID*...

"TO THY OWN SELF BE *TRUE* — AND THOU CANST NOT BE FALSE TO ANY MAN..."

"THE GLORY OF MY BOYHOOD YEARS WAS MY *FATHER*."

The COMPLETE Shakespe

The ILIAD HOMER

ILIAD-HOMER

VERGIL-AEN

PLATO

SHARON RUDAHL 2018

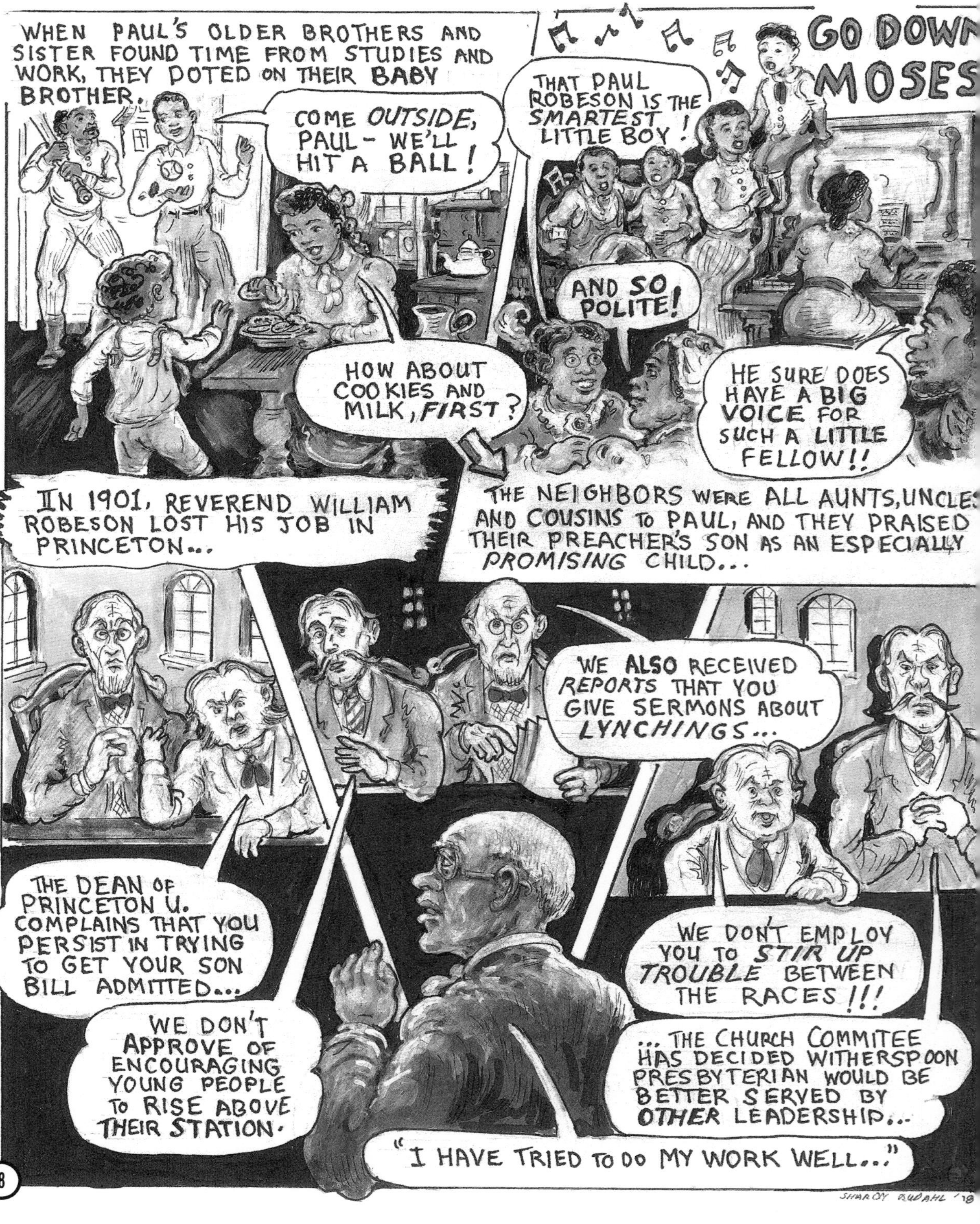
WHEN PAUL'S OLDER BROTHERS AND SISTER FOUND TIME FROM STUDIES AND WORK, THEY DOTED ON THEIR BABY BROTHER.
COME OUTSIDE, PAUL - WE'LL HIT A BALL!
HOW ABOUT COOKIES AND MILK, FIRST?
GO DOWN MOSES
THAT PAUL ROBESON IS THE SMARTEST LITTLE BOY!
AND SO POLITE!
HE SURE DOES HAVE A BIG VOICE FOR SUCH A LITTLE FELLOW!!
THE NEIGHBORS WERE ALL AUNTS, UNCLES AND COUSINS TO PAUL, AND THEY PRAISED THEIR PREACHER'S SON AS AN ESPECIALLY PROMISING CHILD...
IN 1901, REVEREND WILLIAM ROBESON LOST HIS JOB IN PRINCETON...
THE DEAN OF PRINCETON U. COMPLAINS THAT YOU PERSIST IN TRYING TO GET YOUR SON BILL ADMITTED...
WE DON'T APPROVE OF ENCOURAGING YOUNG PEOPLE TO RISE ABOVE THEIR STATION.
WE ALSO RECEIVED REPORTS THAT YOU GIVE SERMONS ABOUT LYNCHINGS...
WE DON'T EMPLOY YOU TO STIR UP TROUBLE BETWEEN THE RACES!!!
... THE CHURCH COMMITEE HAS DECIDED WITHERSPOON PRESBYTERIAN WOULD BE BETTER SERVED BY OTHER LEADERSHIP...
"I HAVE TRIED TO DO MY WORK WELL..."
SHARON RUDAHL '18

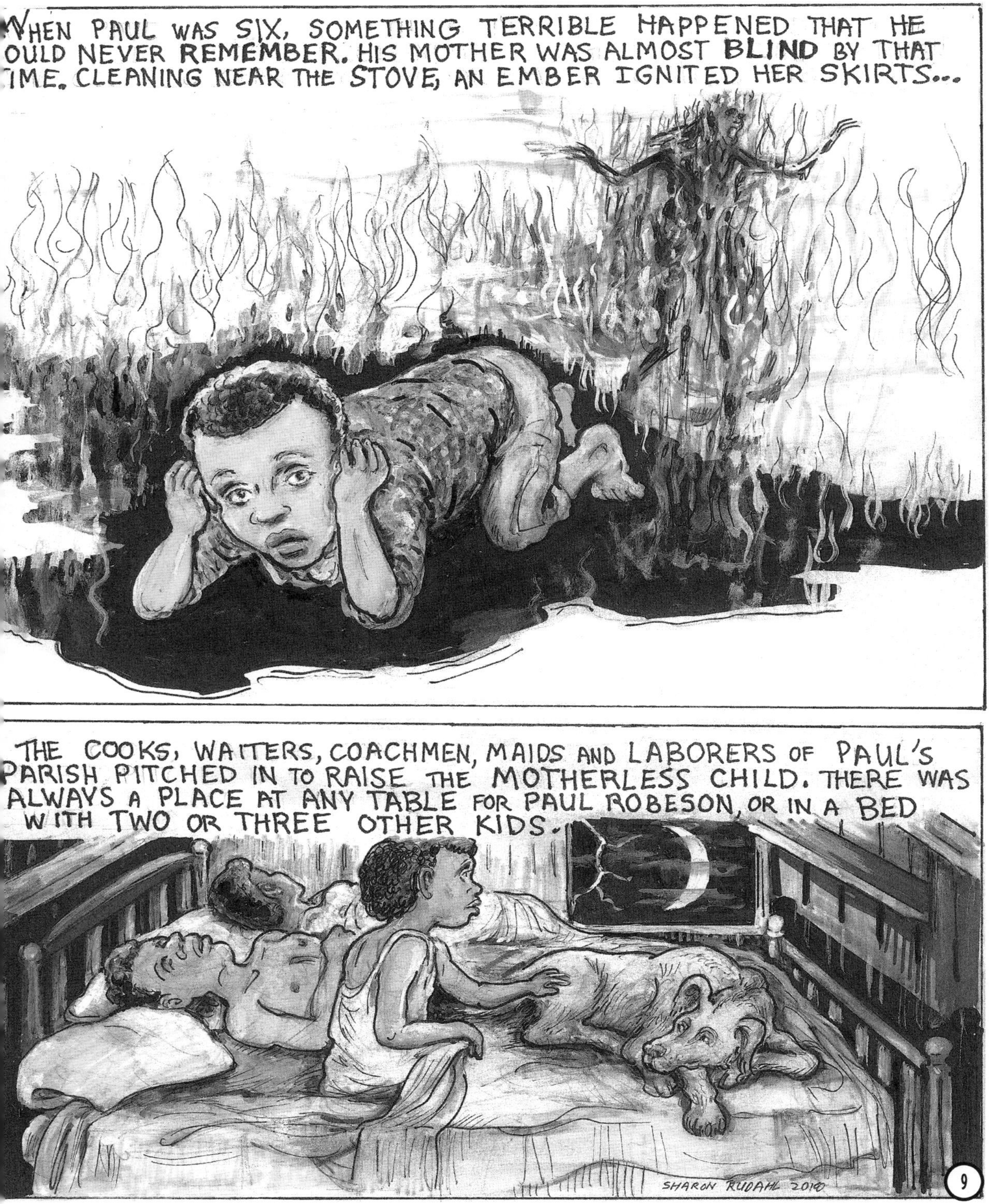
WHEN PAUL WAS SIX, SOMETHING TERRIBLE HAPPENED THAT HE OULD NEVER REMEMBER. HIS MOTHER WAS ALMOST BLIND BY THAT IME. CLEANING NEAR THE STOVE, AN EMBER IGNITED HER SKIRTS...
THE COOKS, WAITERS, COACHMEN, MAIDS AND LABORERS OF PAUL'S PARISH PITCHED IN TO RAISE THE MOTHERLESS CHILD. THERE WAS ALWAYS A PLACE AT ANY TABLE FOR PAUL ROBESON, OR IN A BED WITH TWO OR THREE OTHER KIDS.
SHARON RUDAHL 2010

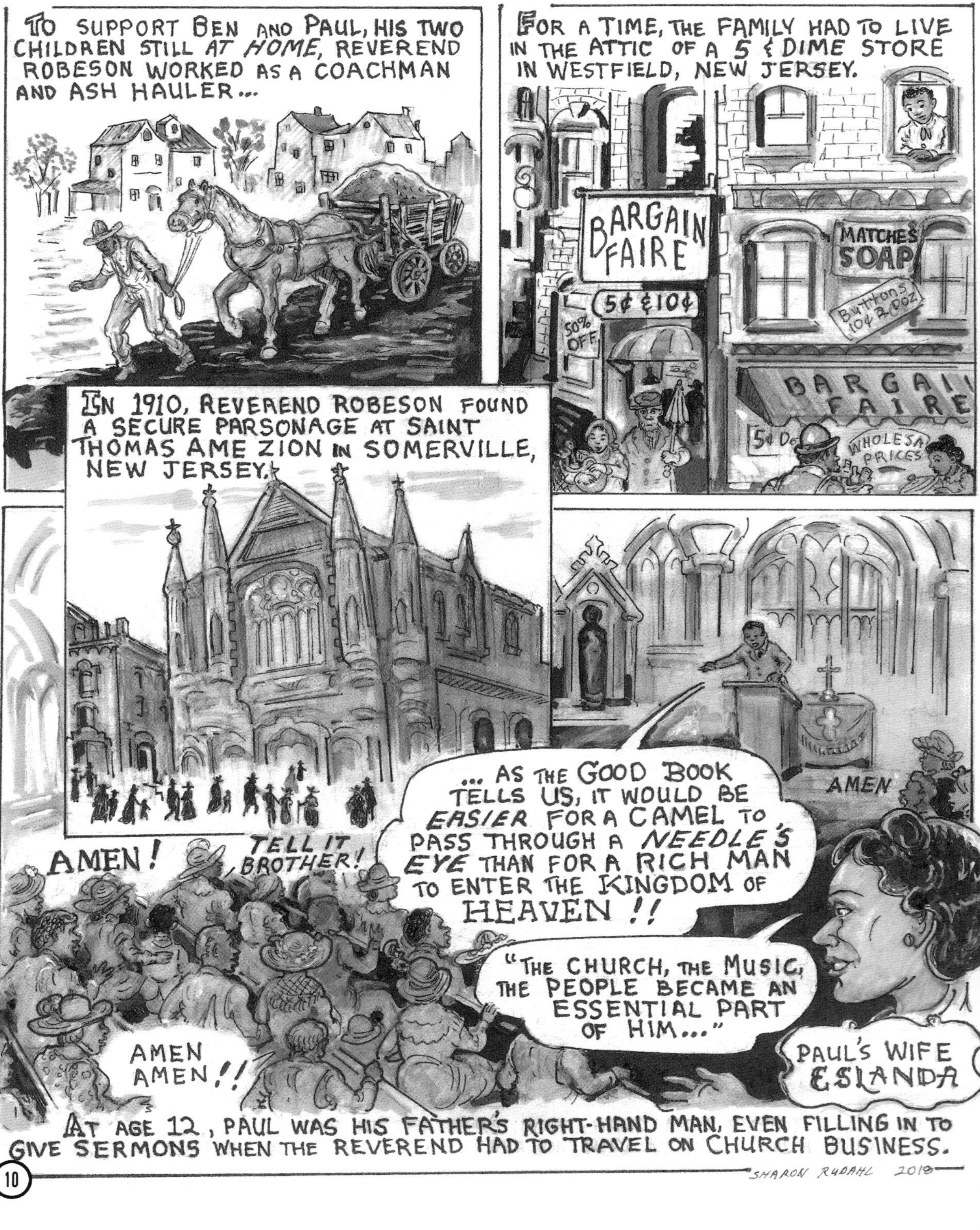

TO SUPPORT BEN AND PAUL, HIS TWO CHILDREN STILL AT HOME, REVEREND ROBESON WORKED AS A COACHMAN AND ASH HAULER...
FOR A TIME, THE FAMILY HAD TO LIVE IN THE ATTIC OF A 5 & DIME STORE IN WESTFIELD, NEW JERSEY.
BARGAIN FAIRE
5¢ & 10¢
50% OFF
MATCHES
SOAP
Buttons 10¢ a Doz
BARGAI FAIRE
WHOLESA PRICES
IN 1910, REVEREND ROBESON FOUND A SECURE PARSONAGE AT SAINT THOMAS AME ZION IN SOMERVILLE, NEW JERSEY.
... AS THE GOOD BOOK TELLS US, IT WOULD BE EASIER FOR A CAMEL TO PASS THROUGH A NEEDLE'S EYE THAN FOR A RICH MAN TO ENTER THE KINGDOM OF HEAVEN !!
AMEN
AMEN!
TELL IT, BROTHER!
"THE CHURCH, THE MUSIC, THE PEOPLE BECAME AN ESSENTIAL PART OF HIM..."
PAUL'S WIFE ESLANDA
AMEN AMEN!!
AT AGE 12, PAUL WAS HIS FATHER'S RIGHT-HAND MAN, EVEN FILLING IN TO GIVE SERMONS WHEN THE REVEREND HAD TO TRAVEL ON CHURCH BUSINESS.
SHARON RUDAHL 2018

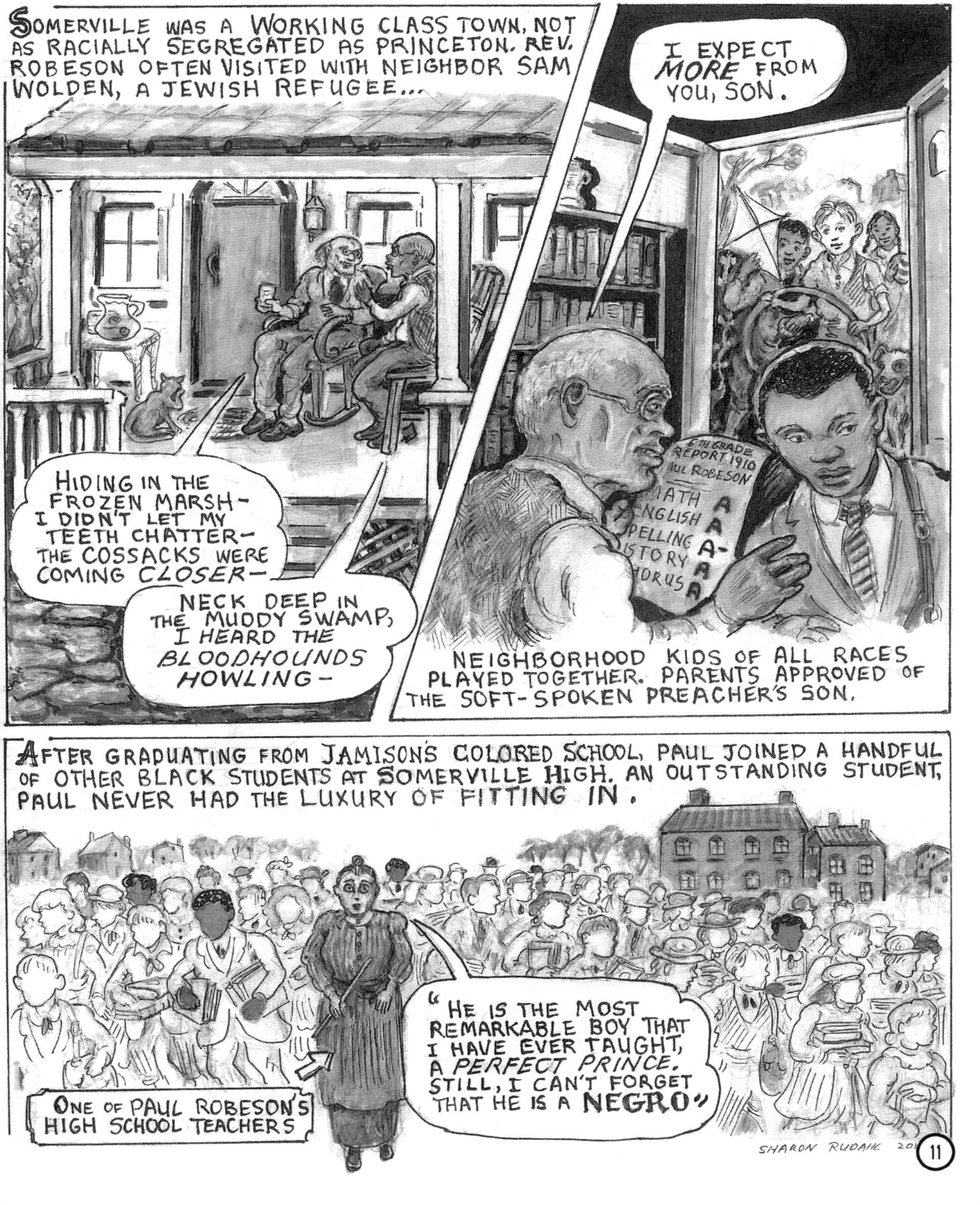
SOMERVILLE WAS A WORKING CLASS TOWN, NOT AS RACIALLY SEGREGATED AS PRINCETON. REV. ROBESON OFTEN VISITED WITH NEIGHBOR SAM WOLDEN, A JEWISH REFUGEE...
HIDING IN THE FROZEN MARSH- I DIDN'T LET MY TEETH CHATTER- THE COSSACKS WERE COMING CLOSER-
NECK DEEP IN THE MUDDY SWAMP, I HEARD THE BLOODHOUNDS HOWLING-
I EXPECT MORE FROM YOU, SON.
6TH GRADE REPORT 1910
NEIGHBORHOOD KIDS OF ALL RACES PLAYED TOGETHER. PARENTS APPROVED OF THE SOFT-SPOKEN PREACHER'S SON.
AFTER GRADUATING FROM JAMISON'S COLORED SCHOOL, PAUL JOINED A HANDFUL OF OTHER BLACK STUDENTS AT SOMERVILLE HIGH. AN OUTSTANDING STUDENT, PAUL NEVER HAD THE LUXURY OF FITTING IN.
"HE IS THE MOST REMARKABLE BOY THAT I HAVE EVER TAUGHT, A PERFECT PRINCE. STILL, I CAN'T FORGET THAT HE IS A NEGRO"
ONE OF PAUL ROBESON'S HIGH SCHOOL TEACHERS
SHARON RUDAHL 201

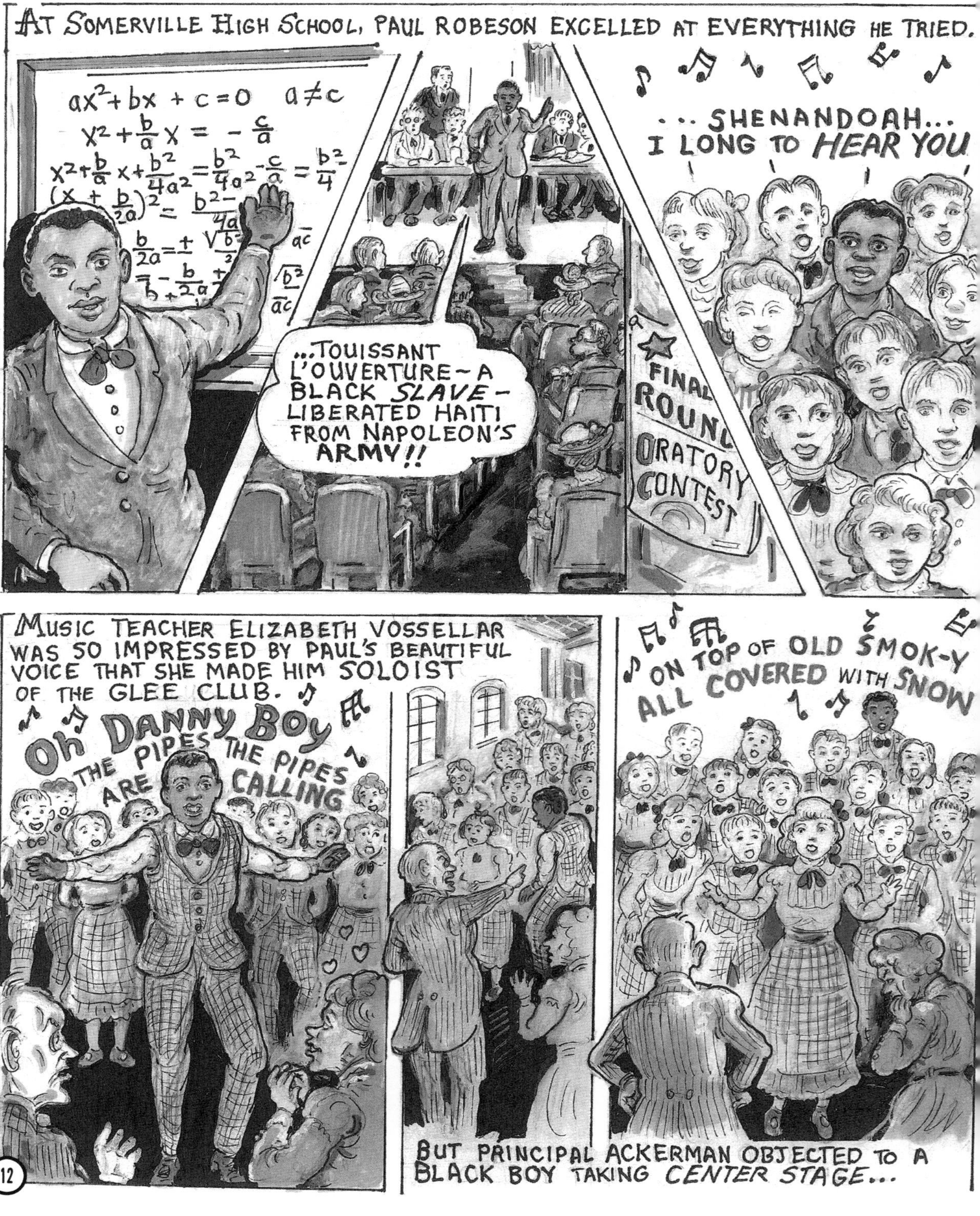
AT SOMERVILLE HIGH SCHOOL, PAUL ROBESON EXCELLED AT EVERYTHING HE TRIED.
...TOUSSANT L'OUVERTURE – A BLACK SLAVE – LIBERATED HAITI FROM NAPOLEON'S ARMY!!
FINAL ROUND ORATORY CONTEST
...SHENANDOAH... I LONG TO HEAR YOU
MUSIC TEACHER ELIZABETH VOSSELLAR WAS SO IMPRESSED BY PAUL'S BEAUTIFUL VOICE THAT SHE MADE HIM SOLOIST OF THE GLEE CLUB.
Oh Danny Boy THE PIPES THE PIPES ARE CALLING
ON TOP OF OLD SMOK-Y ALL COVERED WITH SNOW
BUT PRINCIPAL ACKERMAN OBJECTED TO A BLACK BOY TAKING CENTER STAGE...

THE DRAMA TEACHER CAST PAUL ROBESON IN HIS FIRST DRAMATIC ROLE~ **OTHELLO**, IN A CLASS PARODY OF THE SHAKESPEARE PLAY...

ABOVE ALL, PAUL EXCELLED AT **SPORTS.** HE WAS FAST, GRACEFUL, STRONG. BY HIS SENIOR YEAR IN HIGH SCHOOL, PAUL ROBESON WAS 6 FEET, 190 POUNDS— A HEAD **TALLER** THAN THE AVERAGE ADULT MAN OF THAT TIME.

IN BASEBALL, HE PLAYED SHORTSTOP & CATCHER

HIS HEIGHT AND **DEXTERITY** DOMINATED IN BASKETBALL

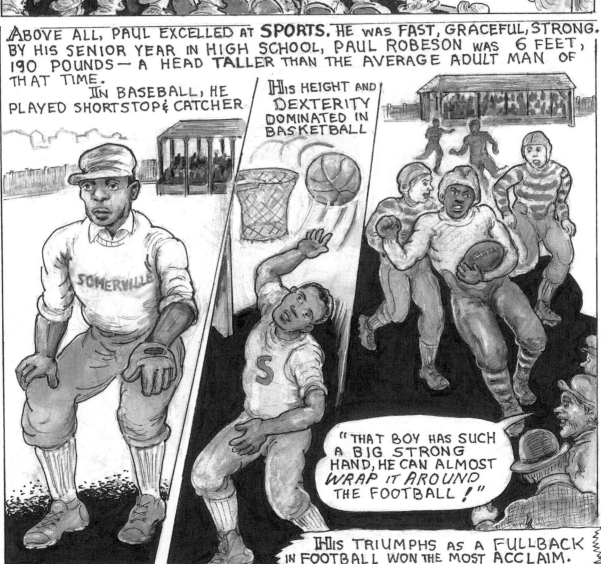

"THAT BOY HAS SUCH A BIG STRONG HAND, HE CAN ALMOST *WRAP IT AROUND* THE FOOTBALL!"

HIS TRIUMPHS AS A **FULLBACK** IN FOOTBALL WON THE MOST **ACCLAIM.**

SHARON RUDAHL 20

DURING BREAKS FROM STUDIES & SPORTS, PAUL WORKED ODD JOBS TO PAY HIS SCHOOL FEES: FARMHAND, BRICKYARD WORKER, KITCHEN BOY.

PAUL ROBESON'S BROTHER BENJAMIN BECAME A MINISTER LIKE HIS FATHER. WILLIAM JR. WAS A DISTINGUISHED DOCTOR. SISTER MARIAN FOLLOWED HER MOTHER'S VOCATION OF TEACHER.

BROTHER REEVE WAS THE BLACK SHEEP, A BRAWLER WHO REFUSED TO TOLERATE RACIAL SLURS...

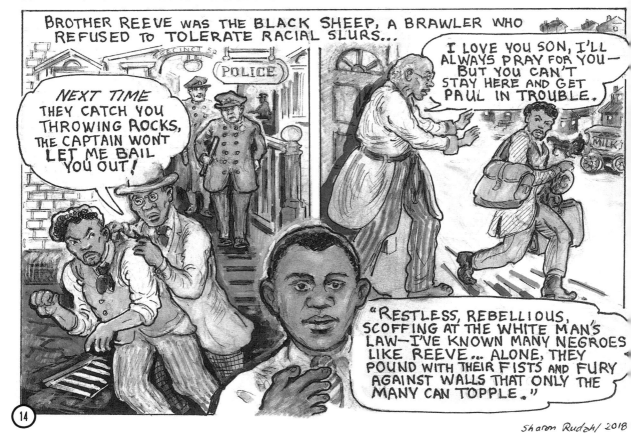

PRECINCT 52 POLICE

NEXT TIME THEY CATCH YOU THROWING ROCKS, THE CAPTAIN WON'T LET ME BAIL YOU OUT!

I LOVE YOU SON, I'LL ALWAYS PRAY FOR YOU— BUT YOU CAN'T STAY HERE AND GET PAUL IN TROUBLE.

MILK

"RESTLESS, REBELLIOUS, SCOFFING AT THE WHITE MAN'S LAW—I'VE KNOWN MANY NEGROES LIKE REEVE... ALONE, THEY POUND WITH THEIR FISTS AND FURY AGAINST WALLS THAT ONLY THE MANY CAN TOPPLE."

14

Sharon Rudahl 2018

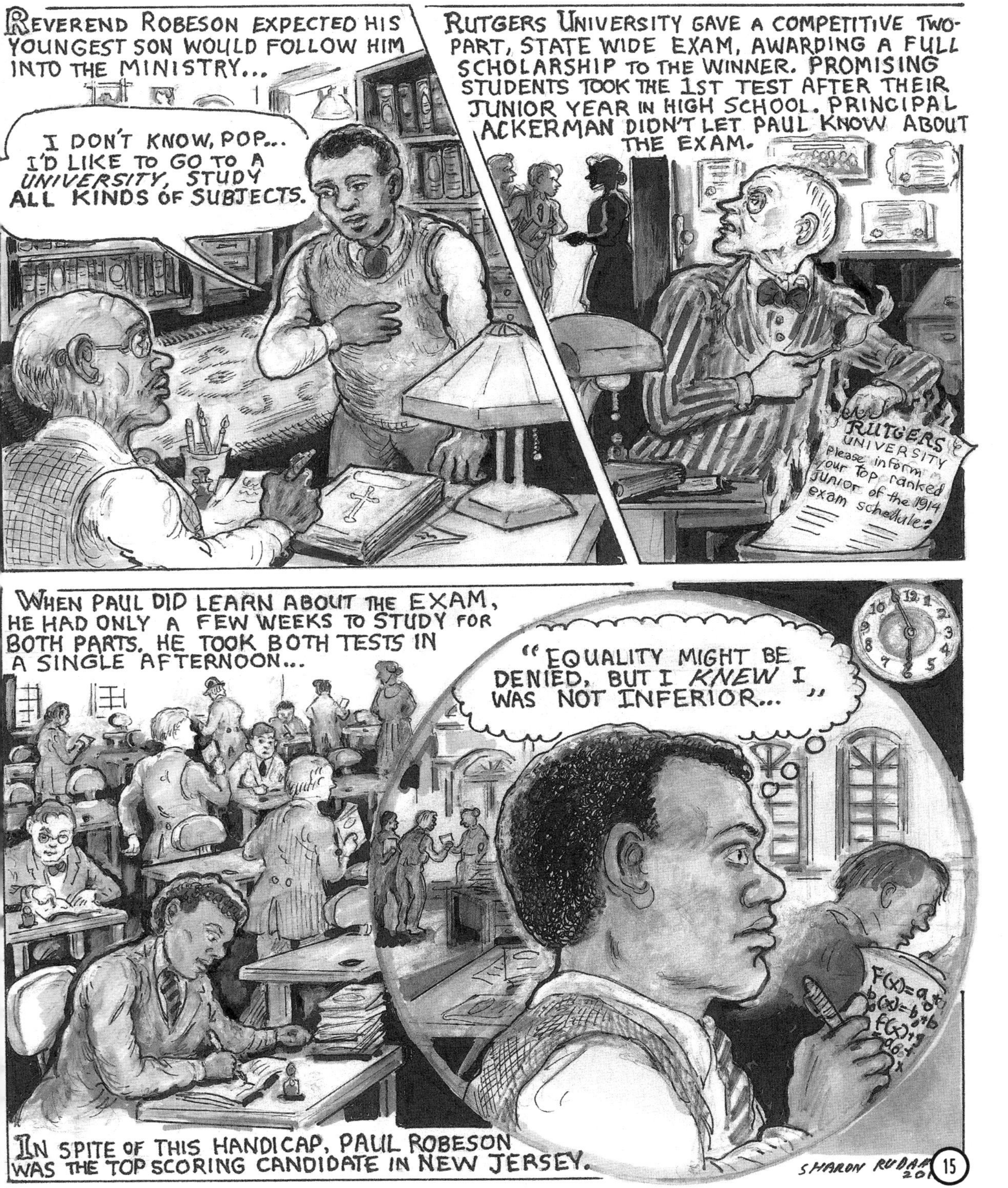

REVEREND ROBESON EXPECTED HIS YOUNGEST SON WOULD FOLLOW HIM INTO THE MINISTRY...
I DON'T KNOW, POP... I'D LIKE TO GO TO A *UNIVERSITY*, STUDY ALL KINDS OF SUBJECTS.
RUTGERS UNIVERSITY GAVE A COMPETITIVE TWO-PART, STATE WIDE EXAM, AWARDING A FULL SCHOLARSHIP TO THE WINNER. PROMISING STUDENTS TOOK THE 1ST TEST AFTER THEIR JUNIOR YEAR IN HIGH SCHOOL. PRINCIPAL ACKERMAN DIDN'T LET PAUL KNOW ABOUT THE EXAM.
RUTGERS UNIVERSITY Please inform your Top ranked Junior of the 1914 exam schedule:
WHEN PAUL DID LEARN ABOUT THE EXAM, HE HAD ONLY A FEW WEEKS TO STUDY FOR BOTH PARTS. HE TOOK BOTH TESTS IN A SINGLE AFTERNOON...
"EQUALITY MIGHT BE DENIED, BUT I *KNEW* I WAS NOT INFERIOR..."
IN SPITE OF THIS HANDICAP, PAUL ROBESON WAS THE TOP SCORING CANDIDATE IN NEW JERSEY.
SHARON RUDAHL

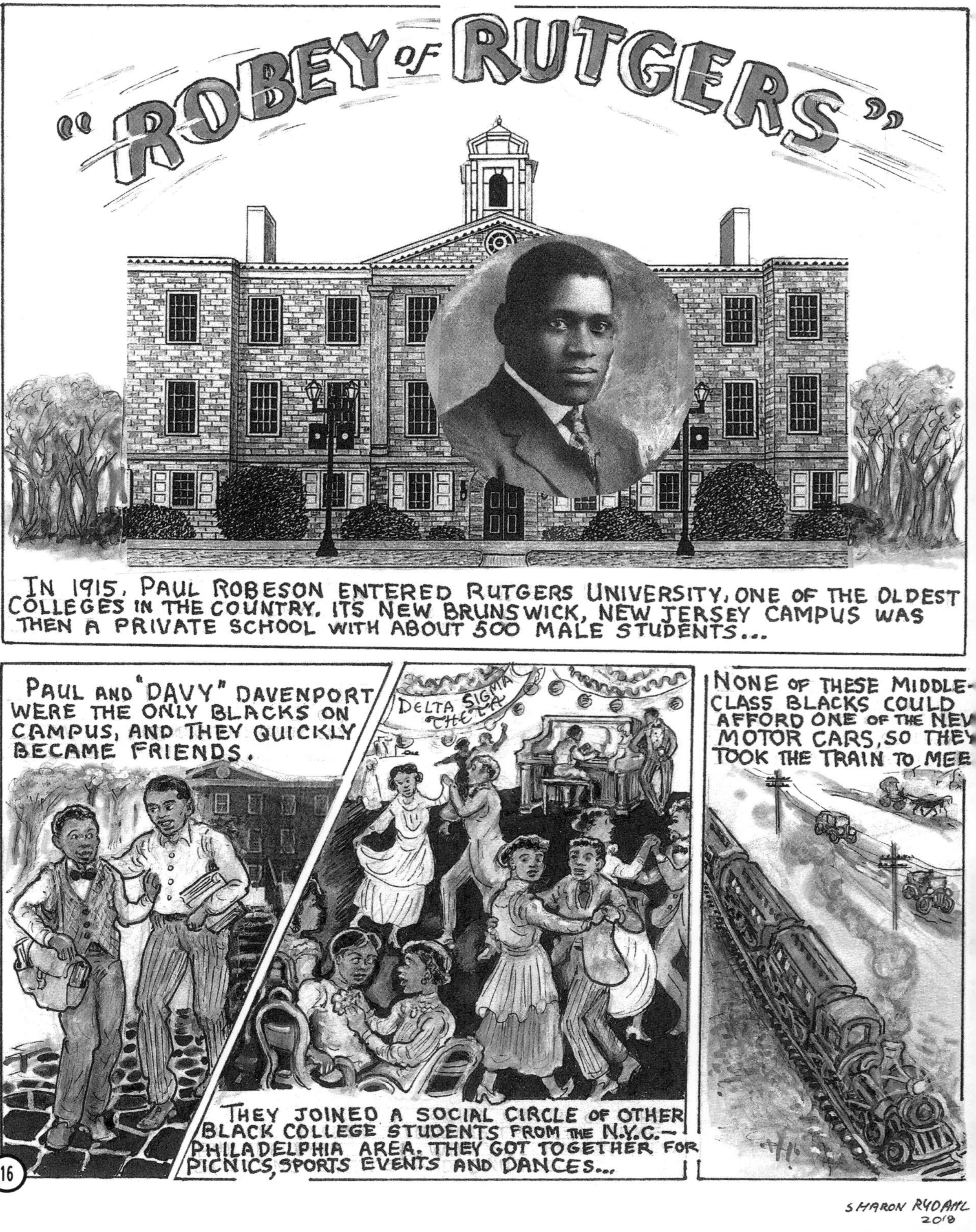
"ROBEY of RUTGERS"
IN 1915, PAUL ROBESON ENTERED RUTGERS UNIVERSITY, ONE OF THE OLDEST COLLEGES IN THE COUNTRY. ITS NEW BRUNSWICK, NEW JERSEY CAMPUS WAS THEN A PRIVATE SCHOOL WITH ABOUT 500 MALE STUDENTS...
PAUL AND "DAVY" DAVENPORT WERE THE ONLY BLACKS ON CAMPUS, AND THEY QUICKLY BECAME FRIENDS.
DELTA SIGMA THETA
THEY JOINED A SOCIAL CIRCLE OF OTHER BLACK COLLEGE STUDENTS FROM THE N.Y.C.–PHILADELPHIA AREA. THEY GOT TOGETHER FOR PICNICS, SPORTS EVENTS AND DANCES...
NONE OF THESE MIDDLE-CLASS BLACKS COULD AFFORD ONE OF THE NEW MOTOR CARS, SO THEY TOOK THE TRAIN TO MEE
SHARON RUDAHL 2018

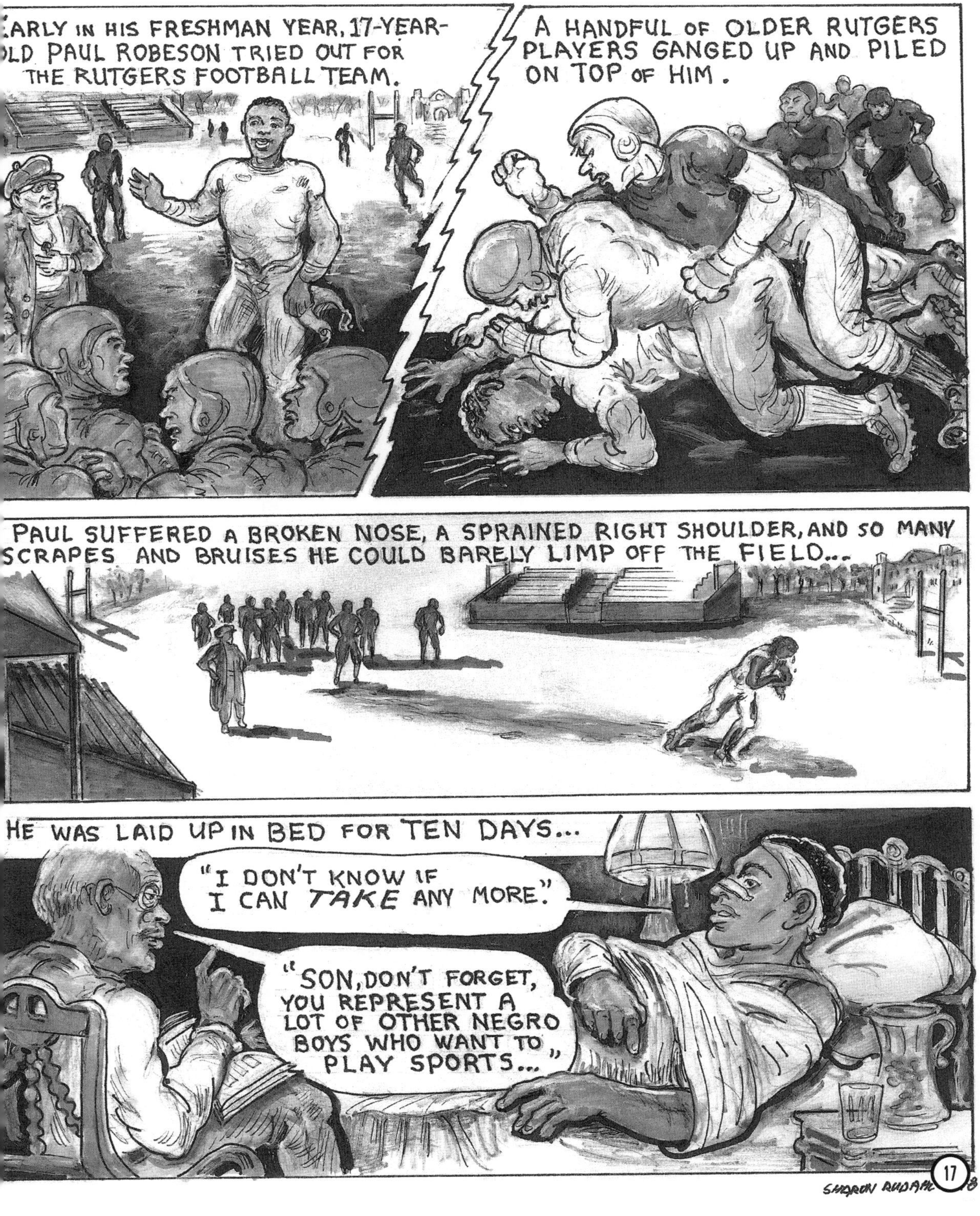
EARLY IN HIS FRESHMAN YEAR, 17-YEAR-OLD PAUL ROBESON TRIED OUT FOR THE RUTGERS FOOTBALL TEAM.
A HANDFUL OF OLDER RUTGERS PLAYERS GANGED UP AND PILED ON TOP OF HIM.
PAUL SUFFERED A BROKEN NOSE, A SPRAINED RIGHT SHOULDER, AND SO MANY SCRAPES AND BRUISES HE COULD BARELY LIMP OFF THE FIELD...
HE WAS LAID UP IN BED FOR TEN DAYS...
"I DON'T KNOW IF I CAN *TAKE* ANY MORE."
"SON, DON'T FORGET, YOU REPRESENT A LOT OF OTHER NEGRO BOYS WHO WANT TO PLAY SPORTS..."

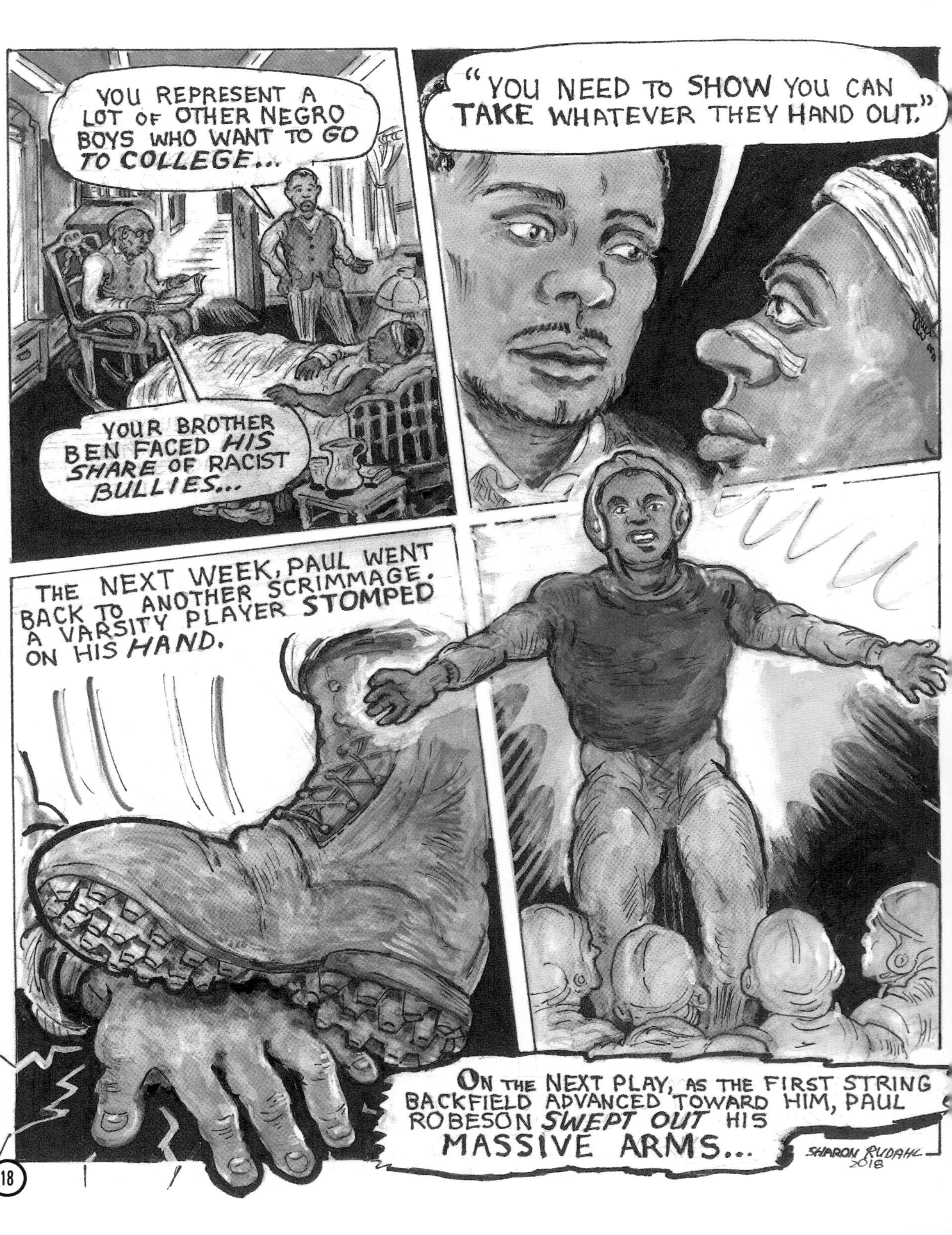
YOU REPRESENT A LOT OF OTHER NEGRO BOYS WHO WANT TO GO TO COLLEGE...
YOUR BROTHER BEN FACED HIS SHARE OF RACIST BULLIES...
"YOU NEED TO SHOW YOU CAN TAKE WHATEVER THEY HAND OUT."
THE NEXT WEEK, PAUL WENT BACK TO ANOTHER SCRIMMAGE. A VARSITY PLAYER STOMPED ON HIS HAND.
ON THE NEXT PLAY, AS THE FIRST STRING BACKFIELD ADVANCED TOWARD HIM, PAUL ROBESON SWEPT OUT HIS MASSIVE ARMS...
SHARON RUDAHL 2018

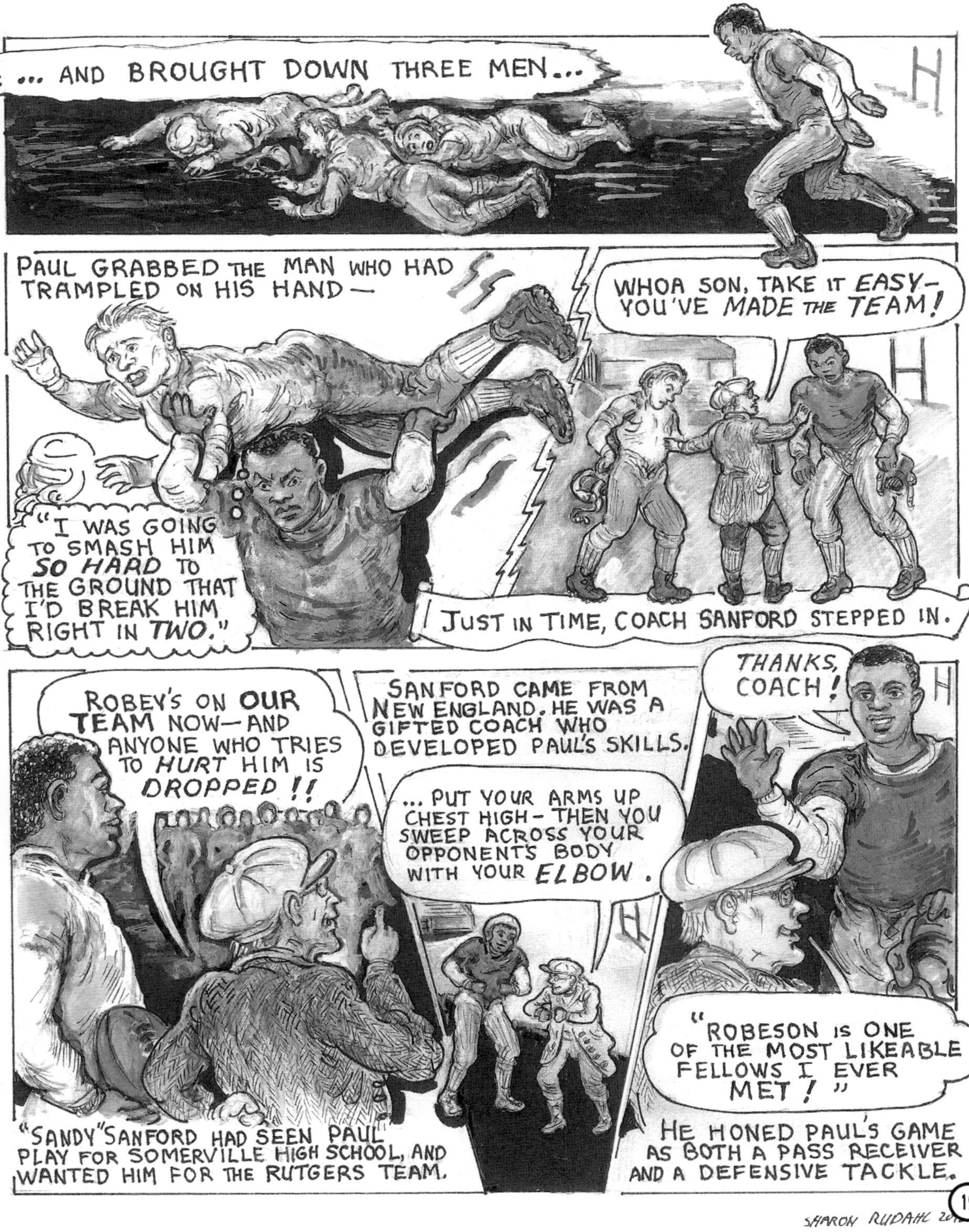
... AND BROUGHT DOWN THREE MEN...
PAUL GRABBED THE MAN WHO HAD TRAMPLED ON HIS HAND—
"I WAS GOING TO SMASH HIM SO HARD TO THE GROUND THAT I'D BREAK HIM RIGHT IN TWO."
WHOA SON, TAKE IT EASY—YOU'VE MADE THE TEAM!
JUST IN TIME, COACH SANFORD STEPPED IN.
ROBEY'S ON OUR TEAM NOW—AND ANYONE WHO TRIES TO HURT HIM IS DROPPED!!
"SANDY" SANFORD HAD SEEN PAUL PLAY FOR SOMERVILLE HIGH SCHOOL, AND WANTED HIM FOR THE RUTGERS TEAM.
SANFORD CAME FROM NEW ENGLAND. HE WAS A GIFTED COACH WHO DEVELOPED PAUL'S SKILLS.
... PUT YOUR ARMS UP CHEST HIGH—THEN YOU SWEEP ACROSS YOUR OPPONENT'S BODY WITH YOUR ELBOW.
THANKS, COACH!
"ROBESON IS ONE OF THE MOST LIKEABLE FELLOWS I EVER MET!"
HE HONED PAUL'S GAME AS BOTH A PASS RECEIVER AND A DEFENSIVE TACKLE.
SHARON RUDAHL

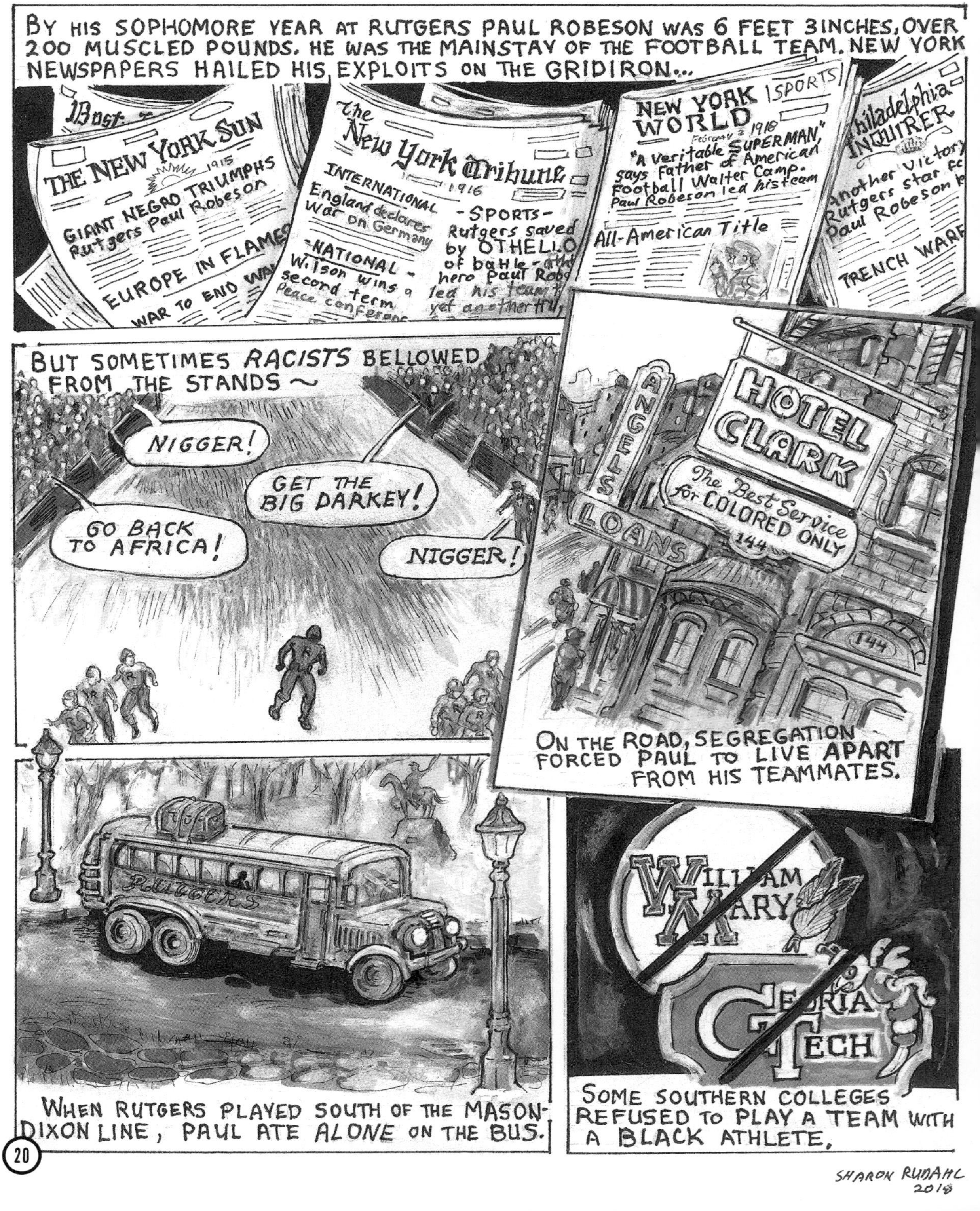

BY HIS SOPHOMORE YEAR AT RUTGERS PAUL ROBESON WAS 6 FEET 3 INCHES, OVER 200 MUSCLED POUNDS. HE WAS THE MAINSTAY OF THE FOOTBALL TEAM. NEW YORK NEWSPAPERS HAILED HIS EXPLOITS ON THE GRIDIRON...
THE NEW YORK SUN
1915
GIANT NEGRO TRIUMPHS
Rutgers Paul Robeson
EUROPE IN FLAMES
WAR TO END WA
The New York Tribune
1916
INTERNATIONAL
England declares War on Germany
-NATIONAL-
Wilson wins a second term
Peace conferenc
-SPORTS-
Rutgers saved by OTHELLO
of battle - athl
hero Paul Rob
led his team t
yet another tr
NEW YORK WORLD
SPORTS
February 2 1918
"A veritable SUPERMAN," says Father of American Football Walter Camp.
Paul Robeson led his team
All-American Title
Philadelphia INQUIRER
Another victory
Rutgers star fo
Paul Robeson le
TRENCH WARF
BUT SOMETIMES RACISTS BELLOWED FROM THE STANDS ~
NIGGER!
GET THE BIG DARKEY!
GO BACK TO AFRICA!
NIGGER!
ANGELS
LOANS
HOTEL CLARK
The Best Service for COLORED ONLY
144
144
ON THE ROAD, SEGREGATION FORCED PAUL TO LIVE APART FROM HIS TEAMMATES.
RUTGERS
WHEN RUTGERS PLAYED SOUTH OF THE MASON-DIXON LINE, PAUL ATE ALONE ON THE BUS.
WILLIAM MARY
GEORGIA TECH
SOME SOUTHERN COLLEGES REFUSED TO PLAY A TEAM WITH A BLACK ATHLETE.
SHARON RUDAHL 2018

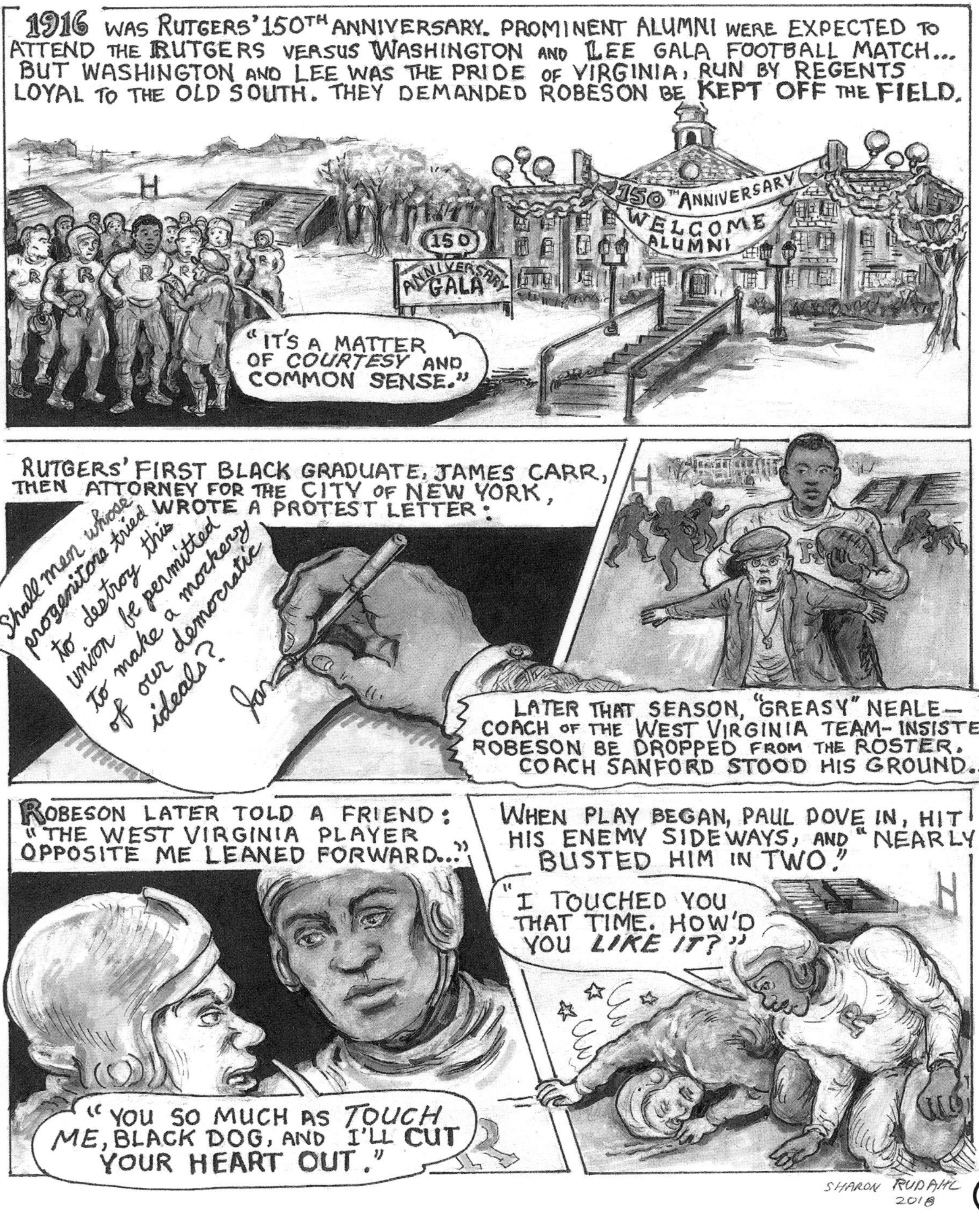
1916 WAS RUTGERS' 150TH ANNIVERSARY. PROMINENT ALUMNI WERE EXPECTED TO ATTEND THE RUTGERS VERSUS WASHINGTON AND LEE GALA FOOTBALL MATCH... BUT WASHINGTON AND LEE WAS THE PRIDE OF VIRGINIA, RUN BY REGENTS LOYAL TO THE OLD SOUTH. THEY DEMANDED ROBESON BE KEPT OFF THE FIELD.
150TH ANNIVERSARY
WELCOME ALUMNI
150
ANNIVERSARY GALA
"IT'S A MATTER OF COURTESY AND COMMON SENSE."
RUTGERS' FIRST BLACK GRADUATE, JAMES CARR, THEN ATTORNEY FOR THE CITY OF NEW YORK, WROTE A PROTEST LETTER:
Shall men whose progenitors tried to destroy this union be permitted to make a mockery of our democratic ideals?
LATER THAT SEASON, "GREASY" NEALE— COACH OF THE WEST VIRGINIA TEAM— INSISTED ROBESON BE DROPPED FROM THE ROSTER. COACH SANFORD STOOD HIS GROUND...
ROBESON LATER TOLD A FRIEND: "THE WEST VIRGINIA PLAYER OPPOSITE ME LEANED FORWARD..."
"YOU SO MUCH AS TOUCH ME, BLACK DOG, AND I'LL CUT YOUR HEART OUT."
WHEN PLAY BEGAN, PAUL DOVE IN, HIT HIS ENEMY SIDEWAYS, AND "NEARLY BUSTED HIM IN TWO."
"I TOUCHED YOU THAT TIME. HOW'D YOU LIKE IT?"
SHARON RUDAHL 2018

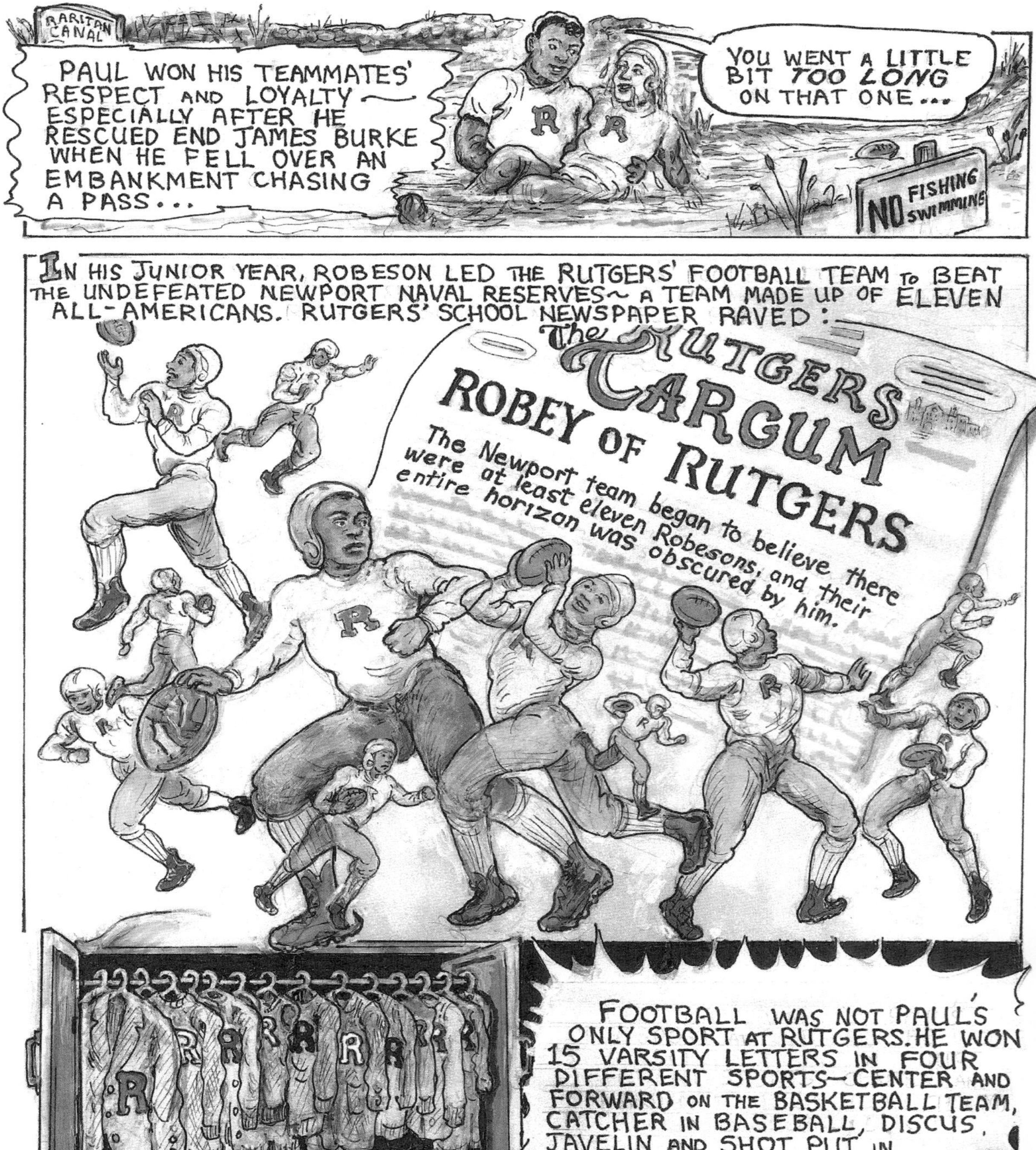
RARITAN CANAL
PAUL WON HIS TEAMMATES' RESPECT AND LOYALTY — ESPECIALLY AFTER HE RESCUED END JAMES BURKE WHEN HE FELL OVER AN EMBANKMENT CHASING A PASS...
YOU WENT A LITTLE BIT TOO LONG ON THAT ONE...
NO FISHING SWIMMING
IN HIS JUNIOR YEAR, ROBESON LED THE RUTGERS' FOOTBALL TEAM TO BEAT THE UNDEFEATED NEWPORT NAVAL RESERVES ~ A TEAM MADE UP OF ELEVEN ALL-AMERICANS. RUTGERS' SCHOOL NEWSPAPER RAVED:
The Rutgers Targum
ROBEY OF RUTGERS
The Newport team began to believe there were at least eleven Robesons, and their entire horizon was obscured by him.
FOOTBALL WAS NOT PAUL'S ONLY SPORT AT RUTGERS. HE WON 15 VARSITY LETTERS IN FOUR DIFFERENT SPORTS—CENTER AND FORWARD ON THE BASKETBALL TEAM, CATCHER IN BASEBALL, DISCUS, JAVELIN AND SHOT PUT IN TRACK AND FIELD...
SHARON RUDAHL 2018

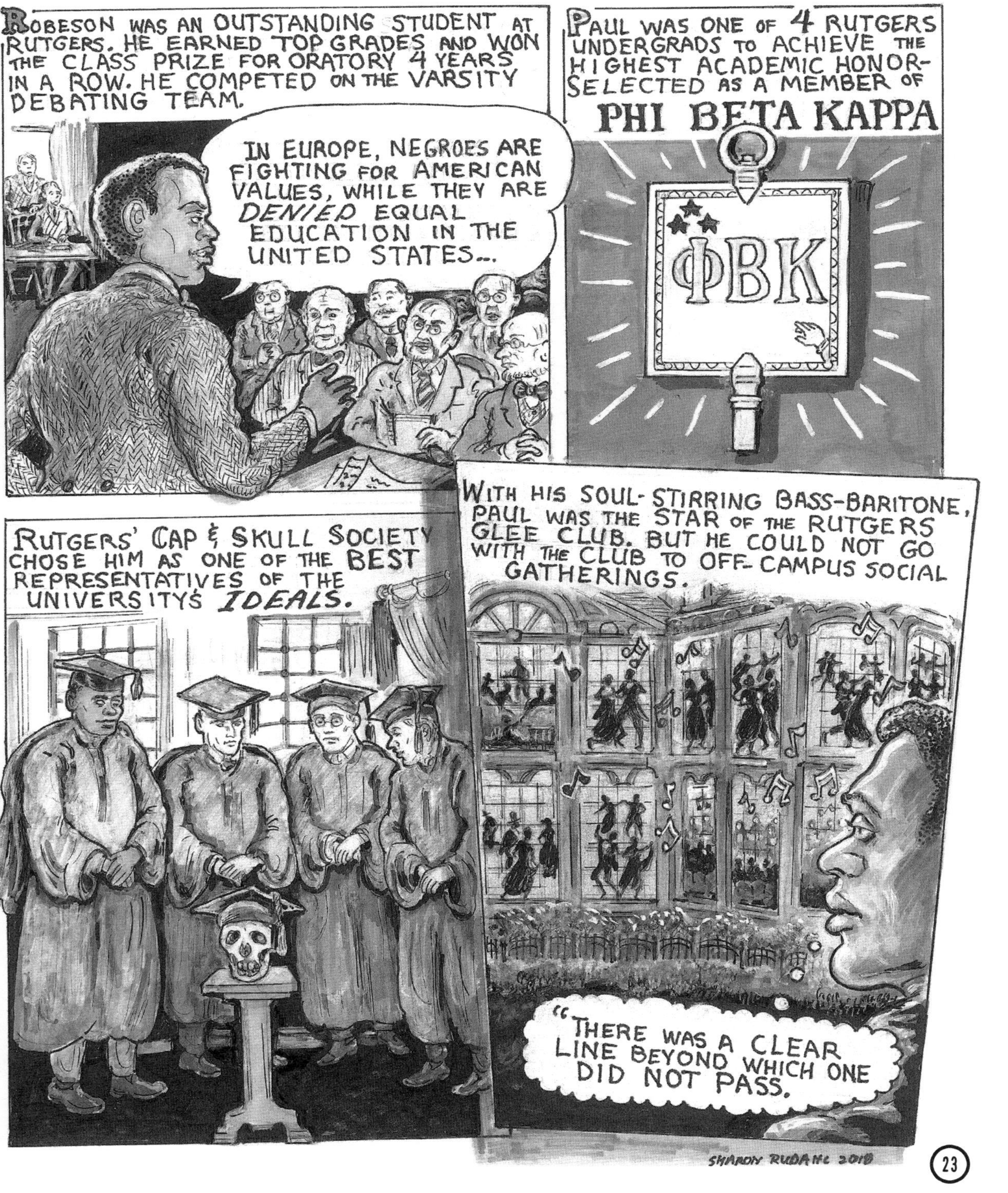
ROBESON WAS AN OUTSTANDING STUDENT AT RUTGERS. HE EARNED TOP GRADES AND WON THE CLASS PRIZE FOR ORATORY 4 YEARS IN A ROW. HE COMPETED ON THE VARSITY DEBATING TEAM.
IN EUROPE, NEGROES ARE FIGHTING FOR AMERICAN VALUES, WHILE THEY ARE DENIED EQUAL EDUCATION IN THE UNITED STATES...
PAUL WAS ONE OF 4 RUTGERS UNDERGRADS TO ACHIEVE THE HIGHEST ACADEMIC HONOR- SELECTED AS A MEMBER OF
PHI BETA KAPPA
ΦBK
RUTGERS' CAP & SKULL SOCIETY CHOSE HIM AS ONE OF THE BEST REPRESENTATIVES OF THE UNIVERSITY'S IDEALS.
WITH HIS SOUL-STIRRING BASS-BARITONE, PAUL WAS THE STAR OF THE RUTGERS GLEE CLUB. BUT HE COULD NOT GO WITH THE CLUB TO OFF-CAMPUS SOCIAL GATHERINGS.
"THERE WAS A CLEAR LINE BEYOND WHICH ONE DID NOT PASS."
SHARON RUDAHL 2018

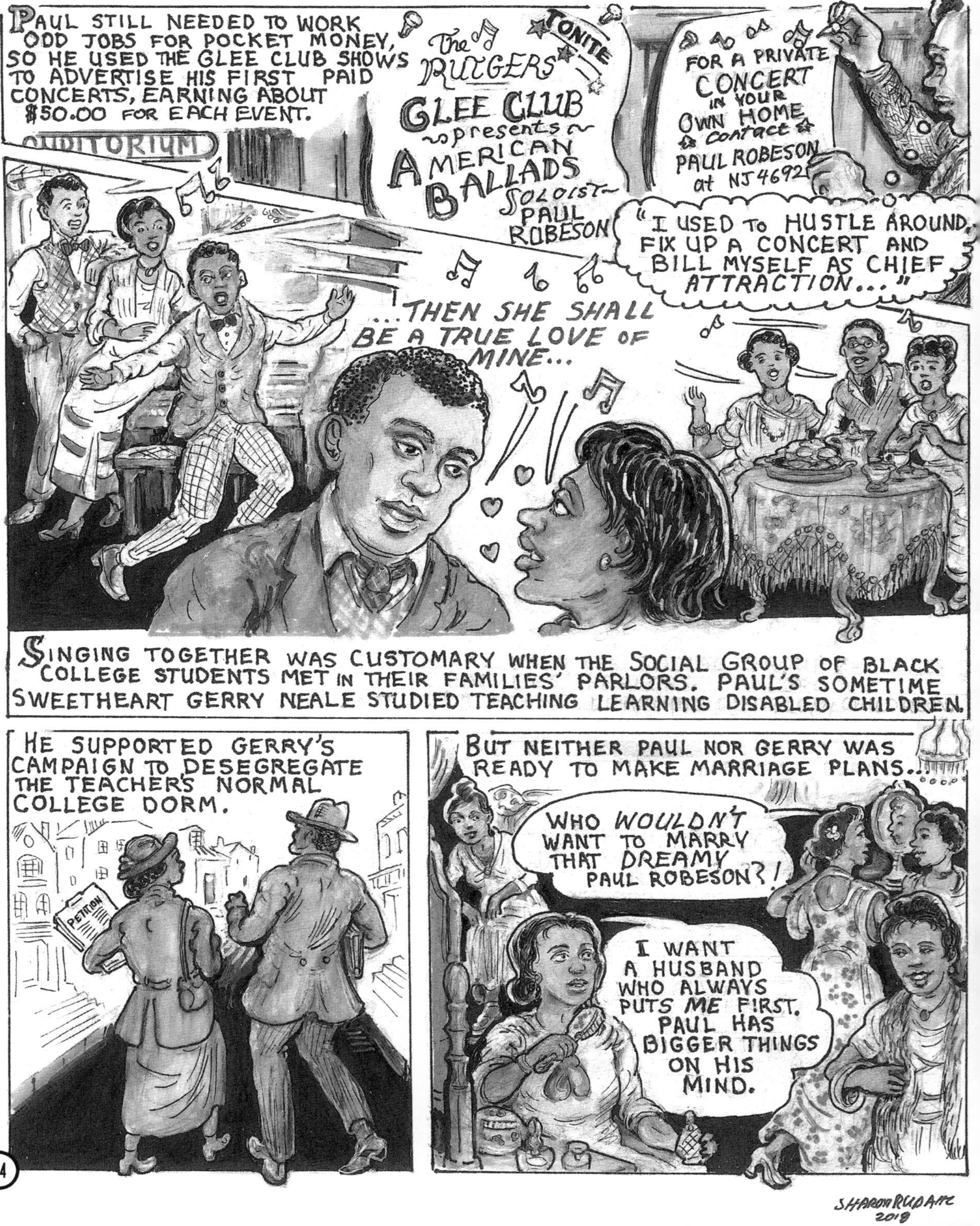
PAUL STILL NEEDED TO WORK ODD JOBS FOR POCKET MONEY, SO HE USED THE GLEE CLUB SHOWS TO ADVERTISE HIS FIRST PAID CONCERTS, EARNING ABOUT $50.00 FOR EACH EVENT.
AUDITORIUM
TONITE
The RUTGERS GLEE CLUB presents AMERICAN BALLADS SOLOIST PAUL ROBESON
FOR A PRIVATE CONCERT IN YOUR OWN HOME CONTACT PAUL ROBESON at NJ 4692
"I USED TO HUSTLE AROUND, FIX UP A CONCERT AND BILL MYSELF AS CHIEF ATTRACTION..."
...THEN SHE SHALL BE A TRUE LOVE OF MINE...
SINGING TOGETHER WAS CUSTOMARY WHEN THE SOCIAL GROUP OF BLACK COLLEGE STUDENTS MET IN THEIR FAMILIES' PARLORS. PAUL'S SOMETIME SWEETHEART GERRY NEALE STUDIED TEACHING LEARNING DISABLED CHILDREN.
HE SUPPORTED GERRY'S CAMPAIGN TO DESEGREGATE THE TEACHER'S NORMAL COLLEGE DORM.
PETITION
BUT NEITHER PAUL NOR GERRY WAS READY TO MAKE MARRIAGE PLANS...
WHO WOULDN'T WANT TO MARRY THAT DREAMY PAUL ROBESON?!
I WANT A HUSBAND WHO ALWAYS PUTS ME FIRST. PAUL HAS BIGGER THINGS ON HIS MIND.
SHARON RUDAHL 2018

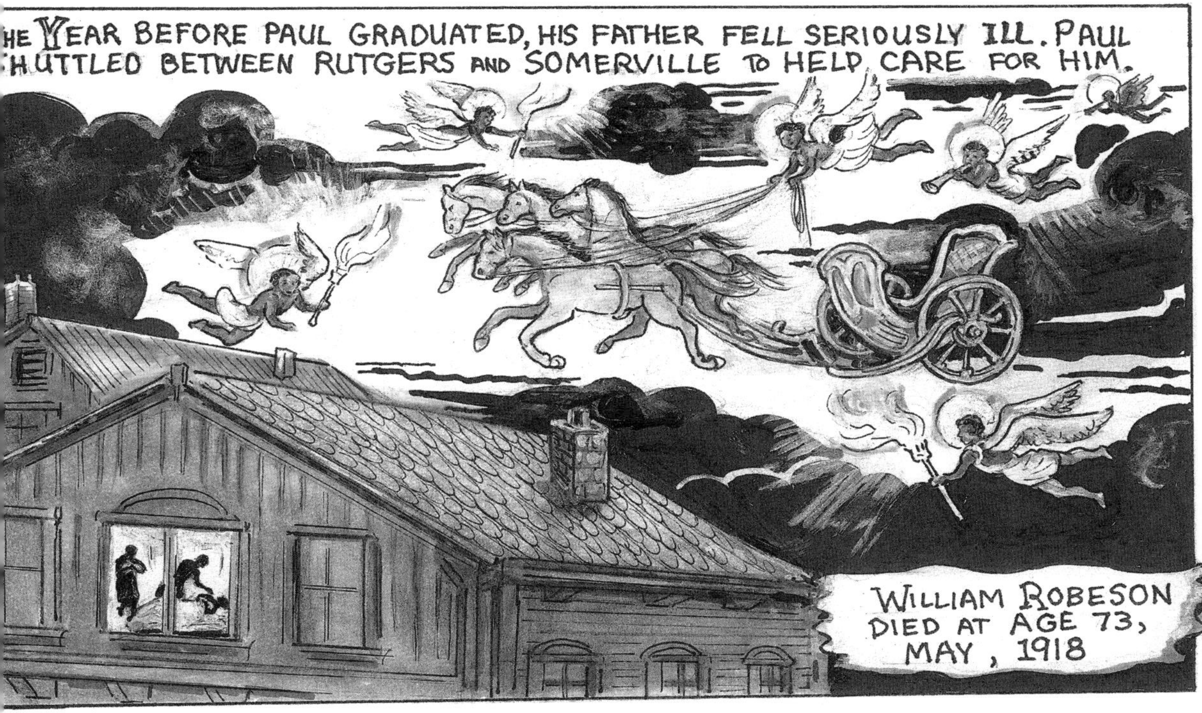
HE YEAR BEFORE PAUL GRADUATED, HIS FATHER FELL SERIOUSLY ILL. PAUL
HUTTLED BETWEEN RUTGERS AND SOMERVILLE TO HELP CARE FOR HIM.
WILLIAM ROBESON DIED AT AGE 73, MAY, 1918

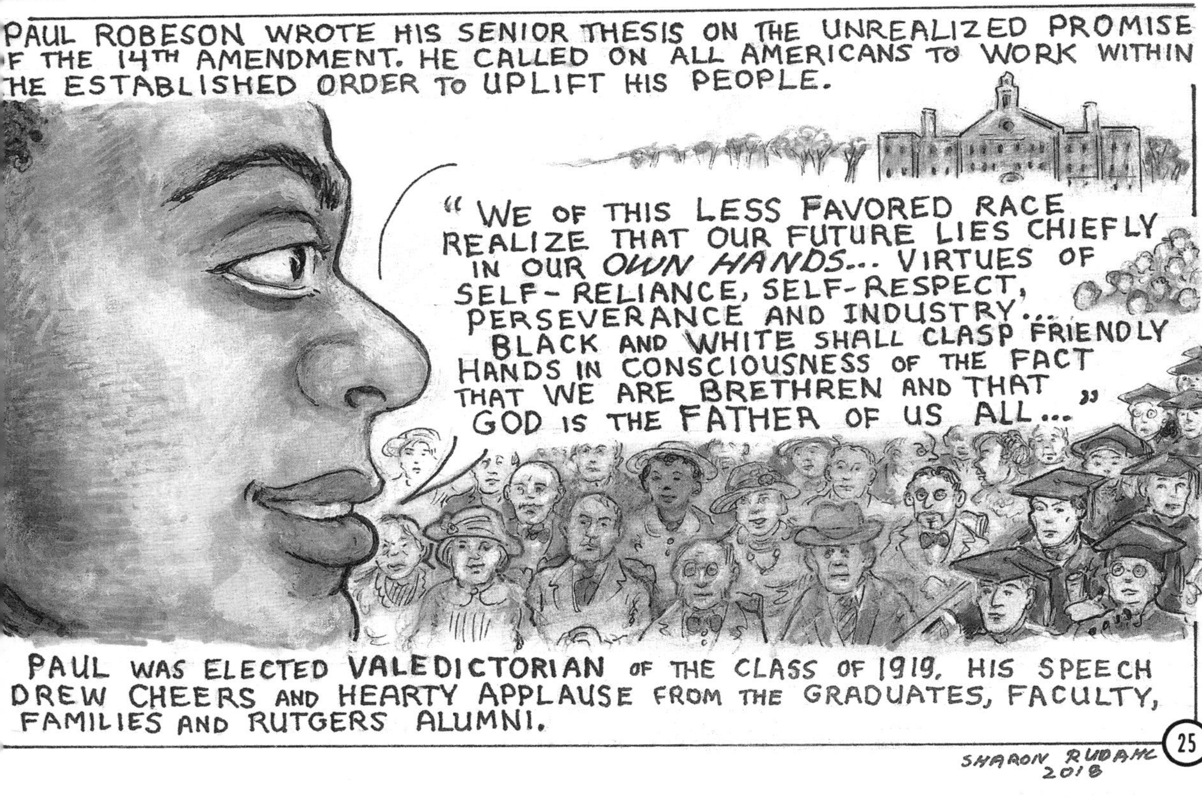
PAUL ROBESON WROTE HIS SENIOR THESIS ON THE UNREALIZED PROMISE
F THE 14TH AMENDMENT. HE CALLED ON ALL AMERICANS TO WORK WITHIN
HE ESTABLISHED ORDER TO UPLIFT HIS PEOPLE.
"WE OF THIS LESS FAVORED RACE REALIZE THAT OUR FUTURE LIES CHIEFLY IN OUR *OWN HANDS*... VIRTUES OF SELF-RELIANCE, SELF-RESPECT, PERSEVERANCE AND INDUSTRY... BLACK AND WHITE SHALL CLASP FRIENDLY HANDS IN CONSCIOUSNESS OF THE FACT THAT WE ARE BRETHREN AND THAT GOD IS THE FATHER OF US ALL..."
PAUL WAS ELECTED VALEDICTORIAN OF THE CLASS OF 1919. HIS SPEECH
DREW CHEERS AND HEARTY APPLAUSE FROM THE GRADUATES, FACULTY,
FAMILIES AND RUTGERS ALUMNI.

SHARON RUDAHL 2018

CHAPTER II

FIRST STEPS ON THE STAGE

AFTER GRADUATING FROM RUTGERS, PAUL ROBESON WENT TO LAW SCHOOL. HE
OPED HIS TALENT FOR DEBATE, HIS KNACK FOR GETTING ALONG WITH PEOPLE, COULD
MOOTH HIS PATH TO SUCCESS AS A LAWYER. HE MOVED TO NEW YORK CITY TO
TTEND COLUMBIA UNIVERSITY, SHARING AN APARTMENT ON 135TH STREET~

HARLEM ~ "THE NEGRO CAPITAL OF THE WORLD"

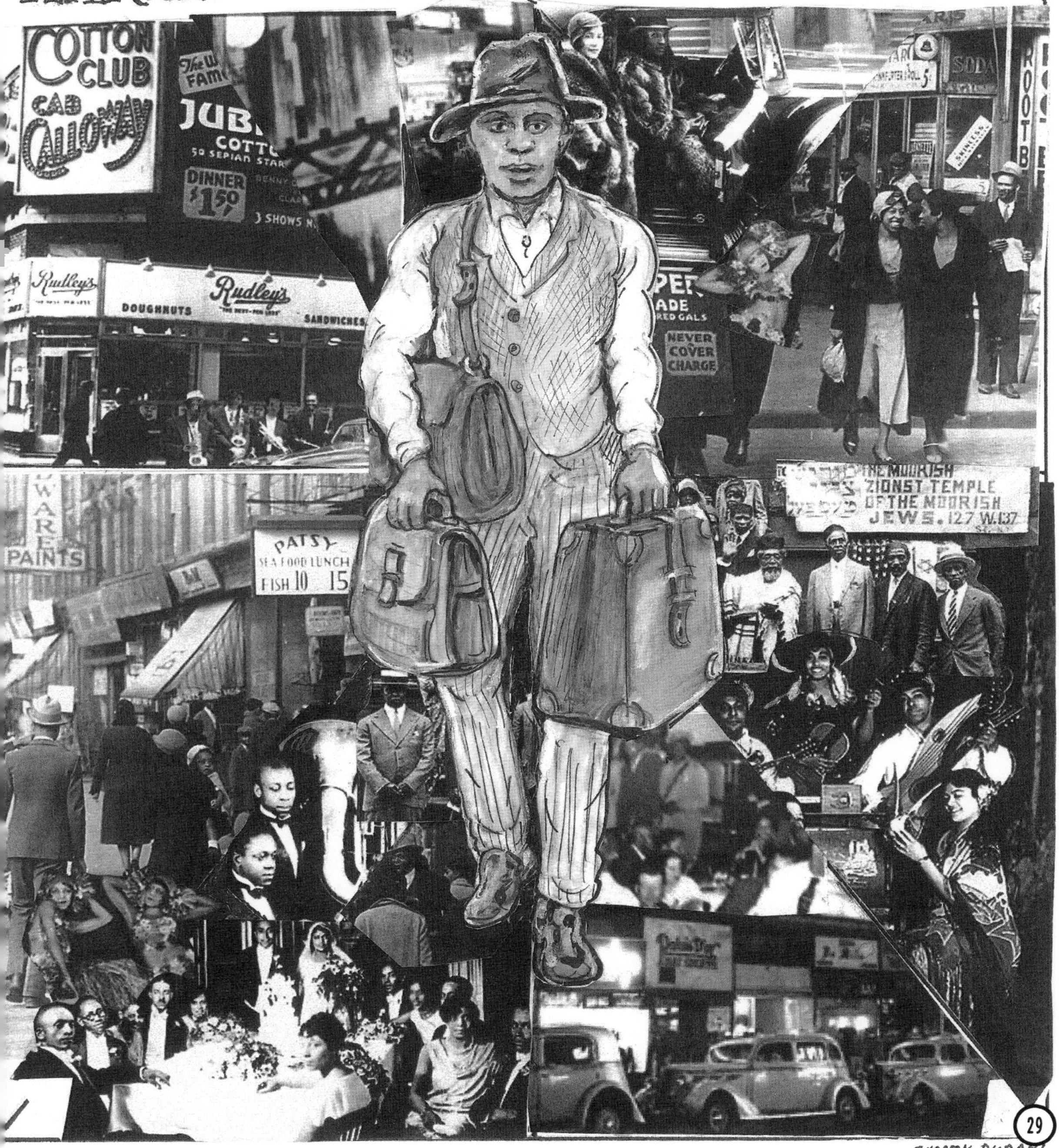
COTTON CLUB
CAB CALLOWAY
DINNER $1.50
Rudley's
DOUGHNUTS
SANDWICHES
NEVER COVER CHARGE
PAINTS
PATSY
SEA FOOD LUNCH
FISH 10 15
THE MOORISH ZIONST TEMPLE OF THE MOORISH JEWS. 127 W.137
SODA

SHARON RUDAHL
2018

IN THE FIRST DECADES OF THE 20TH CENTURY, TWO MILLION BLACKS MIGRATED FROM THE RURAL SOUTH TO NORTHERN CITIES. THEY FOUND NO PROMISED LAND, BUT BETTER HEALTH CARE, EDUCATION AND JOB OPPORTUNITIES... ILLITERACY AND INFANT MORTALITY DECLINED.

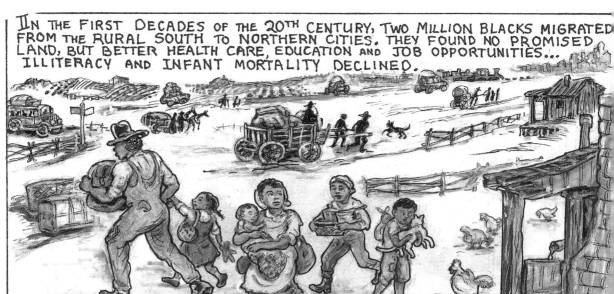

PAUL'S ROOMMATE WAS MUSICIAN JIMMY LIGHTFOOT. WHAT WOULD BE CALLED THE "HARLEM RENAISSANCE" WAS JUST BLOSSOMING, WITH TALENTED BLACK ARTISTS, WRITERS, & PERFORMERS ARRIVING DAILY...

PAUL ROBESON WAS ALREADY KNOWN IN THE NEIGHBORHOOD AS A SPORTS STAR. HE WAS SOON A FAMILIAR FIGURE STROLLING DOWN 7TH AVENUE "WITH A PRETTY GIRL ON HIS ARM."

HOWDY, PAUL!

'MORNING, PAUL.

FISH

SHARON RUDAHL
2018

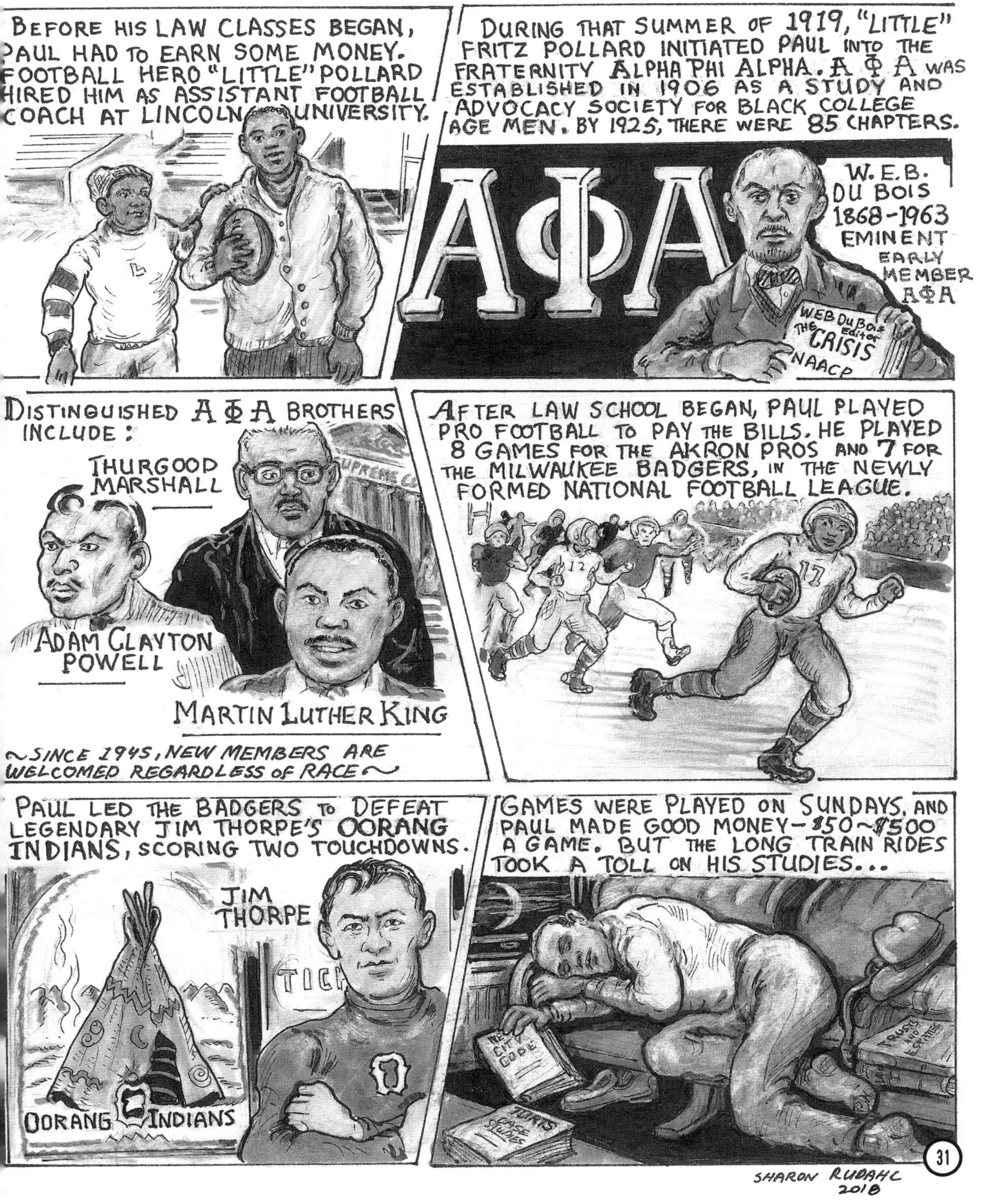
BEFORE HIS LAW CLASSES BEGAN, PAUL HAD TO EARN SOME MONEY. FOOTBALL HERO "LITTLE" POLLARD HIRED HIM AS ASSISTANT FOOTBALL COACH AT LINCOLN UNIVERSITY.
DURING THAT SUMMER OF 1919, "LITTLE" FRITZ POLLARD INITIATED PAUL INTO THE FRATERNITY ALPHA PHI ALPHA. Α Φ Α WAS ESTABLISHED IN 1906 AS A STUDY AND ADVOCACY SOCIETY FOR BLACK COLLEGE AGE MEN. BY 1925, THERE WERE 85 CHAPTERS.
ΑΦΑ
W. E. B. DU BOIS 1868-1963 EMINENT EARLY MEMBER ΑΦΑ
WEB DuBois Editor THE CRISIS NAACP
DISTINGUISHED Α Φ Α BROTHERS INCLUDE:
THURGOOD MARSHALL
ADAM CLAYTON POWELL
MARTIN LUTHER KING
~SINCE 1945, NEW MEMBERS ARE WELCOMED REGARDLESS OF RACE~
AFTER LAW SCHOOL BEGAN, PAUL PLAYED PRO FOOTBALL TO PAY THE BILLS. HE PLAYED 8 GAMES FOR THE AKRON PROS AND 7 FOR THE MILWAUKEE BADGERS, IN THE NEWLY FORMED NATIONAL FOOTBALL LEAGUE.
12
17
PAUL LED THE BADGERS TO DEFEAT LEGENDARY JIM THORPE'S OORANG INDIANS, SCORING TWO TOUCHDOWNS.
JIM THORPE
OORANG INDIANS
GAMES WERE PLAYED ON SUNDAYS, AND PAUL MADE GOOD MONEY—$50~$500 A GAME. BUT THE LONG TRAIN RIDES TOOK A TOLL ON HIS STUDIES...
CITY CODE
TORTS CASE STUDIES
TRUSTS AND ESTATES
SHARON RUDAHL 2018

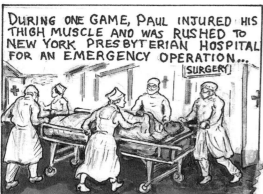

DURING ONE GAME, PAUL INJURED HIS THIGH MUSCLE AND WAS RUSHED TO NEW YORK PRESBYTERIAN HOSPITAL FOR AN EMERGENCY OPERATION... [SURGERY]

PAUL, I'D LIKE YOU TO MEET MY COLLEAGUE, ESLANDA GOODE...

DR. MURRAY, AN ASSISTANT SURGEON IMPRESSED BY PAUL'S COURAGE AND CHARM, INTRODUCED HIM TO A BRIGHT YOUNG LAB TECHNICIAN.

DR. MURRAY *DIDN'T KNOW* PAUL AND ESSIE HAD BUMPED INTO EACH OTHER AT HARLEM PARTIES...

WE CAN'T GO ON MEETING *LIKE THIS*...

ESSIE WAS DELIGHTED TO HAVE PAUL ALL TO HERSELF FOR A CHANGE...

NO VISITO[RS]

... FRESH FRUIT, THE MORNING NEWSPAPERS...

... *OH*, AND HERE ARE NOTES TO THE LECTURES YOU MISSED LAST WEEK.

SHE MADE HERSELF INDISPENSABLE.

32

SHARON RUDAHL 2018

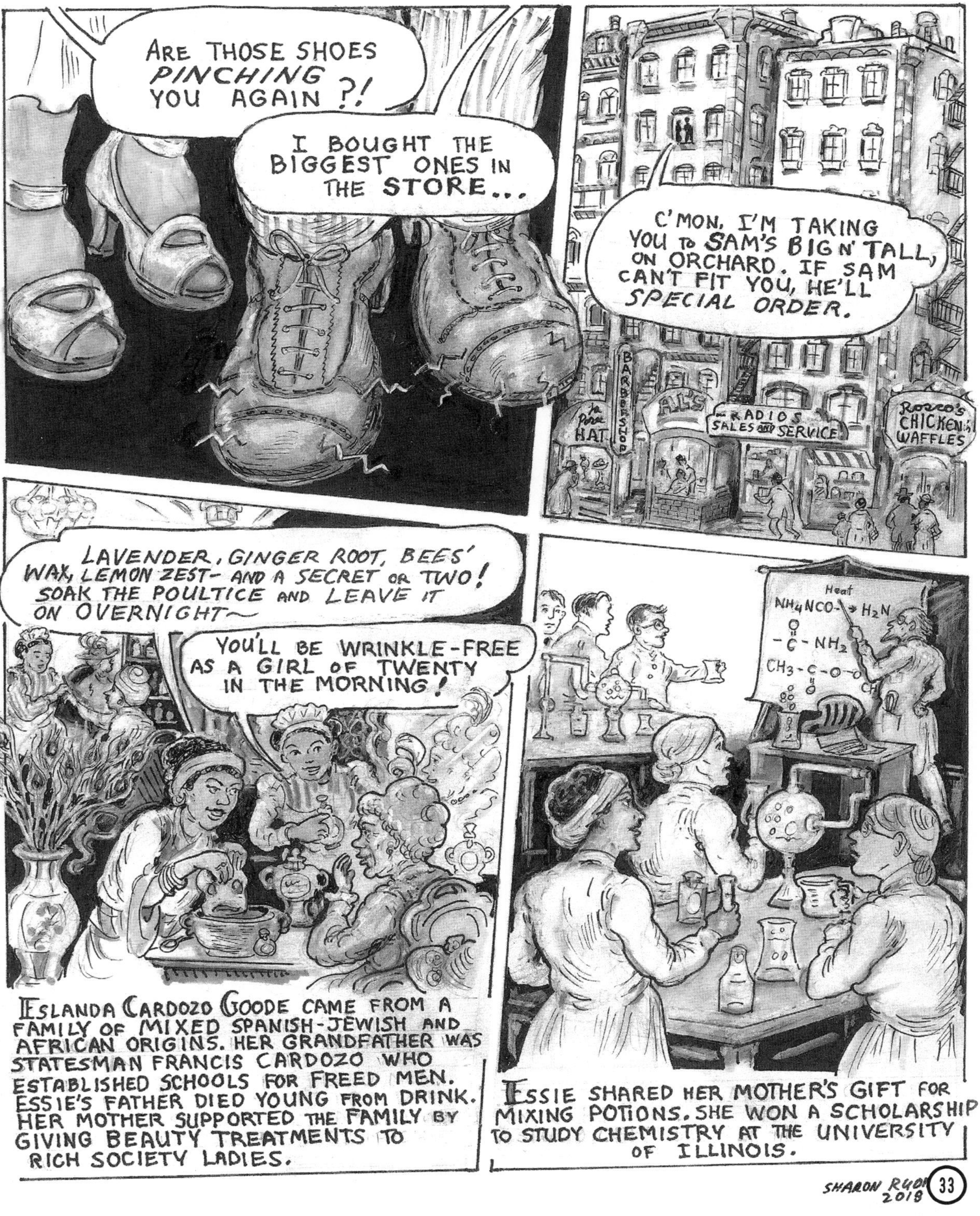
ARE THOSE SHOES *PINCHING* YOU AGAIN ?!
I BOUGHT THE BIGGEST ONES IN THE **STORE**...
C'MON, I'M TAKING YOU TO **SAM'S BIG N' TALL**, ON ORCHARD. IF SAM CAN'T FIT YOU, HE'LL *SPECIAL ORDER.*
BARBERSHOP
AL'S
RADIOS SALES AND SERVICE
ROSCO'S CHICKEN & WAFFLES
LAVENDER, GINGER ROOT, BEES' WAX, LEMON ZEST- AND A SECRET OR TWO! SOAK THE POULTICE AND LEAVE IT ON OVERNIGHT~
YOU'LL BE WRINKLE-FREE AS A GIRL OF TWENTY IN THE MORNING!
ESLANDA CARDOZO GOODE CAME FROM A FAMILY OF MIXED SPANISH-JEWISH AND AFRICAN ORIGINS. HER GRANDFATHER WAS STATESMAN FRANCIS CARDOZO WHO ESTABLISHED SCHOOLS FOR FREED MEN. ESSIE'S FATHER DIED YOUNG FROM DRINK. HER MOTHER SUPPORTED THE FAMILY BY GIVING BEAUTY TREATMENTS TO RICH SOCIETY LADIES.
Heat
ESSIE SHARED HER MOTHER'S GIFT FOR MIXING POTIONS. SHE WON A SCHOLARSHIP TO STUDY CHEMISTRY AT THE UNIVERSITY OF ILLINOIS.
SHARON RUDAHL 2018

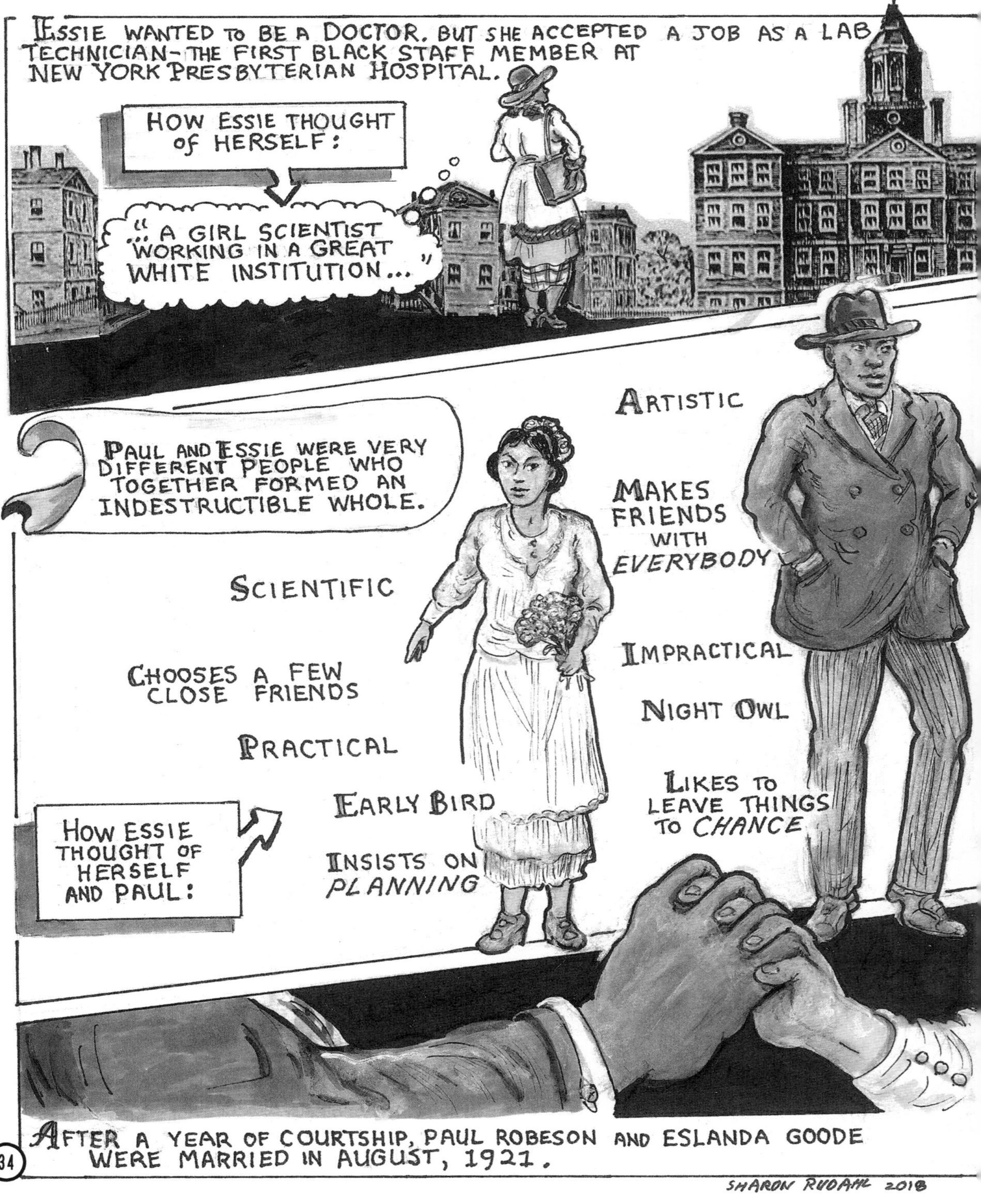
ESSIE WANTED TO BE A DOCTOR, BUT SHE ACCEPTED A JOB AS A LAB TECHNICIAN- THE FIRST BLACK STAFF MEMBER AT NEW YORK PRESBYTERIAN HOSPITAL.
HOW ESSIE THOUGHT OF HERSELF:
"... A GIRL SCIENTIST WORKING IN A GREAT WHITE INSTITUTION..."
PAUL AND ESSIE WERE VERY DIFFERENT PEOPLE WHO TOGETHER FORMED AN INDESTRUCTIBLE WHOLE.
HOW ESSIE THOUGHT OF HERSELF AND PAUL:
SCIENTIFIC
CHOOSES A FEW CLOSE FRIENDS
PRACTICAL
EARLY BIRD
INSISTS ON *PLANNING*
ARTISTIC
MAKES FRIENDS WITH *EVERYBODY*
IMPRACTICAL
NIGHT OWL
LIKES TO LEAVE THINGS TO *CHANCE*
AFTER A YEAR OF COURTSHIP, PAUL ROBESON AND ESLANDA GOODE WERE MARRIED IN AUGUST, 1921.
SHARON RUDAHL 2018

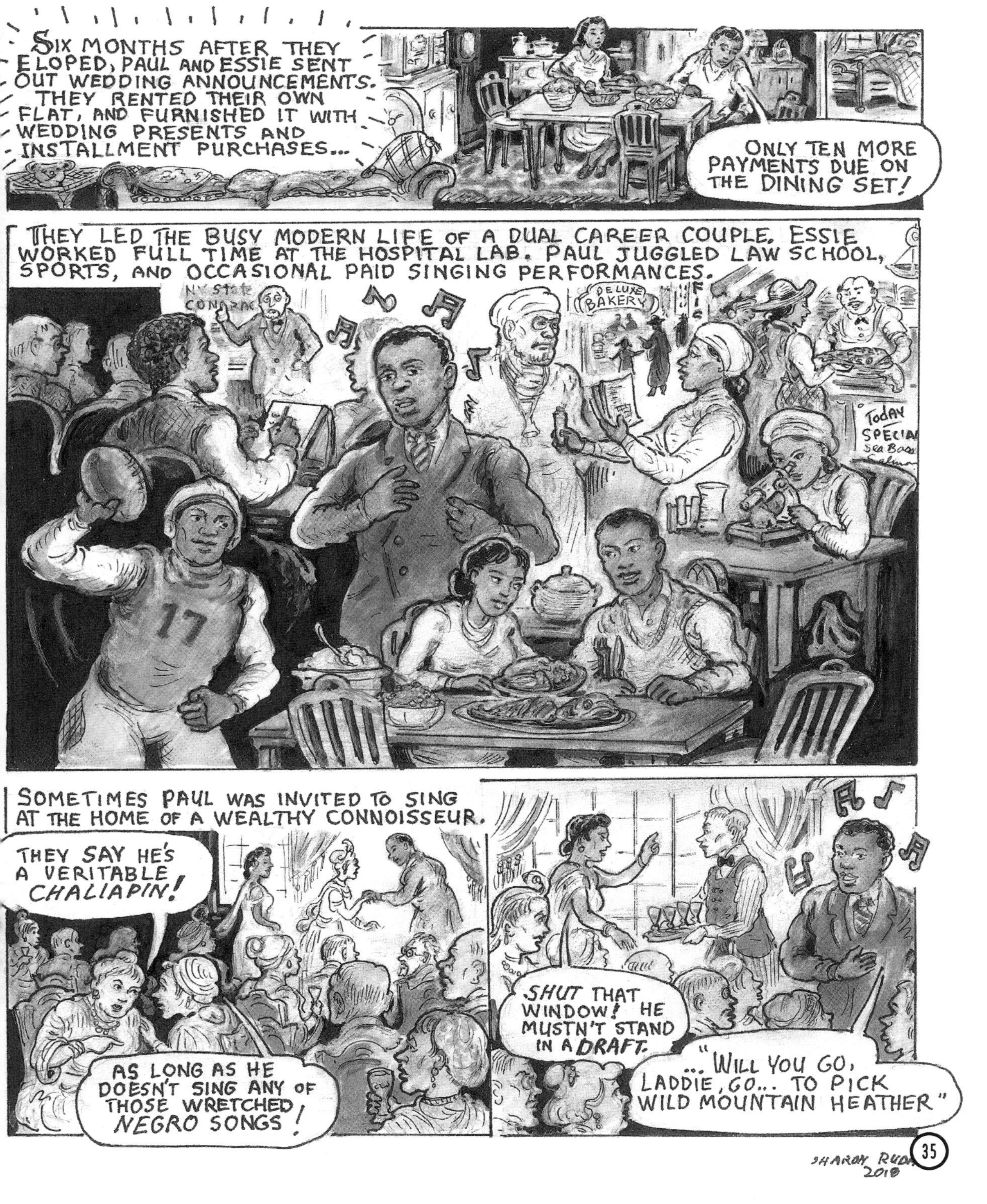

SIX MONTHS AFTER THEY ELOPED, PAUL AND ESSIE SENT OUT WEDDING ANNOUNCEMENTS. THEY RENTED THEIR OWN FLAT, AND FURNISHED IT WITH WEDDING PRESENTS AND INSTALLMENT PURCHASES...
ONLY TEN MORE PAYMENTS DUE ON THE DINING SET!
THEY LED THE BUSY MODERN LIFE OF A DUAL CAREER COUPLE. ESSIE WORKED FULL TIME AT THE HOSPITAL LAB. PAUL JUGGLED LAW SCHOOL, SPORTS, AND OCCASIONAL PAID SINGING PERFORMANCES.
DELUXE BAKERY
17
SOMETIMES PAUL WAS INVITED TO SING AT THE HOME OF A WEALTHY CONNOISSEUR.
THEY SAY HE'S A VERITABLE CHALIAPIN!
AS LONG AS HE DOESN'T SING ANY OF THOSE WRETCHED NEGRO SONGS!
SHUT THAT WINDOW! HE MUSTN'T STAND IN A DRAFT.
..."WILL YOU GO, LADDIE, GO... TO PICK WILD MOUNTAIN HEATHER"
SHARON RUDAHL 2018

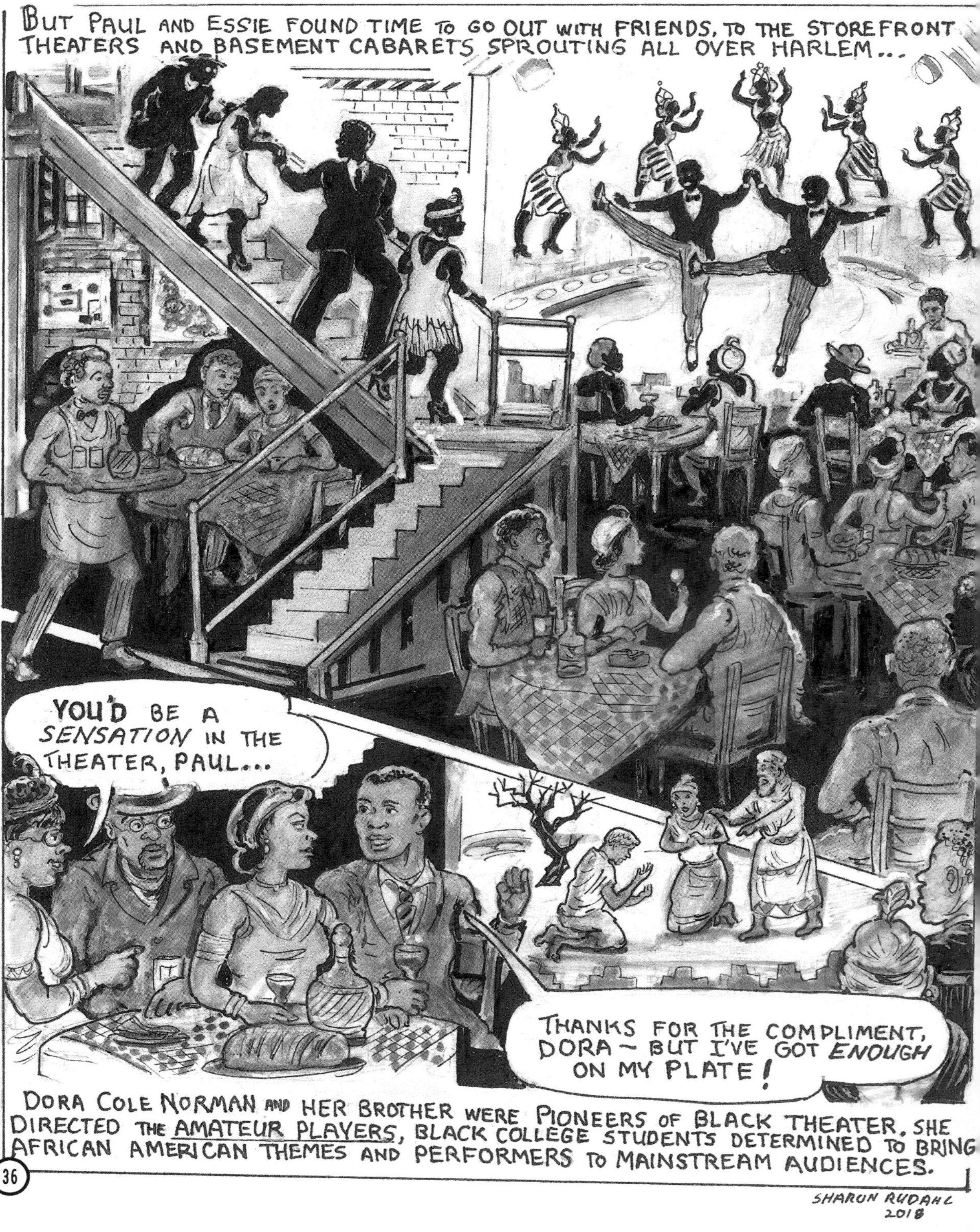
BUT PAUL AND ESSIE FOUND TIME TO GO OUT WITH FRIENDS, TO THE STOREFRONT THEATERS AND BASEMENT CABARETS SPROUTING ALL OVER HARLEM...
YOU'D BE A SENSATION IN THE THEATER, PAUL...
THANKS FOR THE COMPLIMENT, DORA – BUT I'VE GOT ENOUGH ON MY PLATE!
DORA COLE NORMAN AND HER BROTHER WERE PIONEERS OF BLACK THEATER. SHE DIRECTED THE AMATEUR PLAYERS, BLACK COLLEGE STUDENTS DETERMINED TO BRING AFRICAN AMERICAN THEMES AND PERFORMERS TO MAINSTREAM AUDIENCES.
SHARON RUDAHL 2018

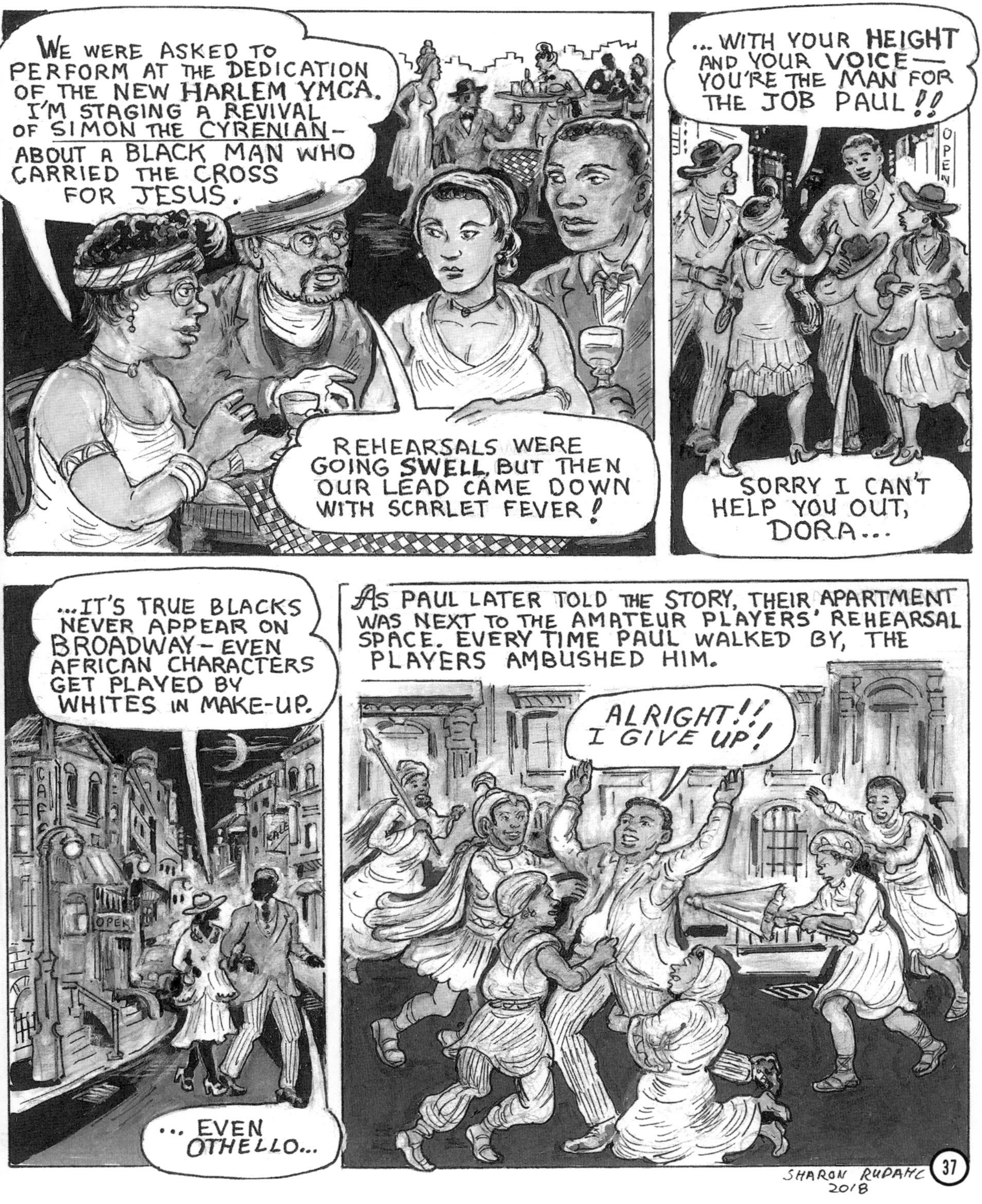
WE WERE ASKED TO PERFORM AT THE DEDICATION OF THE NEW HARLEM YMCA. I'M STAGING A REVIVAL OF SIMON THE CYRENIAN– ABOUT A BLACK MAN WHO CARRIED THE CROSS FOR JESUS.
REHEARSALS WERE GOING SWELL, BUT THEN OUR LEAD CAME DOWN WITH SCARLET FEVER!
...WITH YOUR HEIGHT AND YOUR VOICE— YOU'RE THE MAN FOR THE JOB PAUL!!
OPEN
SORRY I CAN'T HELP YOU OUT, DORA...
...IT'S TRUE BLACKS NEVER APPEAR ON BROADWAY– EVEN AFRICAN CHARACTERS GET PLAYED BY WHITES IN MAKE-UP.
CAFE
OPEN
... EVEN OTHELLO...
AS PAUL LATER TOLD THE STORY, THEIR APARTMENT WAS NEXT TO THE AMATEUR PLAYERS' REHEARSAL SPACE. EVERY TIME PAUL WALKED BY, THE PLAYERS AMBUSHED HIM.
ALRIGHT!! I GIVE UP!
SHARON RUDAHL 2018

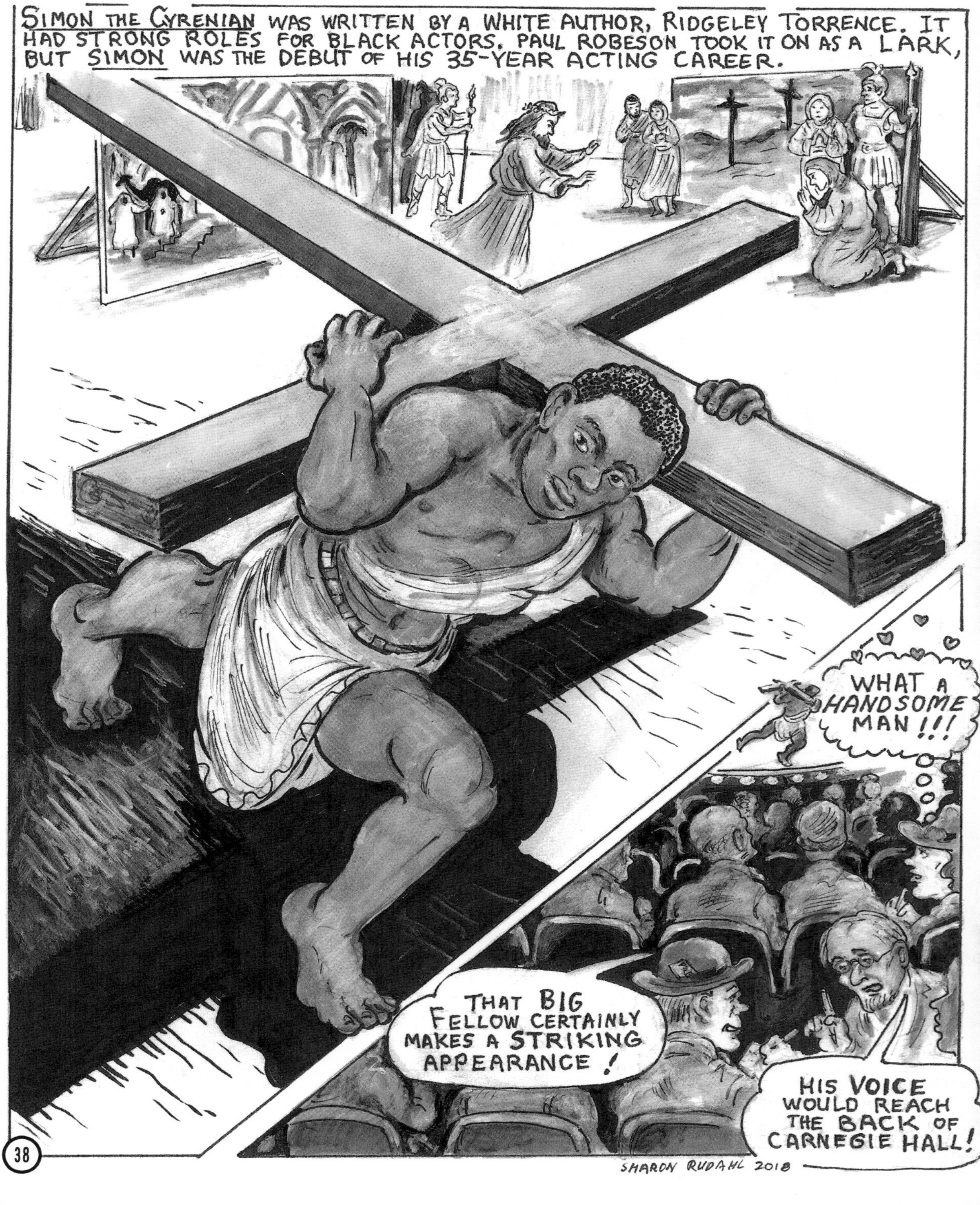
SIMON THE CYRENIAN WAS WRITTEN BY A WHITE AUTHOR, RIDGELEY TORRENCE. IT HAD STRONG ROLES FOR BLACK ACTORS. PAUL ROBESON TOOK IT ON AS A LARK, BUT SIMON WAS THE DEBUT OF HIS 35-YEAR ACTING CAREER.
WHAT A HANDSOME MAN!!!
THAT BIG FELLOW CERTAINLY MAKES A STRIKING APPEARANCE!
HIS VOICE WOULD REACH THE BACK OF CARNEGIE HALL!
SHARON RUDAHL 2018

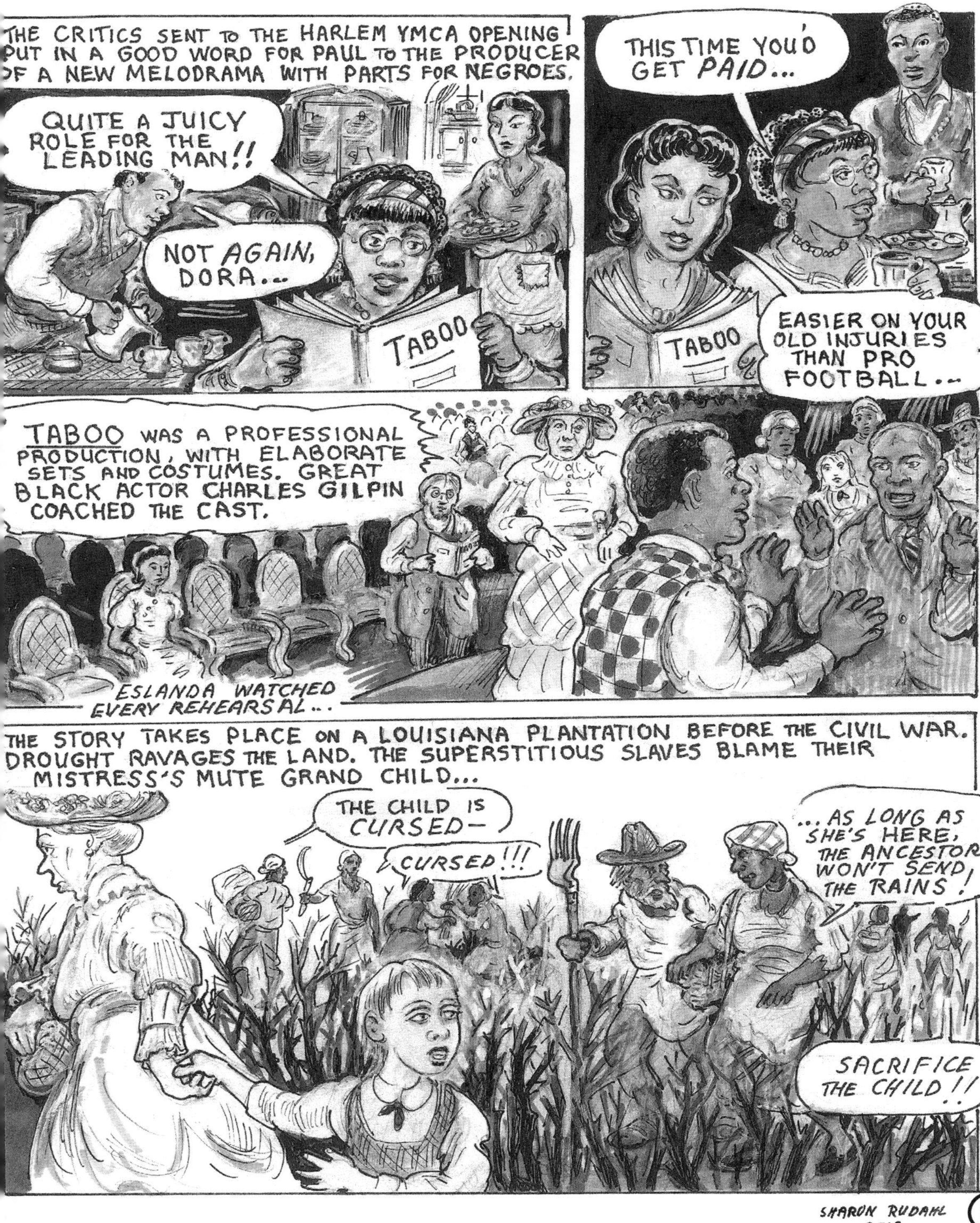
THE CRITICS SENT TO THE HARLEM YMCA OPENING PUT IN A GOOD WORD FOR PAUL TO THE PRODUCER OF A NEW MELODRAMA WITH PARTS FOR NEGROES.
QUITE A JUICY ROLE FOR THE LEADING MAN!!
NOT AGAIN, DORA...
TABOO
THIS TIME YOU'D GET PAID...
TABOO
EASIER ON YOUR OLD INJURIES THAN PRO FOOTBALL...
TABOO WAS A PROFESSIONAL PRODUCTION, WITH ELABORATE SETS AND COSTUMES. GREAT BLACK ACTOR CHARLES GILPIN COACHED THE CAST.
ESLANDA WATCHED EVERY REHEARSAL...
THE STORY TAKES PLACE ON A LOUISIANA PLANTATION BEFORE THE CIVIL WAR. DROUGHT RAVAGES THE LAND. THE SUPERSTITIOUS SLAVES BLAME THEIR MISTRESS'S MUTE GRAND CHILD...
THE CHILD IS CURSED—
CURSED!!!
...AS LONG AS SHE'S HERE, THE ANCESTORS WON'T SEND THE RAINS!
SACRIFICE THE CHILD!!
SHARON RUDAHL 2018

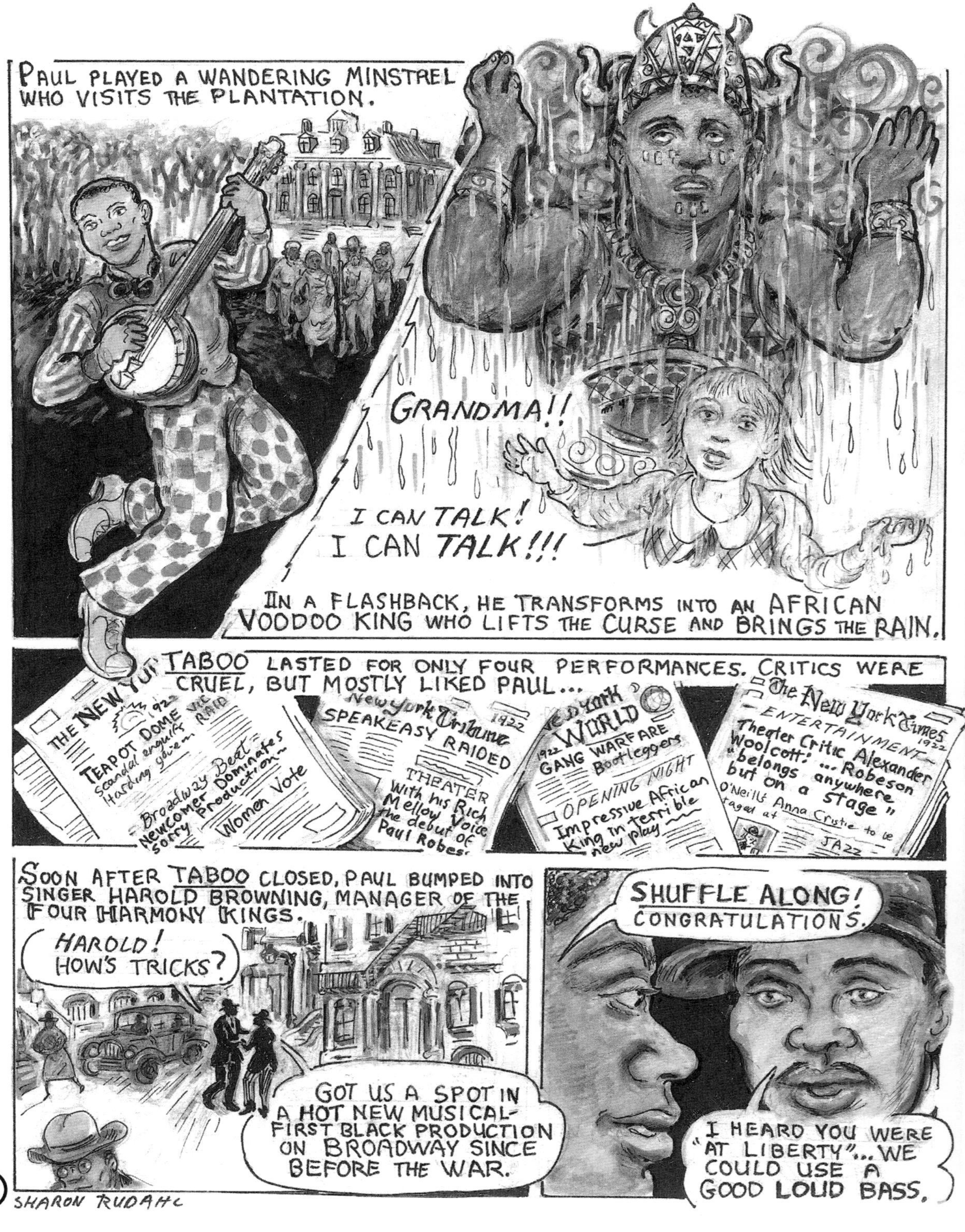
PAUL PLAYED A WANDERING MINSTREL WHO VISITS THE PLANTATION.
GRANDMA!!
I CAN TALK! I CAN TALK!!!
IN A FLASHBACK, HE TRANSFORMS INTO AN AFRICAN VOODOO KING WHO LIFTS THE CURSE AND BRINGS THE RAIN.
TABOO LASTED FOR ONLY FOUR PERFORMANCES. CRITICS WERE CRUEL, BUT MOSTLY LIKED PAUL...
THE NEW YO 1922
TEAPOT DOME scandal engulfs Harding govern
VICE RAID
Broadway Beat Newcomer Dominates sorry Production
Women Vote
New York Tribune 1922
SPEAKEASY RAIDED
THEATER With his Rich Mellow Voice the debut of Paul Robes
New York WORLD 1922
GANG WARFARE Bootleggers
OPENING NIGHT Impressive African King in terrible new play
The New York Times 1922
ENTERTAINMENT
Theater Critic Alexander Woolcott: ... Robeson "belongs anywhere but on a stage"
O'Neill's Anna Cristie to be staged at
JAZZ
SOON AFTER TABOO CLOSED, PAUL BUMPED INTO SINGER HAROLD BROWNING, MANAGER OF THE FOUR HARMONY KINGS.
HAROLD! HOW'S TRICKS?
GOT US A SPOT IN A HOT NEW MUSICAL- FIRST BLACK PRODUCTION ON BROADWAY SINCE BEFORE THE WAR.
SHUFFLE ALONG! CONGRATULATIONS.
I HEARD YOU WERE "AT LIBERTY"... WE COULD USE A GOOD LOUD BASS.

SHARON RUDAHL

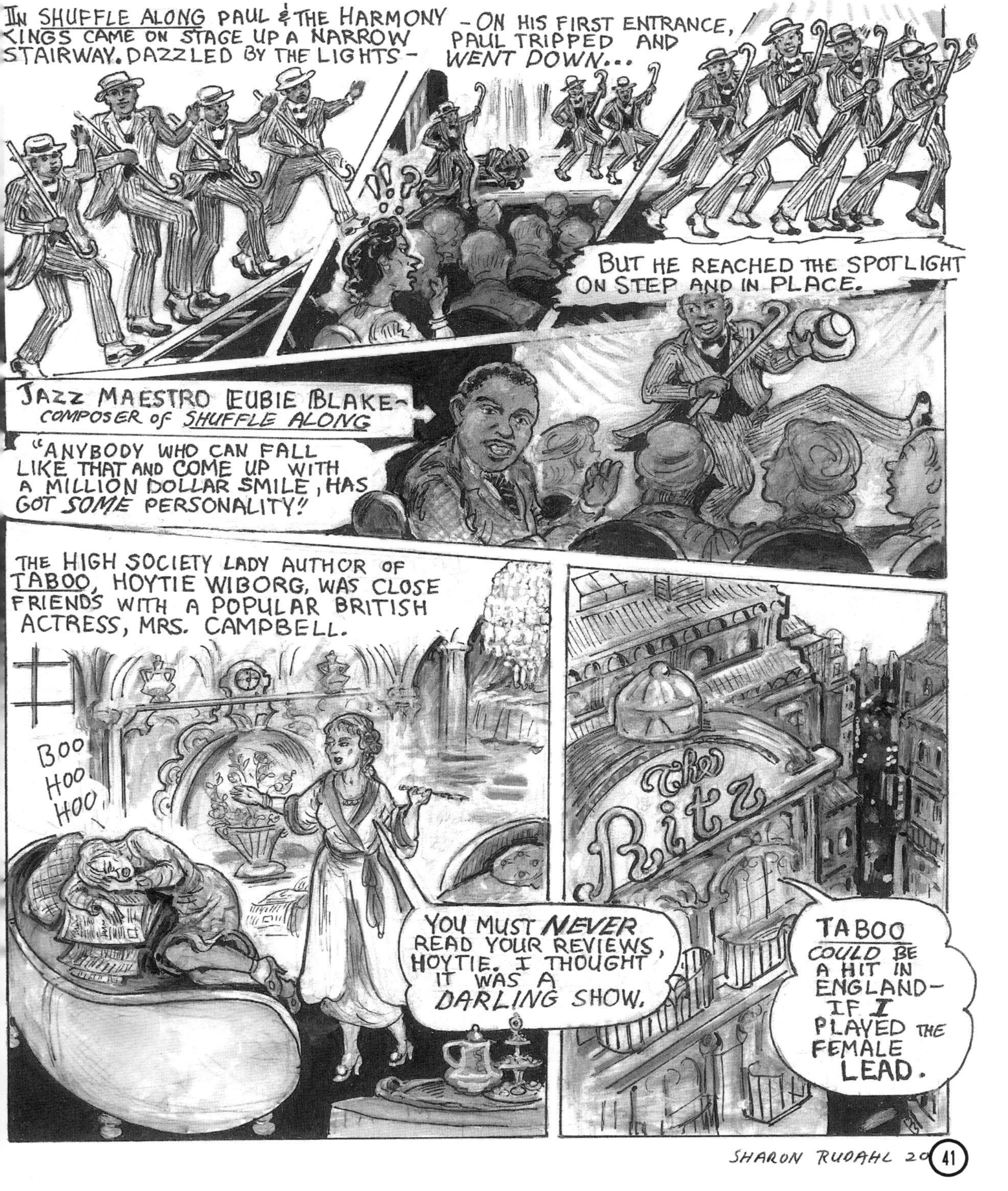
IN SHUFFLE ALONG PAUL & THE HARMONY KINGS CAME ON STAGE UP A NARROW STAIRWAY. DAZZLED BY THE LIGHTS-
-ON HIS FIRST ENTRANCE, PAUL TRIPPED AND WENT DOWN...
!!?
BUT HE REACHED THE SPOTLIGHT ON STEP AND IN PLACE.
JAZZ MAESTRO EUBIE BLAKE- COMPOSER OF SHUFFLE ALONG
"ANYBODY WHO CAN FALL LIKE THAT AND COME UP WITH A MILLION DOLLAR SMILE, HAS GOT SOME PERSONALITY!"
THE HIGH SOCIETY LADY AUTHOR OF TABOO, HOYTIE WIBORG, WAS CLOSE FRIENDS WITH A POPULAR BRITISH ACTRESS, MRS. CAMPBELL.
BOO HOO HOO
YOU MUST NEVER READ YOUR REVIEWS, HOYTIE. I THOUGHT IT WAS A DARLING SHOW.
The Ritz
TABOO COULD BE A HIT IN ENGLAND- IF I PLAYED THE FEMALE LEAD.
SHARON RUDAHL 20

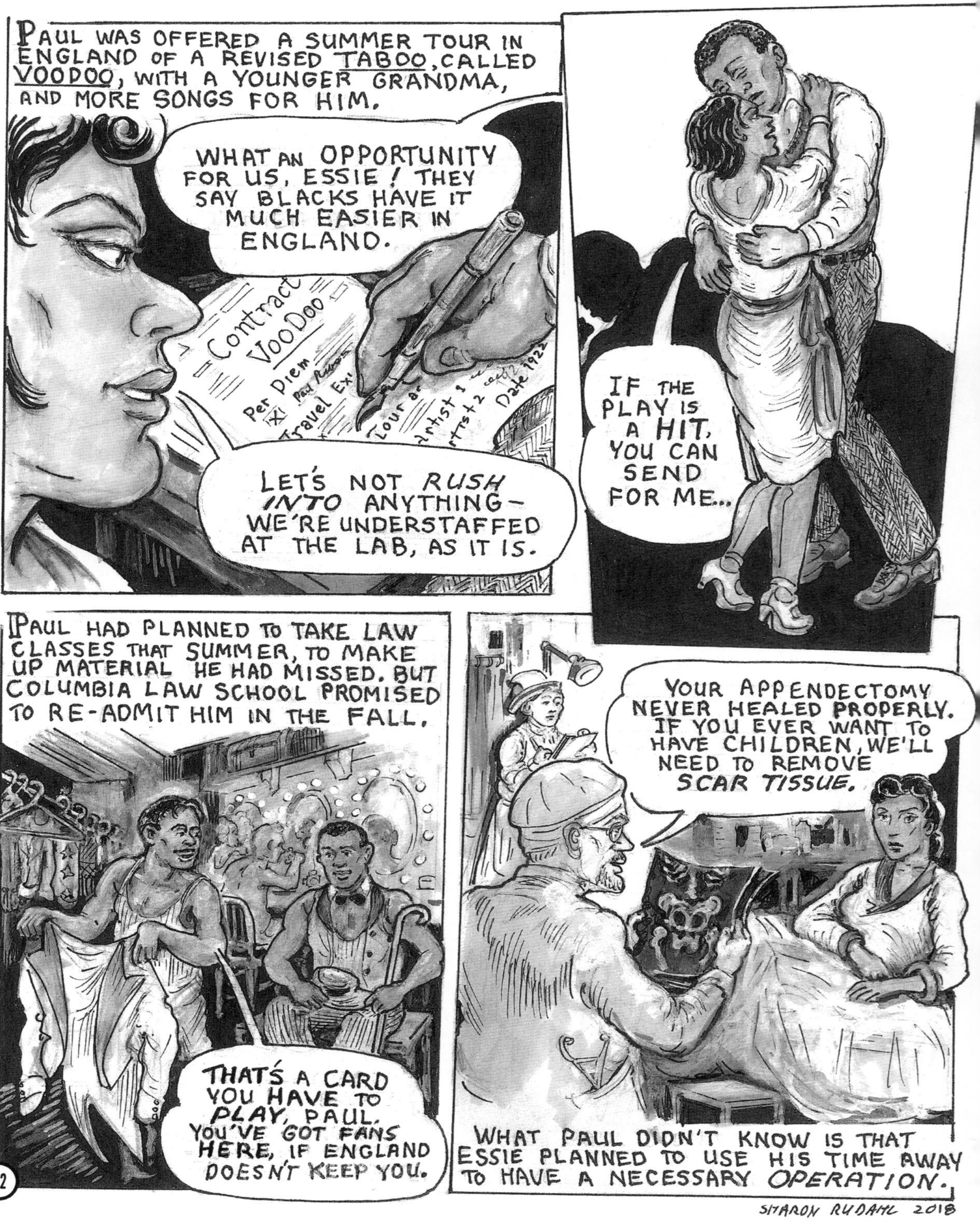
PAUL WAS OFFERED A SUMMER TOUR IN ENGLAND OF A REVISED TABOO, CALLED VOODOO, WITH A YOUNGER GRANDMA, AND MORE SONGS FOR HIM.
WHAT AN OPPORTUNITY FOR US, ESSIE! THEY SAY BLACKS HAVE IT MUCH EASIER IN ENGLAND.
Contract
VooDoo
Per Diem
Date 1922
LET'S NOT RUSH INTO ANYTHING—WE'RE UNDERSTAFFED AT THE LAB, AS IT IS.
IF THE PLAY IS A HIT, YOU CAN SEND FOR ME...
PAUL HAD PLANNED TO TAKE LAW CLASSES THAT SUMMER, TO MAKE UP MATERIAL HE HAD MISSED. BUT COLUMBIA LAW SCHOOL PROMISED TO RE-ADMIT HIM IN THE FALL.
THAT'S A CARD YOU HAVE TO PLAY, PAUL. YOU'VE GOT FANS HERE, IF ENGLAND DOESN'T KEEP YOU.
YOUR APPENDECTOMY NEVER HEALED PROPERLY. IF YOU EVER WANT TO HAVE CHILDREN, WE'LL NEED TO REMOVE SCAR TISSUE.
WHAT PAUL DIDN'T KNOW IS THAT ESSIE PLANNED TO USE HIS TIME AWAY TO HAVE A NECESSARY OPERATION.
SHARON RUDAHL 2018

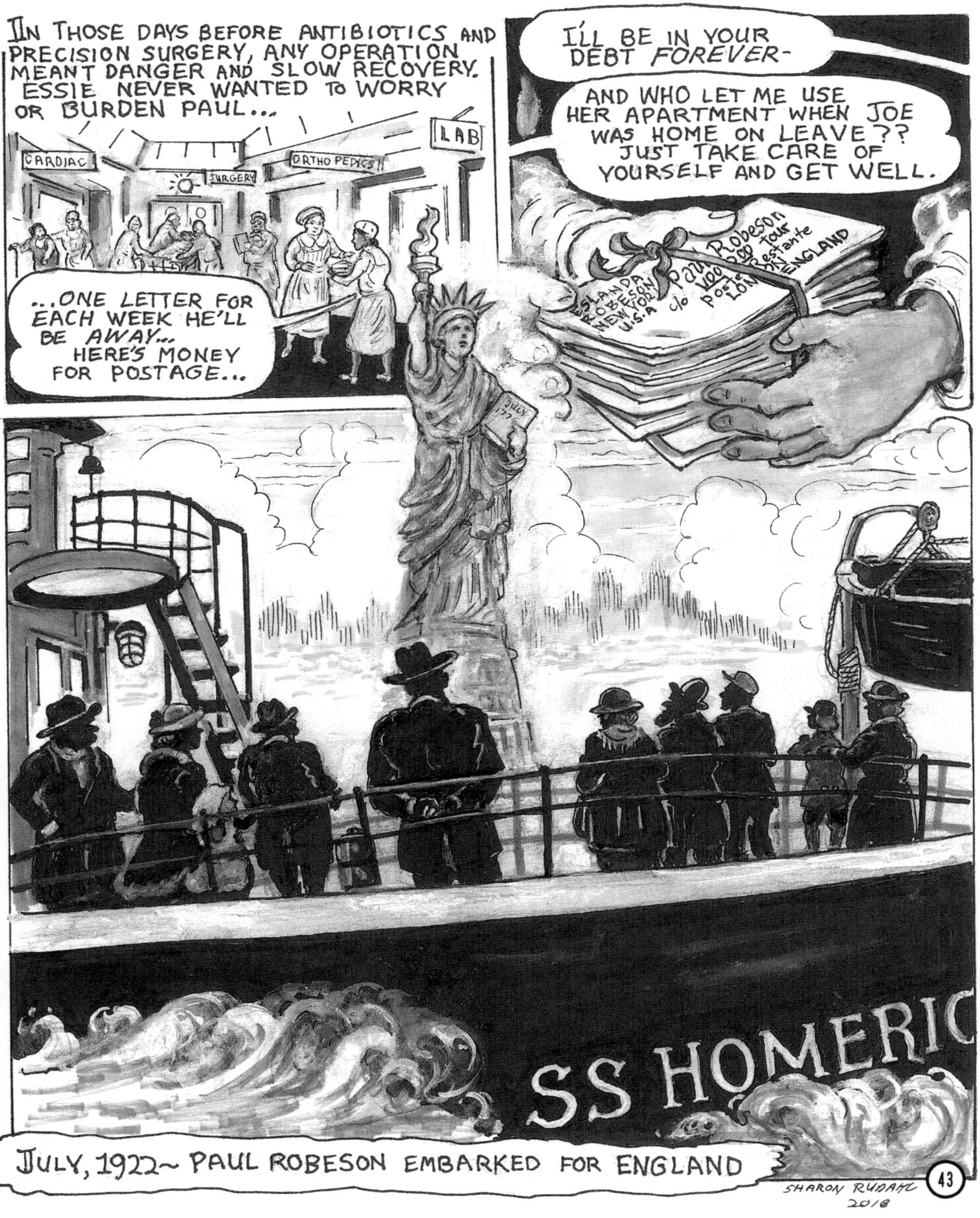

IN THOSE DAYS BEFORE ANTIBIOTICS AND PRECISION SURGERY, ANY OPERATION MEANT DANGER AND SLOW RECOVERY. ESSIE NEVER WANTED TO WORRY OR BURDEN PAUL...
LAB
CARDIAC
ORTHOPEDICS
SURGERY
...ONE LETTER FOR EACH WEEK HE'LL BE *AWAY*... HERE'S MONEY FOR POSTAGE...
I'LL BE IN YOUR DEBT *FOREVER*-
AND WHO LET ME USE HER APARTMENT WHEN JOE WAS HOME ON LEAVE?? JUST TAKE CARE OF YOURSELF AND GET WELL.
ROBESON NEW YORK U.S.A
Robeson
ENGLAND
SS HOMERIC
JULY, 1922~ PAUL ROBESON EMBARKED FOR ENGLAND
SHARON RUDAHL 2018

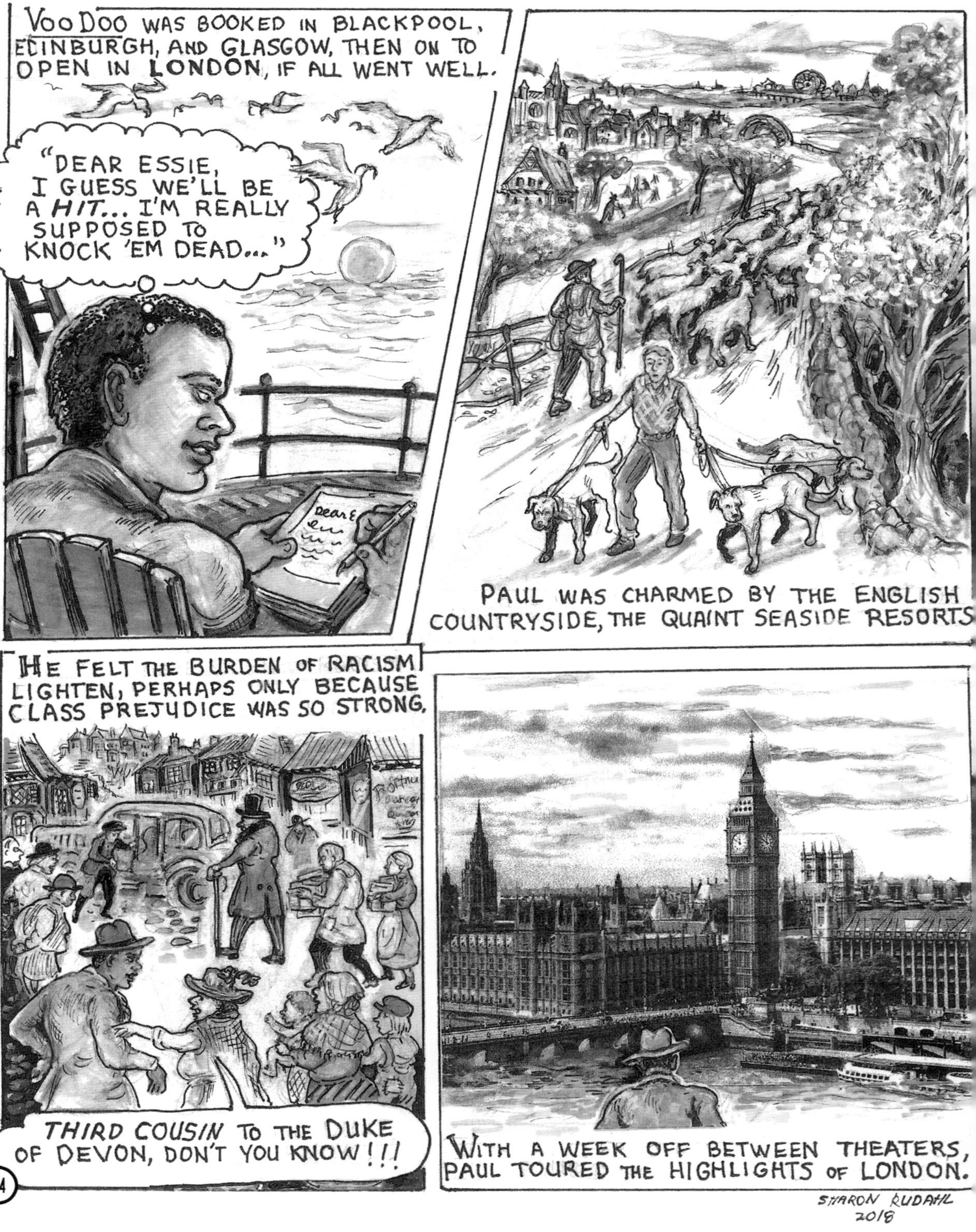
VOODOO WAS BOOKED IN BLACKPOOL, EDINBURGH, AND GLASGOW, THEN ON TO OPEN IN LONDON, IF ALL WENT WELL.
"DEAR ESSIE, I GUESS WE'LL BE A *HIT*... I'M REALLY SUPPOSED TO KNOCK 'EM DEAD..."
Dear E
PAUL WAS CHARMED BY THE ENGLISH COUNTRYSIDE, THE QUAINT SEASIDE RESORTS
HE FELT THE BURDEN OF RACISM LIGHTEN, PERHAPS ONLY BECAUSE CLASS PREJUDICE WAS SO STRONG.
THIRD COUSIN TO THE DUKE OF DEVON, DON'T YOU KNOW!!!
WITH A WEEK OFF BETWEEN THEATERS, PAUL TOURED THE HIGHLIGHTS OF LONDON.
SHARON RUDAHL 2018

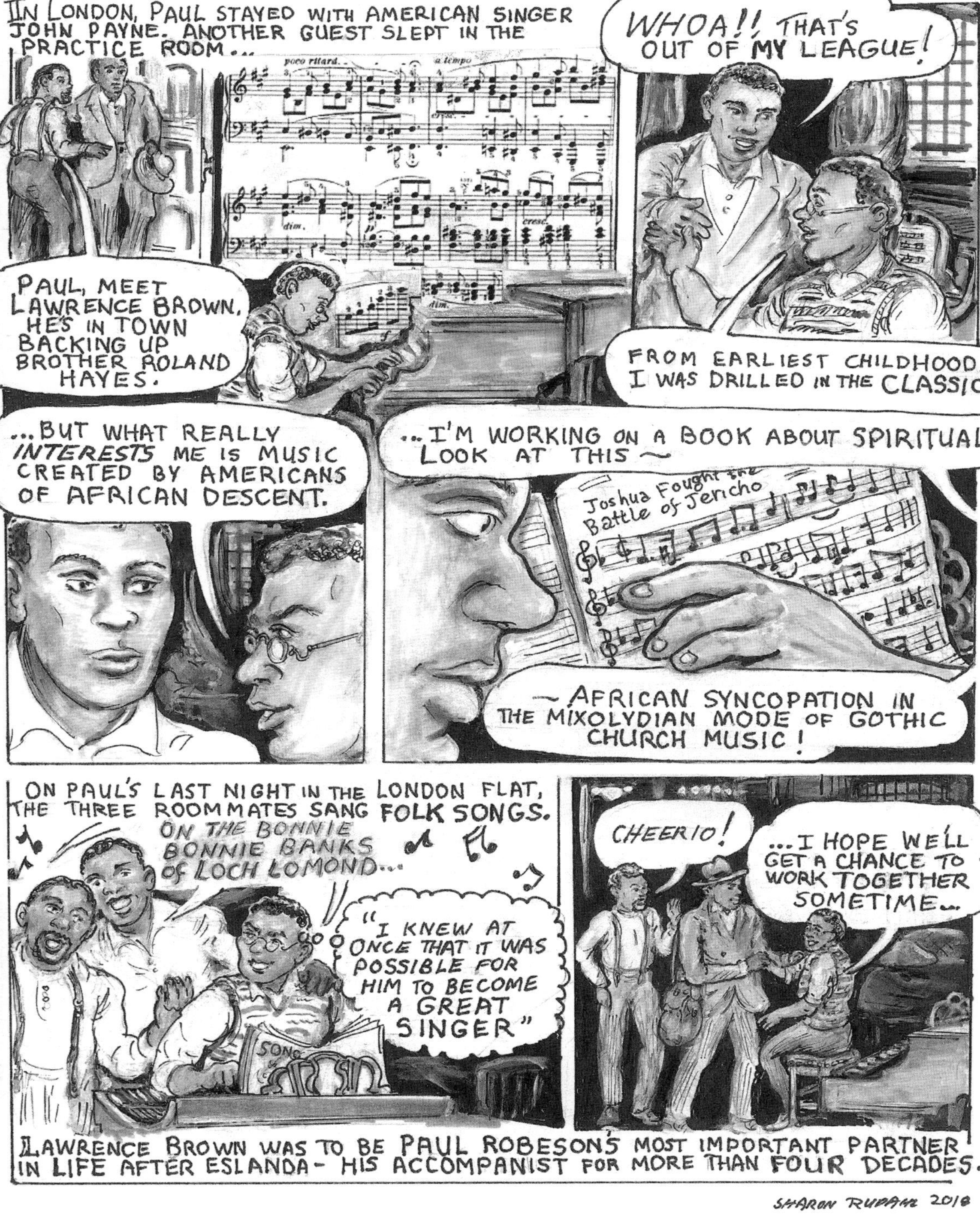
IN LONDON, PAUL STAYED WITH AMERICAN SINGER JOHN PAYNE. ANOTHER GUEST SLEPT IN THE PRACTICE ROOM...
PAUL, MEET LAWRENCE BROWN. HE'S IN TOWN BACKING UP BROTHER ROLAND HAYES.
WHOA!! THAT'S OUT OF MY LEAGUE!
FROM EARLIEST CHILDHOOD, I WAS DRILLED IN THE CLASSICS...
...BUT WHAT REALLY INTERESTS ME IS MUSIC CREATED BY AMERICANS OF AFRICAN DESCENT.
...I'M WORKING ON A BOOK ABOUT SPIRITUALS. LOOK AT THIS~
Joshua Fought the Battle of Jericho
~AFRICAN SYNCOPATION IN THE MIXOLYDIAN MODE OF GOTHIC CHURCH MUSIC!
ON PAUL'S LAST NIGHT IN THE LONDON FLAT, THE THREE ROOMMATES SANG FOLK SONGS.
ON THE BONNIE BONNIE BANKS OF LOCH LOMOND...
"I KNEW AT ONCE THAT IT WAS POSSIBLE FOR HIM TO BECOME A GREAT SINGER"
CHEERIO!
...I HOPE WE'LL GET A CHANCE TO WORK TOGETHER SOMETIME...
LAWRENCE BROWN WAS TO BE PAUL ROBESON'S MOST IMPORTANT PARTNER IN LIFE AFTER ESLANDA- HIS ACCOMPANIST FOR MORE THAN FOUR DECADES.
SHARON RUDAHL 2018

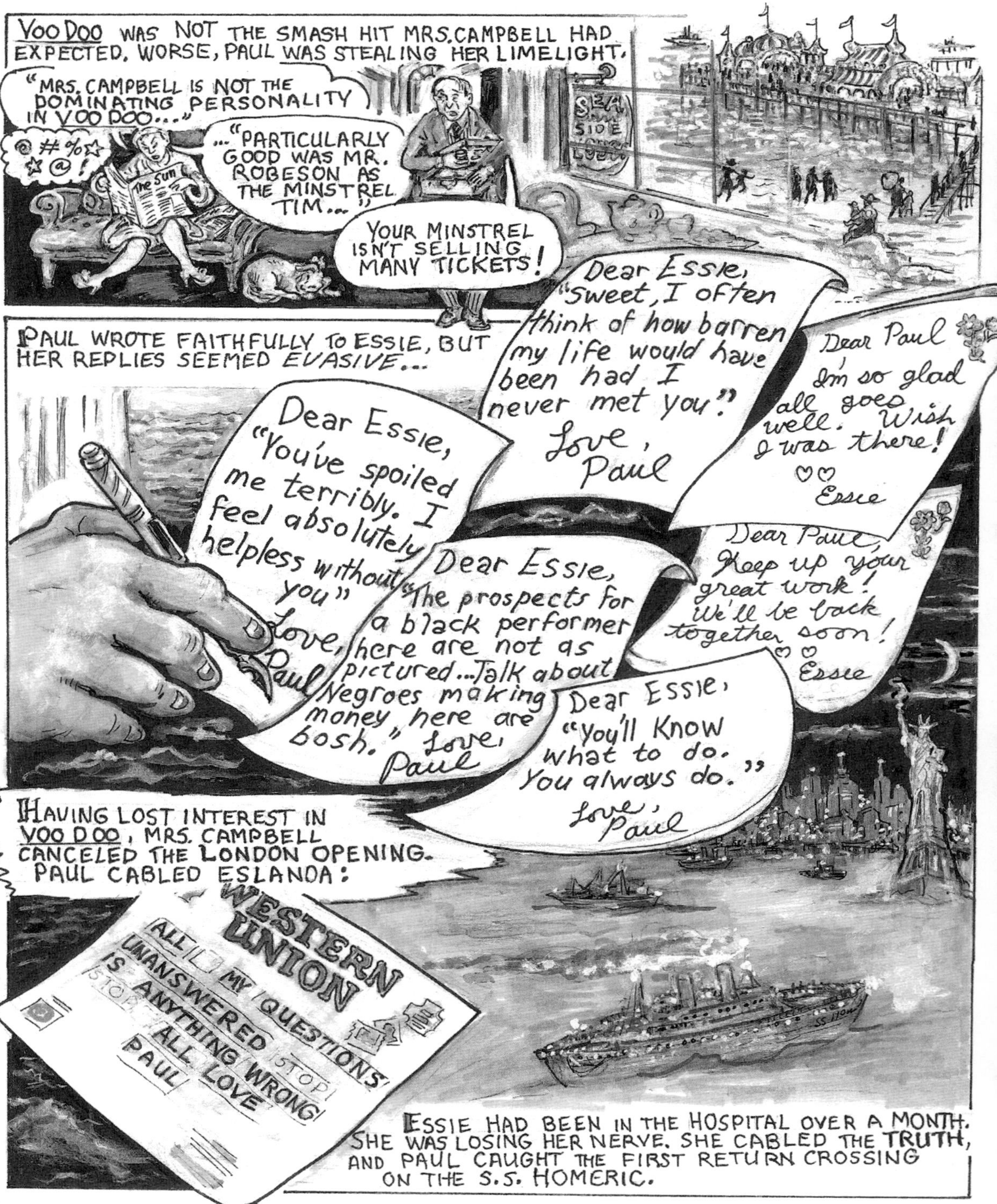
VOO DOO WAS NOT THE SMASH HIT MRS. CAMPBELL HAD EXPECTED. WORSE, PAUL WAS STEALING HER LIMELIGHT.
"MRS. CAMPBELL IS NOT THE DOMINATING PERSONALITY IN VOO DOO..."
@#%☆ ☆@!
THE SUN
..."PARTICULARLY GOOD WAS MR. ROBESON AS THE MINSTREL TIM..."
YOUR MINSTREL ISN'T SELLING MANY TICKETS!
SEA SIDE
PAUL WROTE FAITHFULLY TO ESSIE, BUT HER REPLIES SEEMED EVASIVE...
Dear Essie, "Sweet, I often think of how barren my life would have been had I never met you." Love, Paul
Dear Paul I'm so glad all goes well. Wish I was there! Essie
Dear Essie, "You've spoiled me terribly. I feel absolutely helpless without you" Love, Paul
Dear Essie, "The prospects for a black performer here are not as pictured...Talk about Negroes making money here are bosh." Love, Paul
Dear Paul, Keep up your great work! We'll be back together soon! Essie
Dear Essie, "You'll know what to do. You always do." Love, Paul
HAVING LOST INTEREST IN VOO DOO, MRS. CAMPBELL CANCELED THE LONDON OPENING. PAUL CABLED ESLANDA:
WESTERN UNION
ALL MY QUESTIONS UNANSWERED STOP IS ANYTHING WRONG STOP ALL LOVE PAUL
ESSIE HAD BEEN IN THE HOSPITAL OVER A MONTH. SHE WAS LOSING HER NERVE. SHE CABLED THE TRUTH, AND PAUL CAUGHT THE FIRST RETURN CROSSING ON THE S.S. HOMERIC.

SHARON RUDAHL 2018

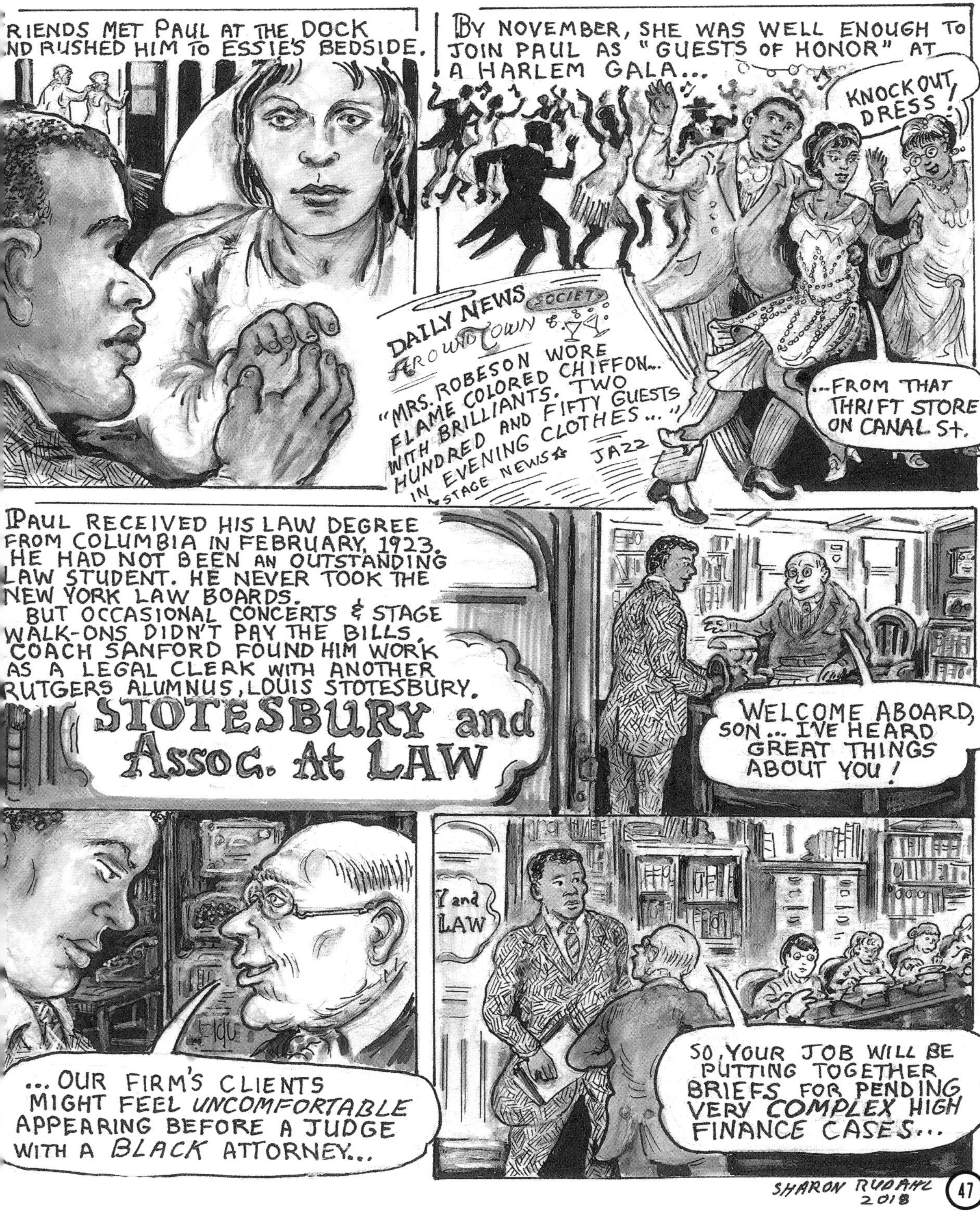

RIENDS MET PAUL AT THE DOCK
ND RUSHED HIM TO ESSIE'S BEDSIDE.
BY NOVEMBER, SHE WAS WELL ENOUGH TO JOIN PAUL AS "GUESTS OF HONOR" AT A HARLEM GALA...
KNOCKOUT DRESS!
DAILY NEWS SOCIETY
AROUND TOWN
"MRS. ROBESON WORE FLAME COLORED CHIFFON... WITH BRILLIANTS. TWO HUNDRED AND FIFTY GUESTS IN EVENING CLOTHES..."
STAGE NEWS
JAZZ
...FROM THAT THRIFT STORE ON CANAL St.
PAUL RECEIVED HIS LAW DEGREE FROM COLUMBIA IN FEBRUARY, 1923. HE HAD NOT BEEN AN OUTSTANDING LAW STUDENT. HE NEVER TOOK THE NEW YORK LAW BOARDS.
BUT OCCASIONAL CONCERTS & STAGE WALK-ONS DIDN'T PAY THE BILLS. COACH SANFORD FOUND HIM WORK AS A LEGAL CLERK WITH ANOTHER RUTGERS ALUMNUS, LOUIS STOTESBURY.
STOTESBURY and Assoc. At LAW
WELCOME ABOARD, SON... I'VE HEARD GREAT THINGS ABOUT YOU!
...OUR FIRM'S CLIENTS MIGHT FEEL UNCOMFORTABLE APPEARING BEFORE A JUDGE WITH A BLACK ATTORNEY...
Y and LAW
SO, YOUR JOB WILL BE PUTTING TOGETHER BRIEFS FOR PENDING VERY COMPLEX HIGH FINANCE CASES...
SHARON RUDAHL 2018

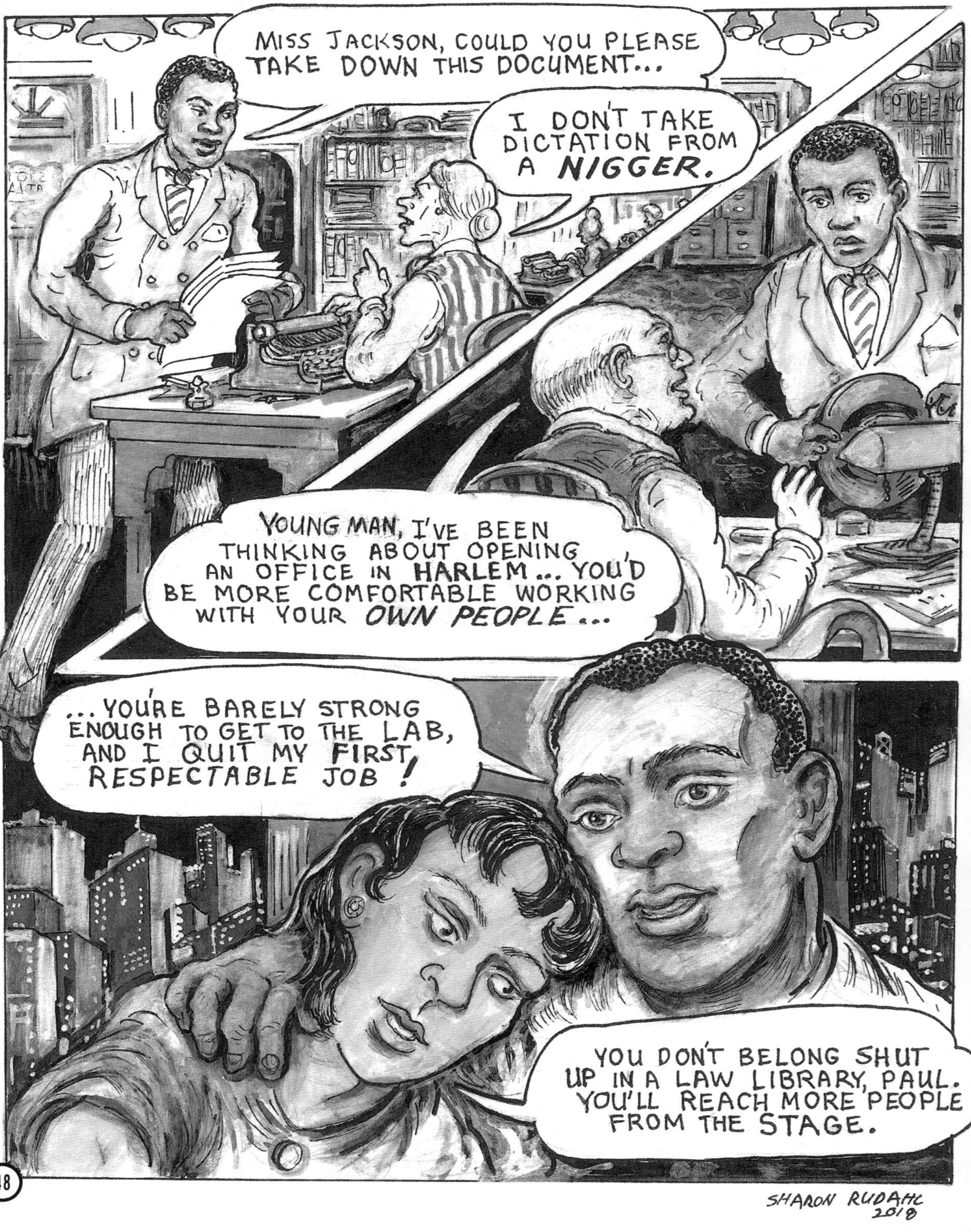
MISS JACKSON, COULD YOU PLEASE TAKE DOWN THIS DOCUMENT...
I DON'T TAKE DICTATION FROM A NIGGER.
YOUNG MAN, I'VE BEEN THINKING ABOUT OPENING AN OFFICE IN HARLEM... YOU'D BE MORE COMFORTABLE WORKING WITH YOUR OWN PEOPLE...
...YOU'RE BARELY STRONG ENOUGH TO GET TO THE LAB, AND I QUIT MY FIRST, RESPECTABLE JOB!
YOU DON'T BELONG SHUT UP IN A LAW LIBRARY, PAUL. YOU'LL REACH MORE PEOPLE FROM THE STAGE.
SHARON RUDAHL 2018

CHAPTER III

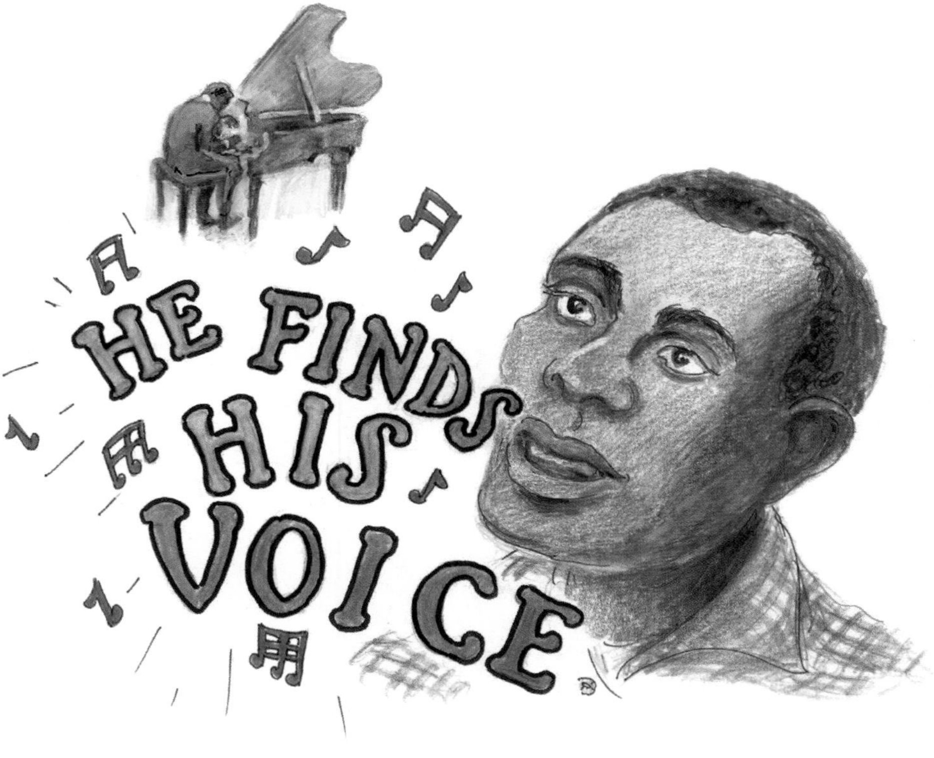
HE FINDS HIS VOICE

SHARON RUDAHL 2019

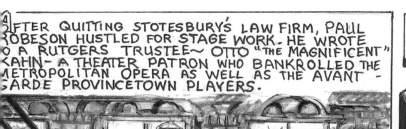

AFTER QUITTING STOTESBURY'S LAW FIRM, PAUL ROBESON HUSTLED FOR STAGE WORK. HE WROTE TO A RUTGERS TRUSTEE~ OTTO "THE MAGNIFICENT" KAHN- A THEATER PATRON WHO BANKROLLED THE METROPOLITAN OPERA AS WELL AS THE AVANT-GARDE PROVINCETOWN PLAYERS.

EUGENE O'NEILL 1888 ~ 1953

RESPECTED U.S. PLAYWRIGHT~ WINNER NOBEL AND PULITZER PRIZES

"I AM VERY ANXIOUS TO GET BEFORE ANY MANAGERS AND AGENTS WHO MIGHT HAVE NEGRO ROLES"

IN HIS LETTER TO KAHN, ROBESON CITED EUGENE O'NEILL'S THE EMPEROR JONES AS A PLAY THAT MIGHT EMPLOY HIM.

WHEN I WRITE 'NIGGER', I DON'T WANT YOU TO KEEP CHANGING IT TO 'NEGRO'!

JUST WHEN PAUL HAD GIVEN UP ON HEARING BACK FROM OTTO KAHN, HE RECEIVED A LETTER FROM THE PROVINCETOWN PLAYERS.

THEN YOU'LL HAVE TO FIND ANOTHER NEGRO TO READ YOUR LINES...

...THEY WANT ME TO AUDITION FOR A NEW EUGENE O'NEILL PLAY~ ALL GOD'S CHILLUN GOT WINGS...

CHARLES GILPIN, WHO COACHED PAUL FOR TABOO, WAS A SENSATION AS BRUTUS THE EMPEROR IN THE ORIGINAL 1920 PRODUCTION. BUT GILPIN AND O'NEILL HAD A FALLING OUT.

SHARON RUDAHL 2010

51

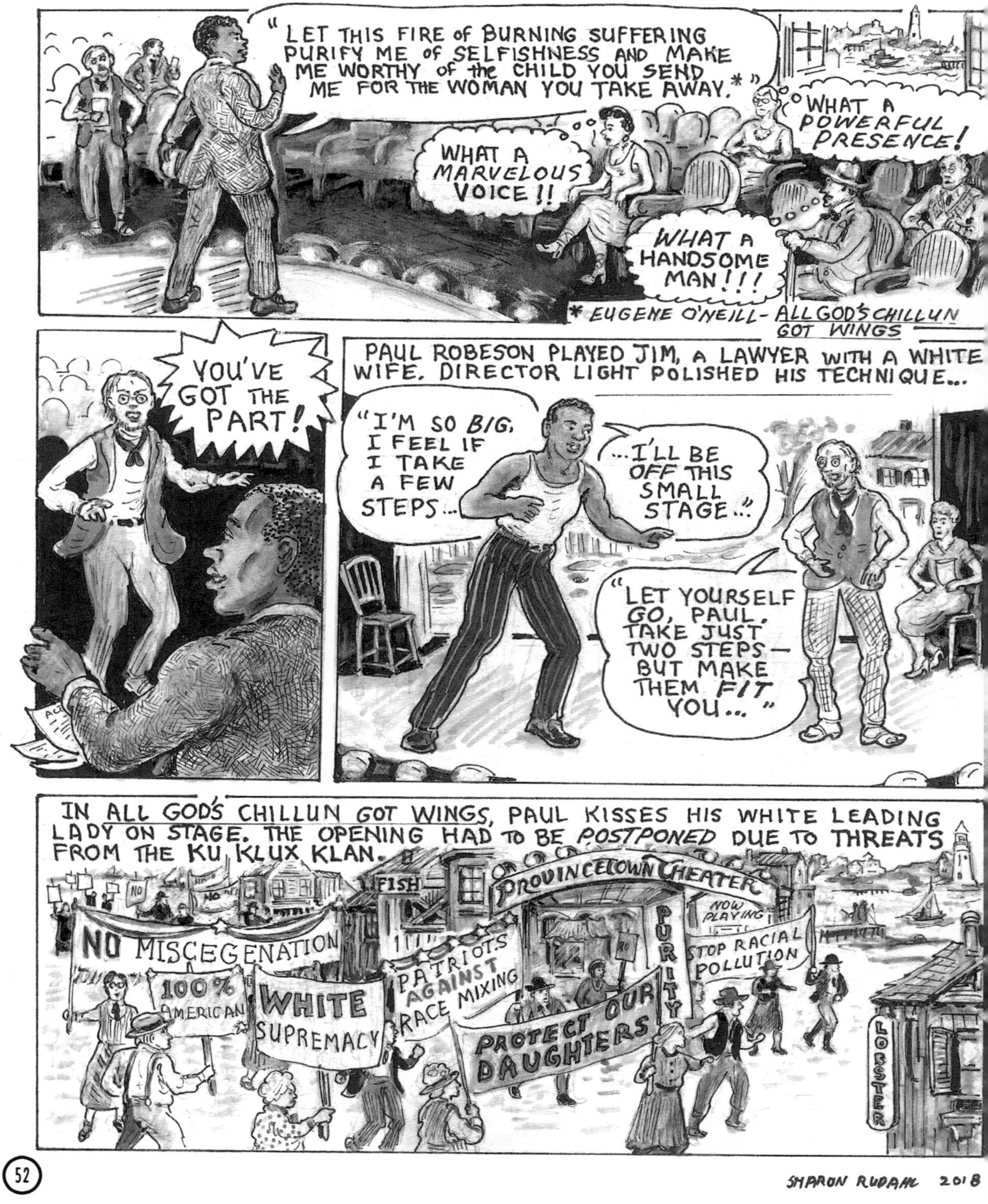
"LET THIS FIRE OF BURNING SUFFERING PURIFY ME OF SELFISHNESS AND MAKE ME WORTHY OF THE CHILD YOU SEND ME FOR THE WOMAN YOU TAKE AWAY.*"
WHAT A MARVELOUS VOICE!!
WHAT A POWERFUL PRESENCE!
WHAT A HANDSOME MAN!!!
* EUGENE O'NEILL - ALL GOD'S CHILLUN GOT WINGS
YOU'VE GOT THE PART!
PAUL ROBESON PLAYED JIM, A LAWYER WITH A WHITE WIFE. DIRECTOR LIGHT POLISHED HIS TECHNIQUE...
"I'M SO BIG, I FEEL IF I TAKE A FEW STEPS...
...I'LL BE OFF THIS SMALL STAGE..."
"LET YOURSELF GO, PAUL, TAKE JUST TWO STEPS— BUT MAKE THEM FIT YOU..."
IN ALL GOD'S CHILLUN GOT WINGS, PAUL KISSES HIS WHITE LEADING LADY ON STAGE. THE OPENING HAD TO BE POSTPONED DUE TO THREATS FROM THE KU KLUX KLAN.
FISH
PROVINCETOWN THEATER
NOW PLAYING
NO MISCEGENATION
100% AMERICAN
WHITE SUPREMACY
PATRIOTS AGAINST RACE MIXING
PROTECT OUR DAUGHTERS
PURITY
STOP RACIAL POLLUTION
LOBSTER
SHARON RUDAHL 2018

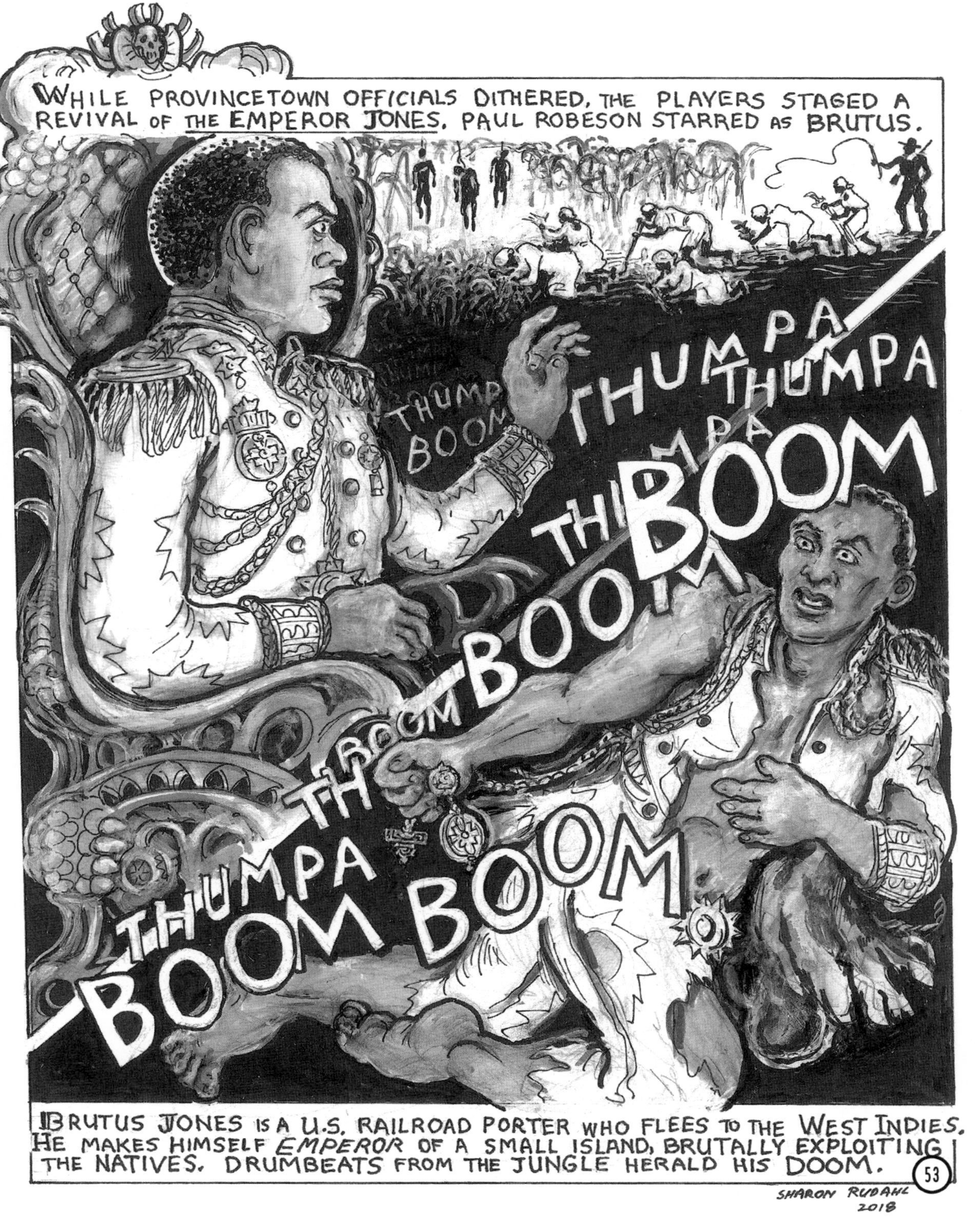
WHILE PROVINCETOWN OFFICIALS DITHERED, THE PLAYERS STAGED A REVIVAL OF THE EMPEROR JONES. PAUL ROBESON STARRED AS BRUTUS.
THUMP BOOM
THUMPA THUMPA
BOOM
BOOM
THUMPA
BOOM BOOM
BRUTUS JONES IS A U.S. RAILROAD PORTER WHO FLEES TO THE WEST INDIES. HE MAKES HIMSELF EMPEROR OF A SMALL ISLAND, BRUTALLY EXPLOITING THE NATIVES. DRUMBEATS FROM THE JUNGLE HERALD HIS DOOM.
SHARON RUDAHL 2018

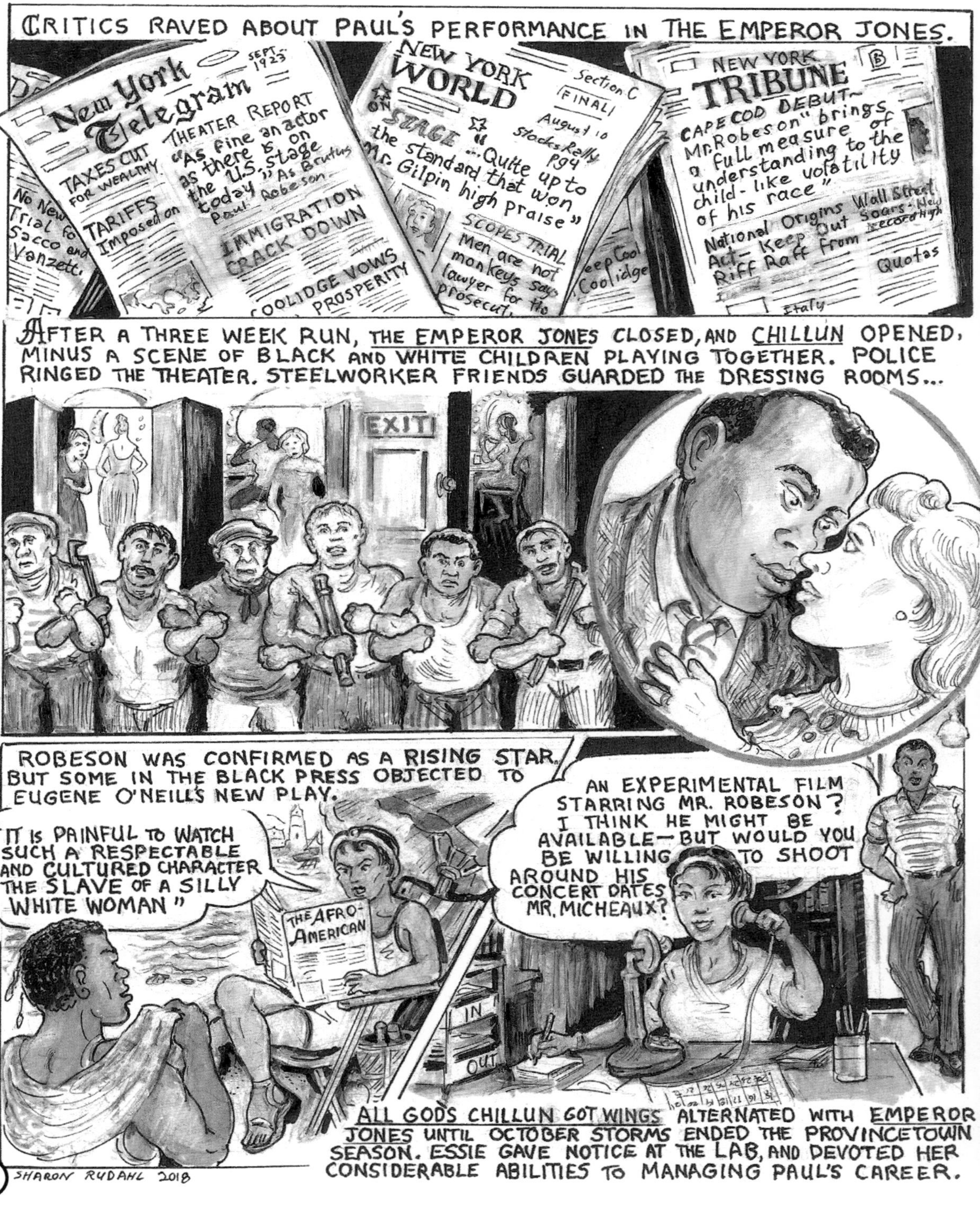

CRITICS RAVED ABOUT PAUL'S PERFORMANCE IN THE EMPEROR JONES.
New York Telegram
SEPT. 1923
THEATER REPORT
"As fine an actor as there is on the U.S. stage today" As Brutus Paul Robeson
TAXES CUT FOR WEALTHY
TARIFFS Imposed on
IMMIGRATION CRACK DOWN
COOLIDGE VOWS PROSPERITY
No New Trial for Sacco and Vanzetti
NEW YORK WORLD
Section C
FINAL
August 10
Stocks Rally Pg 4
ON STAGE
"...Quite up to the standard that won Mr. Gilpin high praise"
SCOPES TRIAL
Men are not monkeys says lawyer for the prosecut...
Keep Cool Coolidge
NEW YORK TRIBUNE
CAPE COD DEBUT—
Mr. Robeson" brings a full measure of understanding to the child-like volatility of his race"
National Origins Act — Keep Out Riff Raff from
Wall Street Soars - New record High
Quotas
Italy
AFTER A THREE WEEK RUN, THE EMPEROR JONES CLOSED, AND CHILLUN OPENED, MINUS A SCENE OF BLACK AND WHITE CHILDREN PLAYING TOGETHER. POLICE RINGED THE THEATER. STEELWORKER FRIENDS GUARDED THE DRESSING ROOMS...
EXIT
ROBESON WAS CONFIRMED AS A RISING STAR. BUT SOME IN THE BLACK PRESS OBJECTED TO EUGENE O'NEILL'S NEW PLAY.
"IT IS PAINFUL TO WATCH SUCH A RESPECTABLE AND CULTURED CHARACTER THE SLAVE OF A SILLY WHITE WOMAN"
THE AFRO-AMERICAN
AN EXPERIMENTAL FILM STARRING MR. ROBESON? I THINK HE MIGHT BE AVAILABLE— BUT WOULD YOU BE WILLING TO SHOOT AROUND HIS CONCERT DATES MR. MICHEAUX?
IN
OUT
ALL GOD'S CHILLUN GOT WINGS ALTERNATED WITH EMPEROR JONES UNTIL OCTOBER STORMS ENDED THE PROVINCETOWN SEASON. ESSIE GAVE NOTICE AT THE LAB, AND DEVOTED HER CONSIDERABLE ABILITIES TO MANAGING PAUL'S CAREER.
SHARON RUDAHL 2018

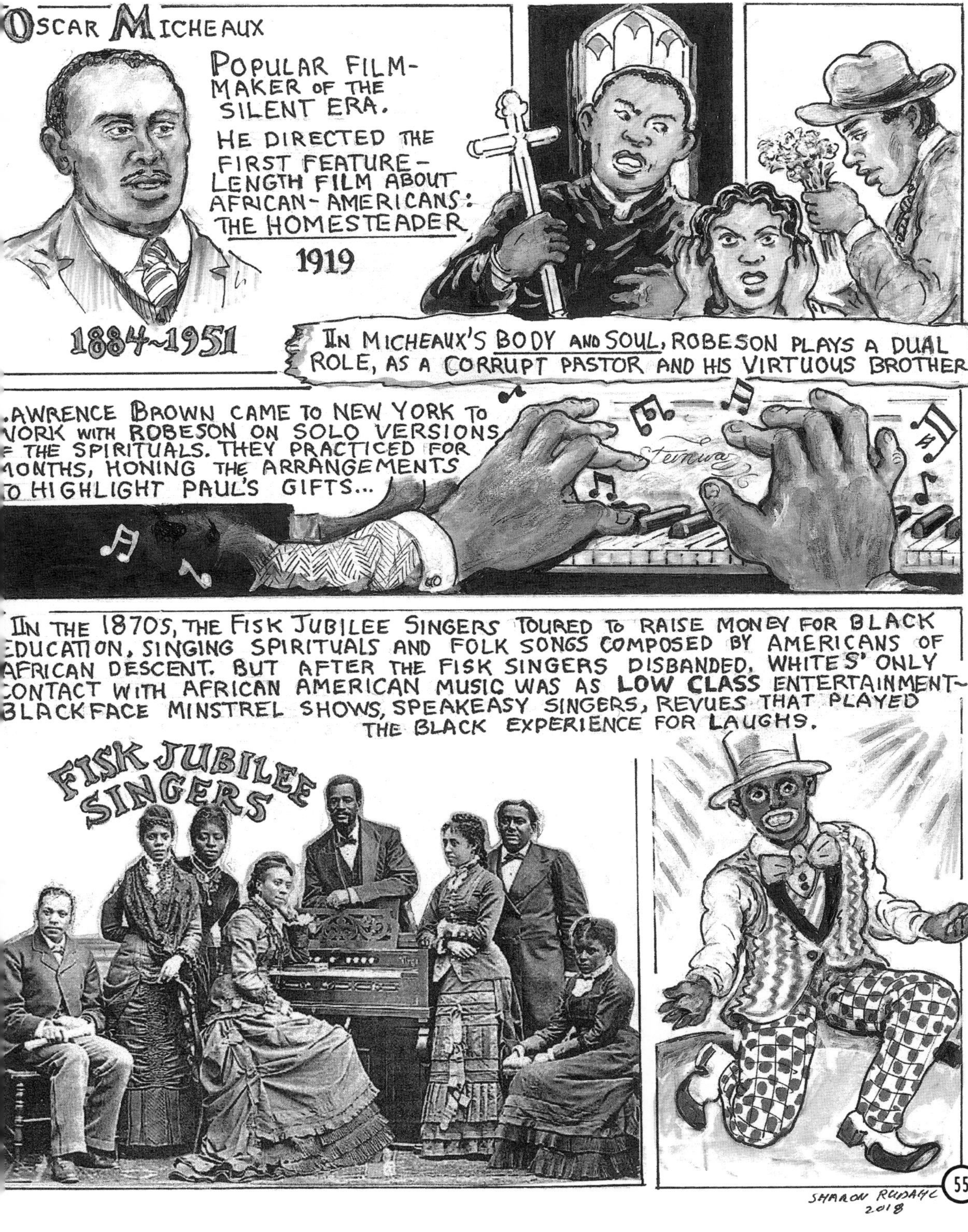
OSCAR MICHEAUX
POPULAR FILM-MAKER OF THE SILENT ERA.
HE DIRECTED THE FIRST FEATURE-LENGTH FILM ABOUT AFRICAN-AMERICANS: THE HOMESTEADER
1919
1884~1951
IN MICHEAUX'S BODY AND SOUL, ROBESON PLAYS A DUAL ROLE, AS A CORRUPT PASTOR AND HIS VIRTUOUS BROTHER.
AWRENCE BROWN CAME TO NEW YORK TO VORK WITH ROBESON ON SOLO VERSIONS F THE SPIRITUALS. THEY PRACTICED FOR MONTHS, HONING THE ARRANGEMENTS O HIGHLIGHT PAUL'S GIFTS...
Steinway
IN THE 1870S, THE FISK JUBILEE SINGERS TOURED TO RAISE MONEY FOR BLACK EDUCATION, SINGING SPIRITUALS AND FOLK SONGS COMPOSED BY AMERICANS OF AFRICAN DESCENT. BUT AFTER THE FISK SINGERS DISBANDED, WHITES' ONLY CONTACT WITH AFRICAN AMERICAN MUSIC WAS AS LOW CLASS ENTERTAINMENT– BLACKFACE MINSTREL SHOWS, SPEAKEASY SINGERS, REVUES THAT PLAYED THE BLACK EXPERIENCE FOR LAUGHS.
FISK JUBILEE SINGERS
SHARON RUDAHL 2018

PAUL ROBESON GAVE HIS FIRST SOLO CONCERT OF SPIRITUALS AT COPLEY PLAZA IN BOSTON, NOVEMBER 1924. HE WORE AN ELEGANT TUXEDO. UNDER A SINGLE CONCENTRATED LIGHT, "SONGS OF SORROW" OF THE AFRICAN DIASPORA WERE PRESENTED WITH THE DIGNITY OF EUROPEAN ART SONGS.

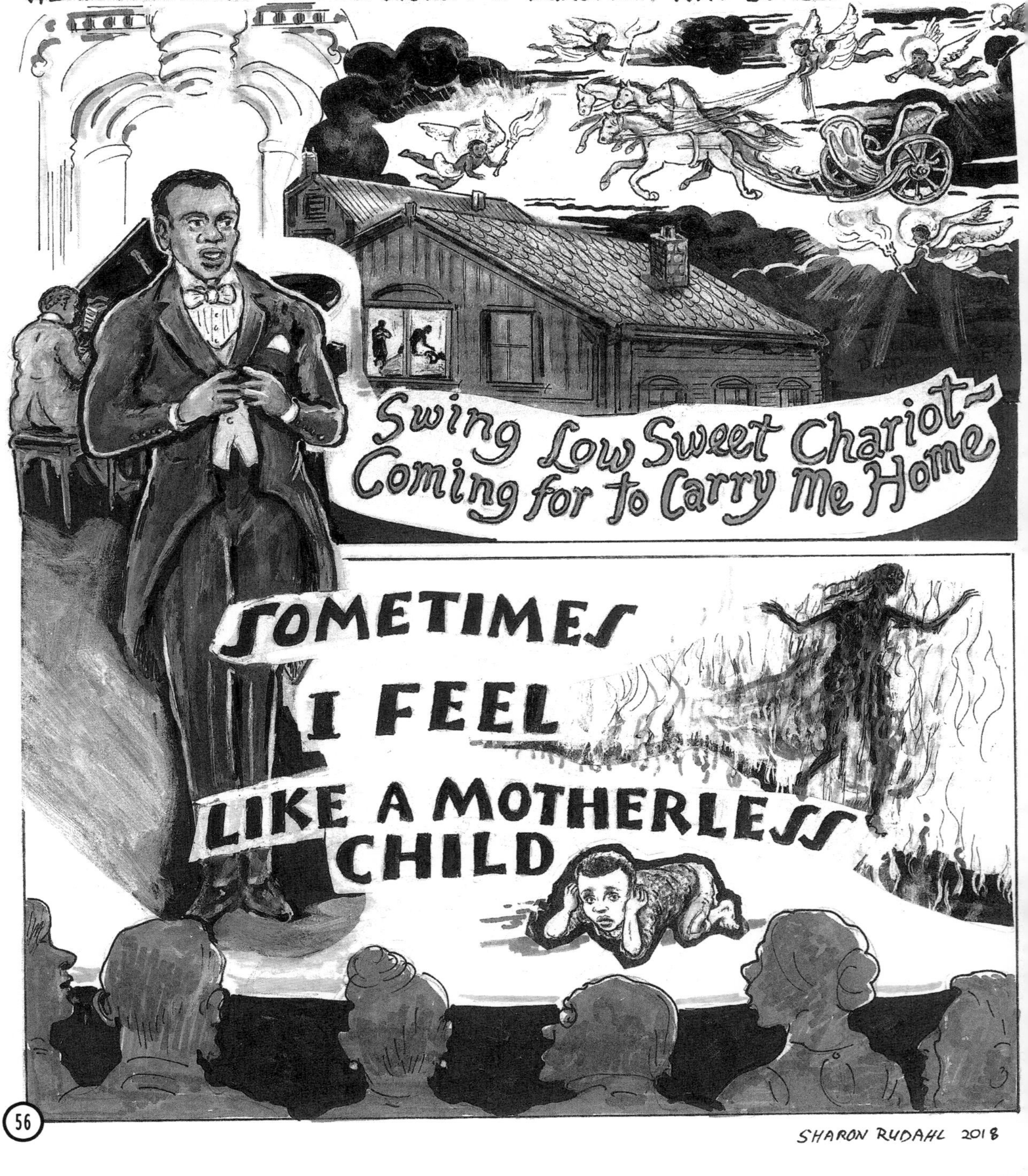

Swing Low Sweet Chariot–
Coming for to Carry Me Home
SOMETIMES
I FEEL
LIKE A MOTHERLESS
CHILD

SHARON RUDAHL 2018

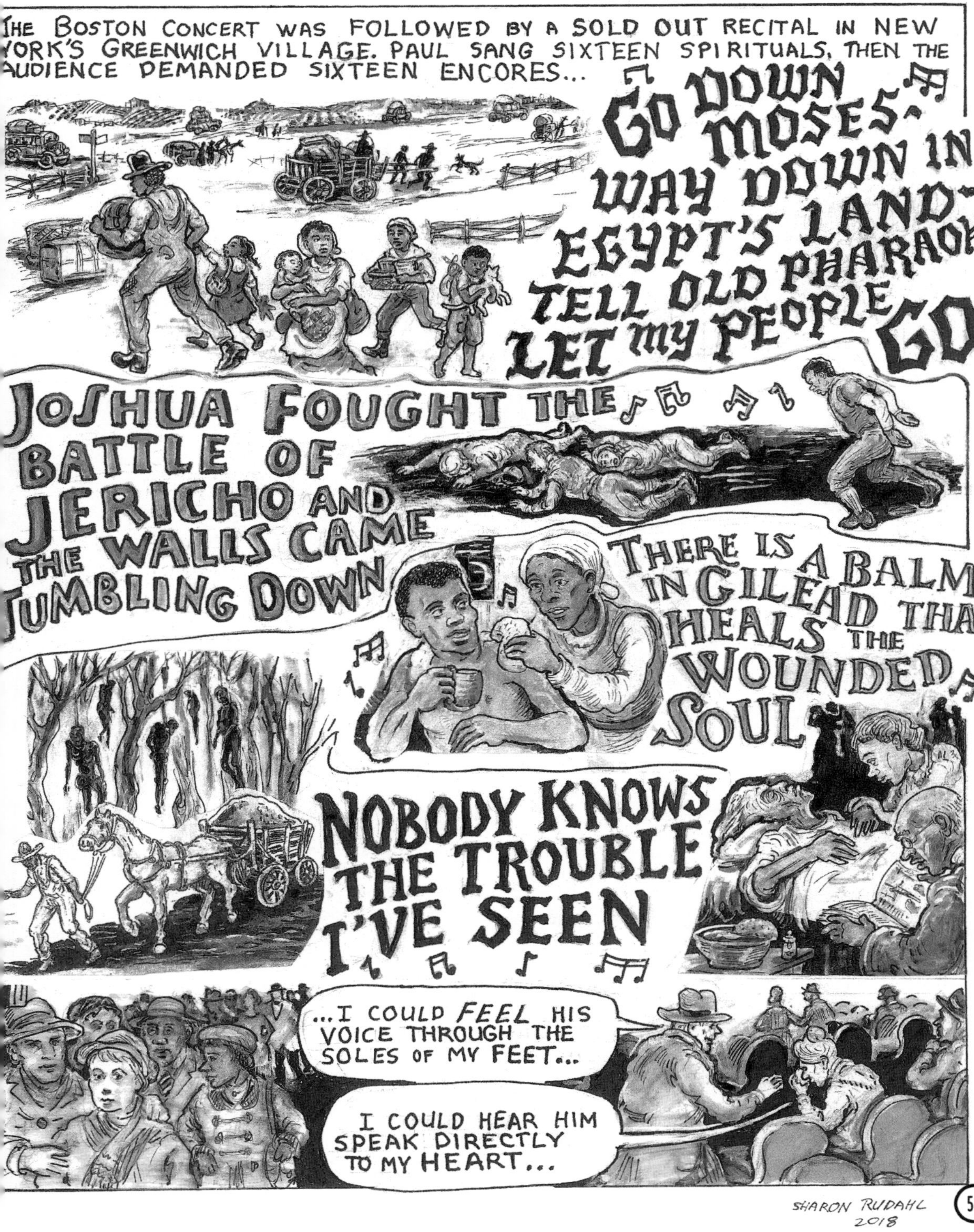
THE BOSTON CONCERT WAS FOLLOWED BY A SOLD OUT RECITAL IN NEW YORK'S GREENWICH VILLAGE. PAUL SANG SIXTEEN SPIRITUALS, THEN THE AUDIENCE DEMANDED SIXTEEN ENCORES...
GO DOWN MOSES- WAY DOWN IN EGYPT'S LAND- TELL OLD PHARAOH LET MY PEOPLE GO
JOSHUA FOUGHT THE BATTLE OF JERICHO AND THE WALLS CAME TUMBLING DOWN
THERE IS A BALM IN GILEAD THAT HEALS THE WOUNDED SOUL
NOBODY KNOWS THE TROUBLE I'VE SEEN
...I COULD FEEL HIS VOICE THROUGH THE SOLES OF MY FEET...
I COULD HEAR HIM SPEAK DIRECTLY TO MY HEART...
SHARON RUDAHL 2018

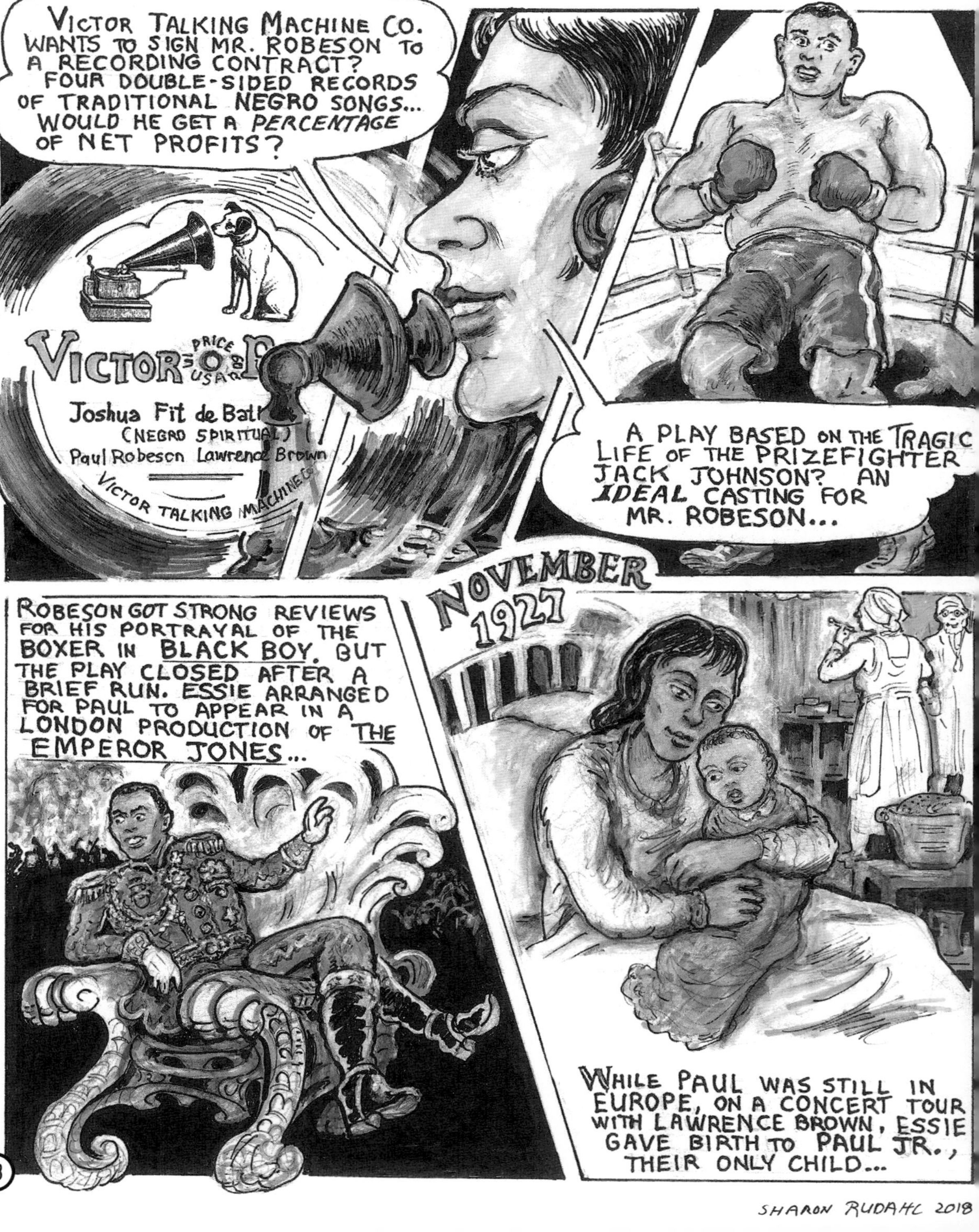
VICTOR TALKING MACHINE CO. WANTS TO SIGN MR. ROBESON TO A RECORDING CONTRACT? FOUR DOUBLE-SIDED RECORDS OF TRADITIONAL NEGRO SONGS... WOULD HE GET A *PERCENTAGE* OF NET PROFITS?
VICTOR
PRICE
USA
Joshua Fit de Batt
(NEGRO SPIRITUAL)
Paul Robeson Lawrence Brown
VICTOR TALKING MACHINE CO.
A PLAY BASED ON THE TRAGIC LIFE OF THE PRIZEFIGHTER JACK JOHNSON? AN *IDEAL* CASTING FOR MR. ROBESON...
ROBESON GOT STRONG REVIEWS FOR HIS PORTRAYAL OF THE BOXER IN BLACK BOY. BUT THE PLAY CLOSED AFTER A BRIEF RUN. ESSIE ARRANGED FOR PAUL TO APPEAR IN A LONDON PRODUCTION OF THE EMPEROR JONES...
NOVEMBER 1927
WHILE PAUL WAS STILL IN EUROPE, ON A CONCERT TOUR WITH LAWRENCE BROWN, ESSIE GAVE BIRTH TO PAUL JR., THEIR ONLY CHILD...
SHARON RUDAHL 2018

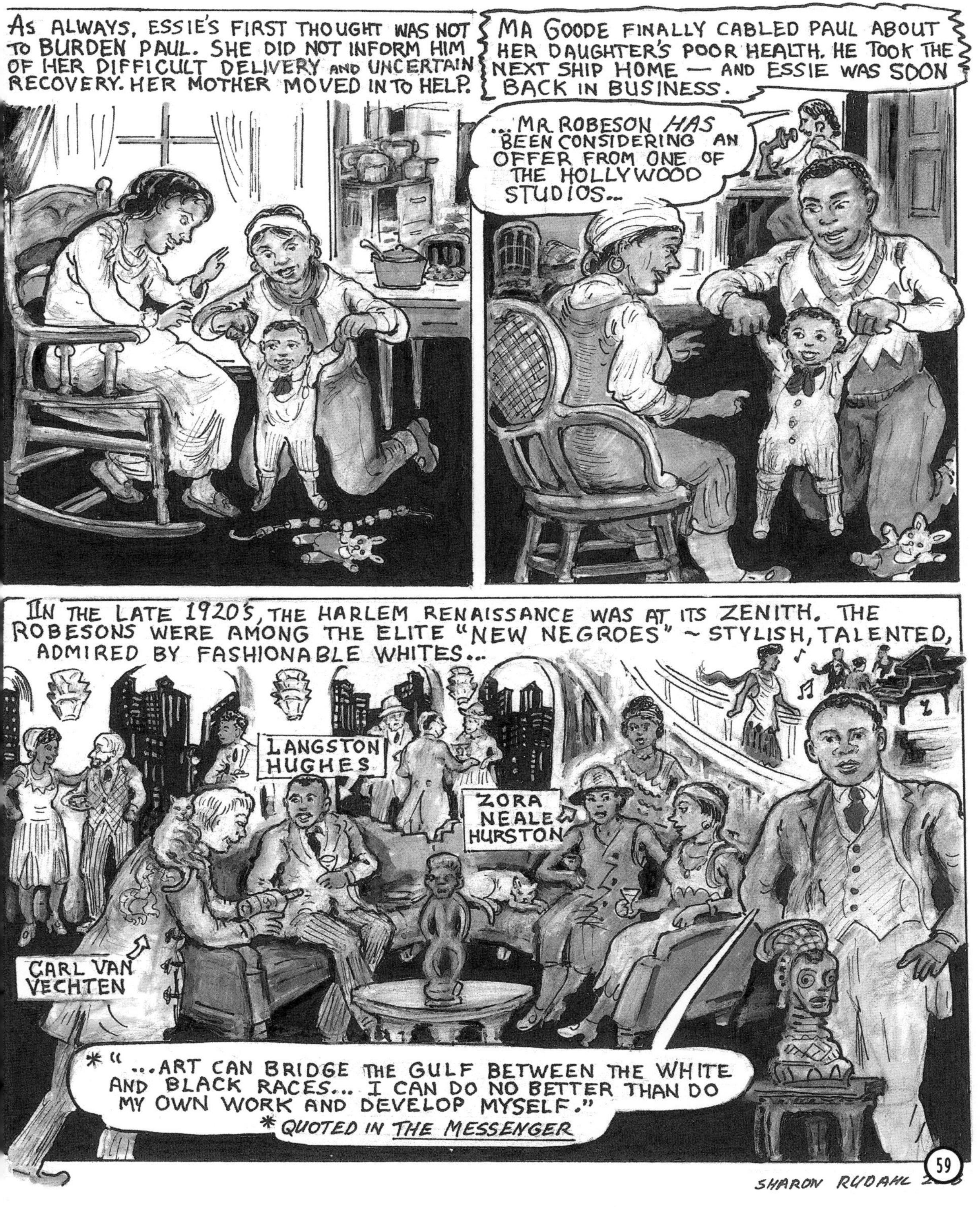
AS ALWAYS, ESSIE'S FIRST THOUGHT WAS NOT TO BURDEN PAUL. SHE DID NOT INFORM HIM OF HER DIFFICULT DELIVERY AND UNCERTAIN RECOVERY. HER MOTHER MOVED IN TO HELP.
MA GOODE FINALLY CABLED PAUL ABOUT HER DAUGHTER'S POOR HEALTH. HE TOOK THE NEXT SHIP HOME — AND ESSIE WAS SOON BACK IN BUSINESS.
...MR. ROBESON HAS BEEN CONSIDERING AN OFFER FROM ONE OF THE HOLLYWOOD STUDIOS...
IN THE LATE 1920'S, THE HARLEM RENAISSANCE WAS AT ITS ZENITH. THE ROBESONS WERE AMONG THE ELITE "NEW NEGROES" ~ STYLISH, TALENTED, ADMIRED BY FASHIONABLE WHITES...
LANGSTON HUGHES
ZORA NEALE HURSTON
CARL VAN VECHTEN
*"...ART CAN BRIDGE THE GULF BETWEEN THE WHITE AND BLACK RACES... I CAN DO NO BETTER THAN DO MY OWN WORK AND DEVELOP MYSELF."
*QUOTED IN THE MESSENGER
SHARON RUDAHL

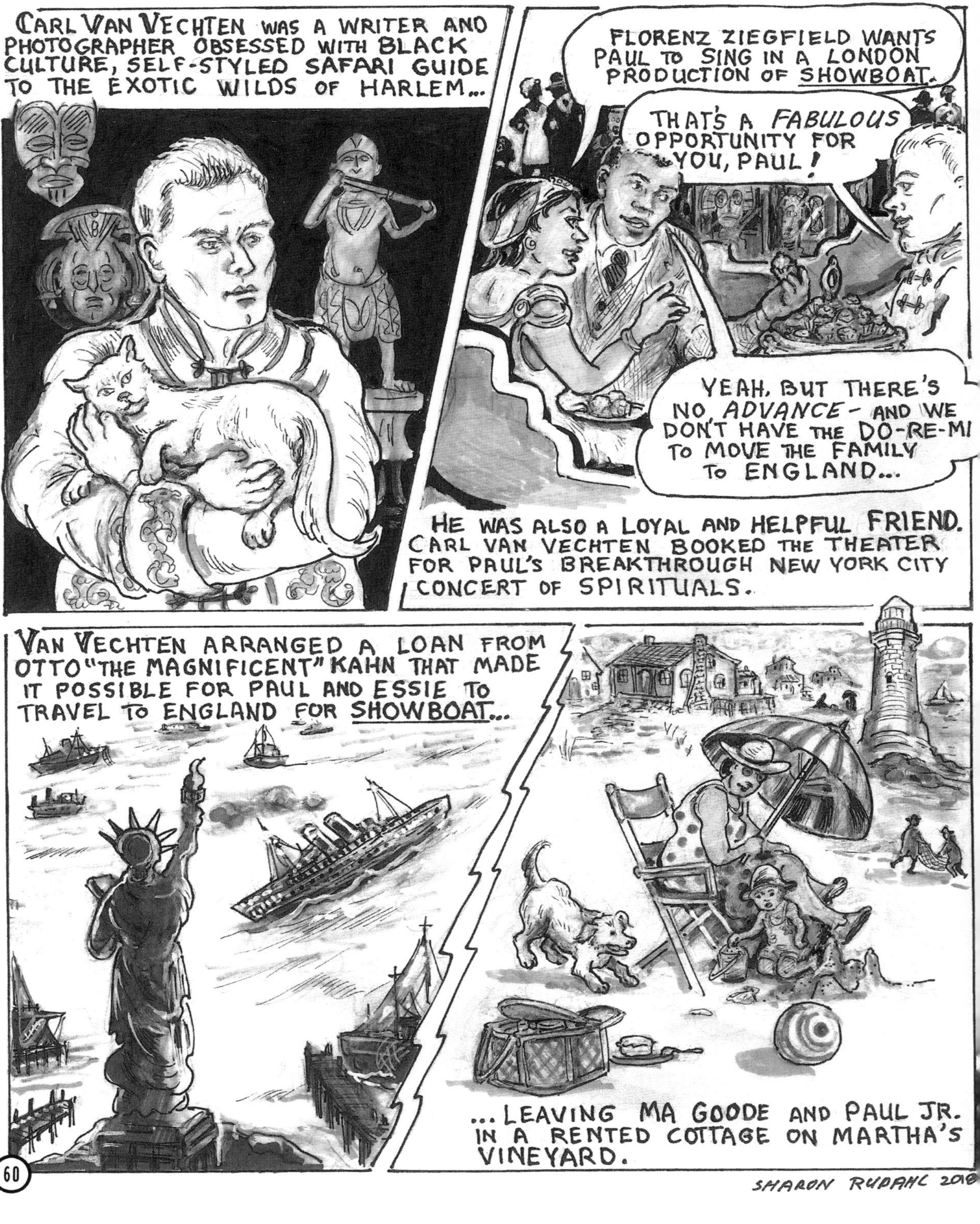
CARL VAN VECHTEN WAS A WRITER AND PHOTOGRAPHER OBSESSED WITH BLACK CULTURE, SELF-STYLED SAFARI GUIDE TO THE EXOTIC WILDS OF HARLEM...
FLORENZ ZIEGFIELD WANTS PAUL TO SING IN A LONDON PRODUCTION OF SHOWBOAT.
THAT'S A FABULOUS OPPORTUNITY FOR YOU, PAUL!
YEAH, BUT THERE'S NO ADVANCE - AND WE DON'T HAVE THE DO-RE-MI TO MOVE THE FAMILY TO ENGLAND...
HE WAS ALSO A LOYAL AND HELPFUL FRIEND. CARL VAN VECHTEN BOOKED THE THEATER FOR PAUL'S BREAKTHROUGH NEW YORK CITY CONCERT OF SPIRITUALS.
VAN VECHTEN ARRANGED A LOAN FROM OTTO "THE MAGNIFICENT" KAHN THAT MADE IT POSSIBLE FOR PAUL AND ESSIE TO TRAVEL TO ENGLAND FOR SHOWBOAT...
...LEAVING MA GOODE AND PAUL JR. IN A RENTED COTTAGE ON MARTHA'S VINEYARD.
SHARON RUDAHL 2018

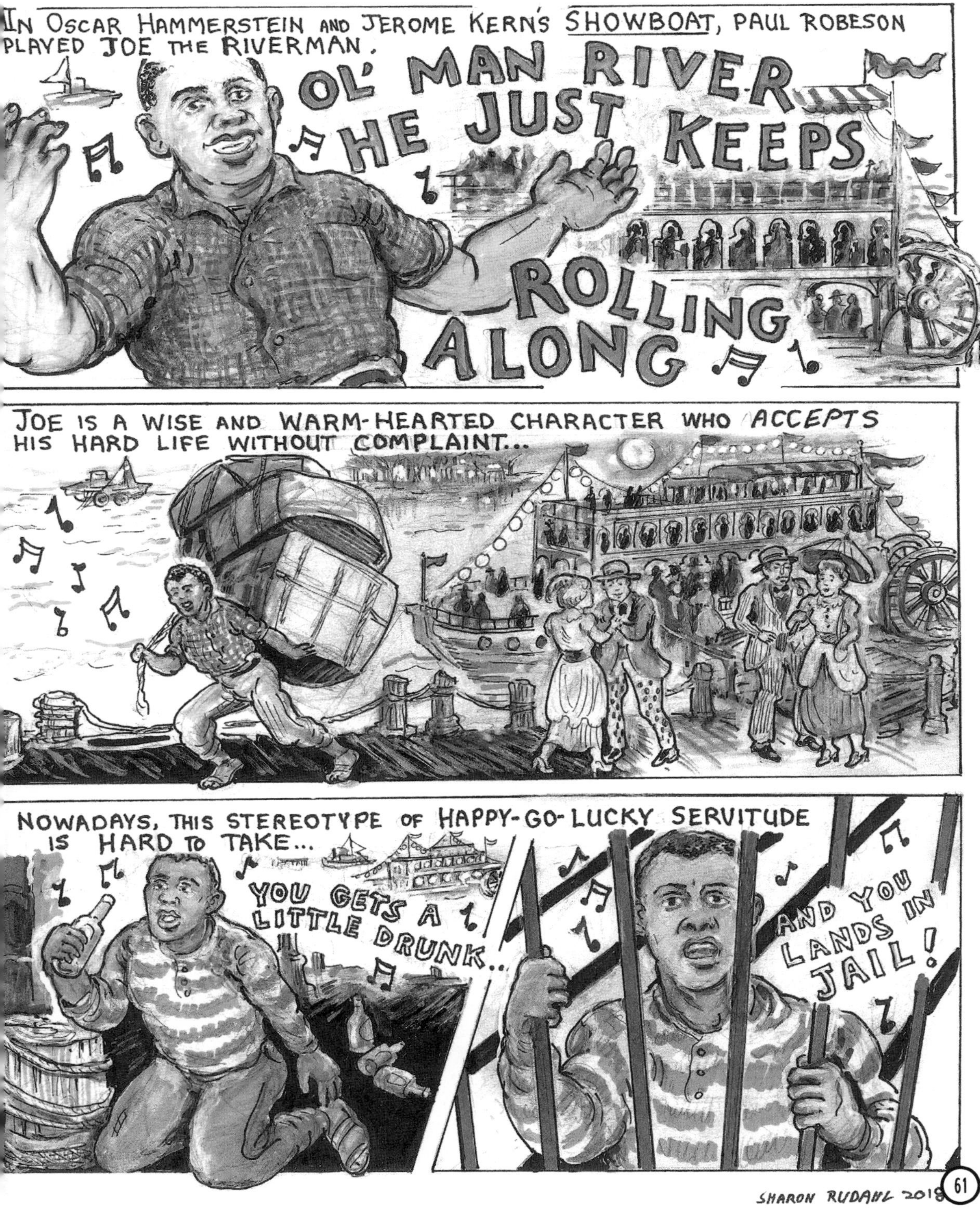

IN OSCAR HAMMERSTEIN AND JEROME KERN'S SHOWBOAT, PAUL ROBESON PLAYED JOE THE RIVERMAN.
OL' MAN RIVER HE JUST KEEPS ROLLING ALONG
JOE IS A WISE AND WARM-HEARTED CHARACTER WHO ACCEPTS HIS HARD LIFE WITHOUT COMPLAINT...
NOWADAYS, THIS STEREOTYPE OF HAPPY-GO-LUCKY SERVITUDE IS HARD TO TAKE...
YOU GETS A LITTLE DRUNK...
AND YOU LANDS IN JAIL!
SHARON RUDAHL 2018

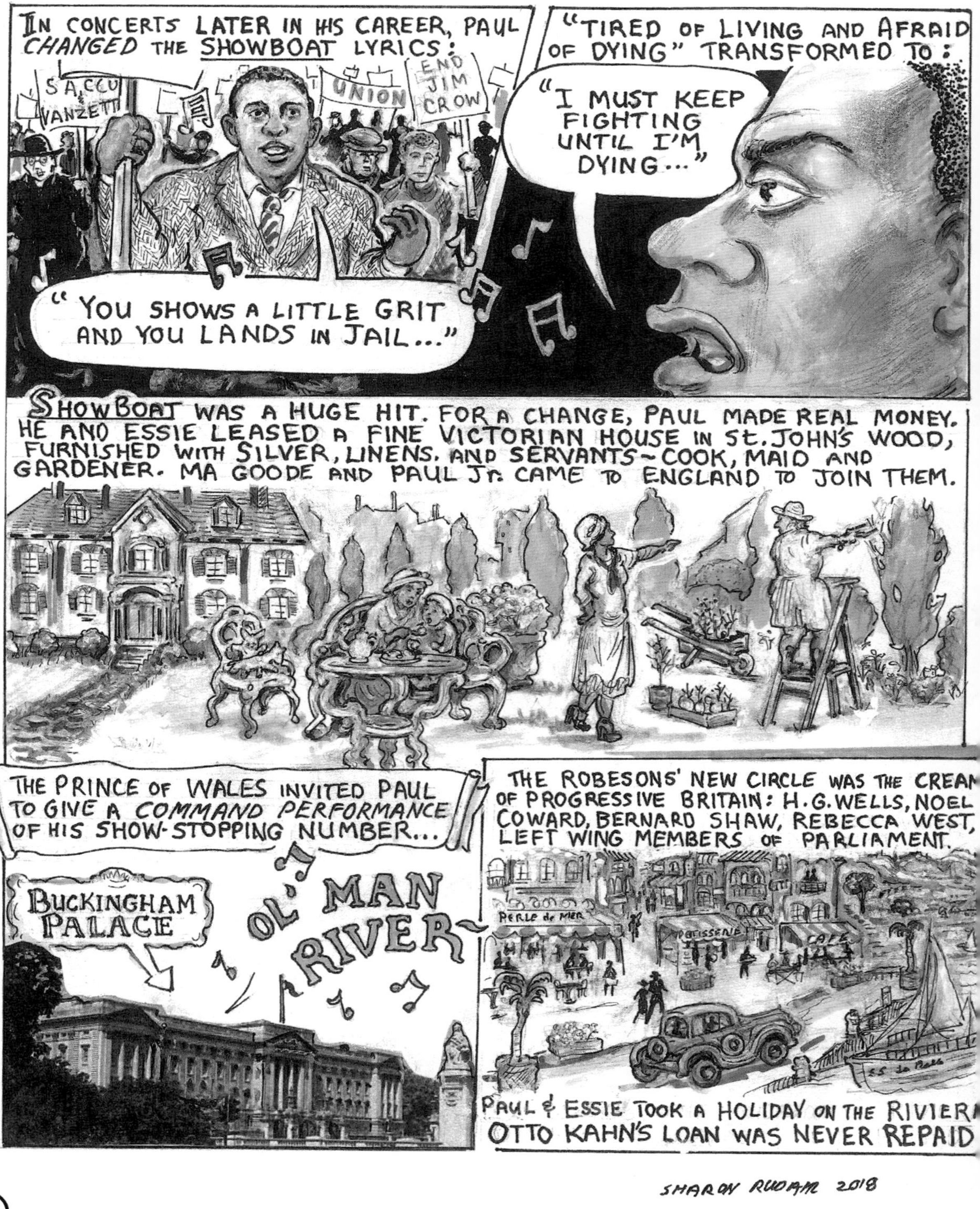
IN CONCERTS LATER IN HIS CAREER, PAUL CHANGED THE SHOWBOAT LYRICS:
SACCO & VANZETTI
UNION
END JIM CROW
"YOU SHOWS A LITTLE GRIT AND YOU LANDS IN JAIL..."
"TIRED OF LIVING AND AFRAID OF DYING" TRANSFORMED TO:
"I MUST KEEP FIGHTING UNTIL I'M DYING..."
SHOWBOAT WAS A HUGE HIT. FOR A CHANGE, PAUL MADE REAL MONEY. HE AND ESSIE LEASED A FINE VICTORIAN HOUSE IN St. JOHN'S WOOD, FURNISHED WITH SILVER, LINENS, AND SERVANTS ~ COOK, MAID AND GARDENER. MA GOODE AND PAUL Jr. CAME TO ENGLAND TO JOIN THEM.
THE PRINCE OF WALES INVITED PAUL TO GIVE A COMMAND PERFORMANCE OF HIS SHOW-STOPPING NUMBER...
BUCKINGHAM PALACE
OL' MAN RIVER
THE ROBESONS' NEW CIRCLE WAS THE CREAM OF PROGRESSIVE BRITAIN: H.G. WELLS, NOEL COWARD, BERNARD SHAW, REBECCA WEST, LEFT WING MEMBERS OF PARLIAMENT.
PERLE de MER
PATISSERIE
CAFE
PAUL & ESSIE TOOK A HOLIDAY ON THE RIVIERA
OTTO KAHN'S LOAN WAS NEVER REPAID
SHARON RUDAHL 2018

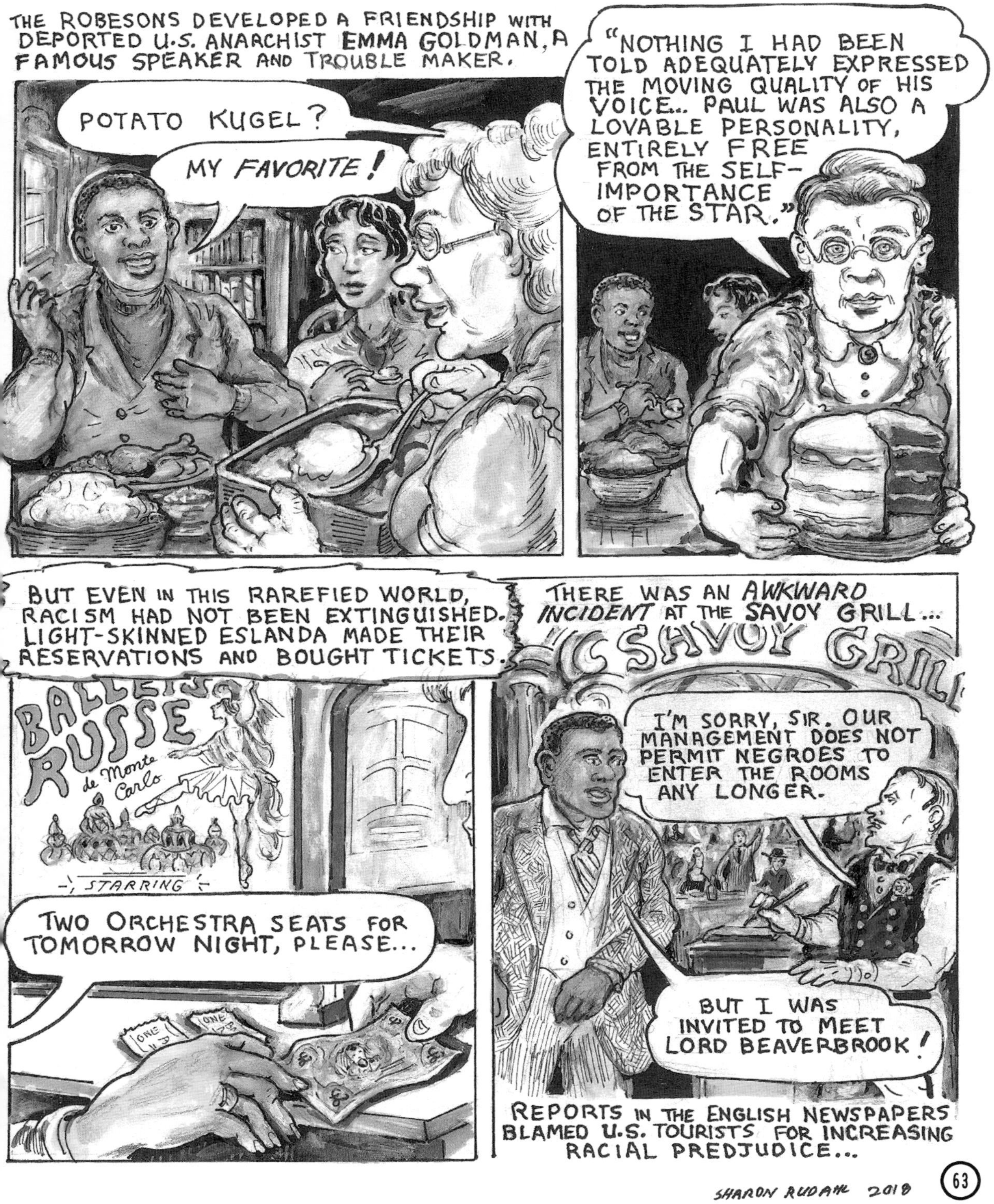
THE ROBESONS DEVELOPED A FRIENDSHIP WITH DEPORTED U.S. ANARCHIST EMMA GOLDMAN, A FAMOUS SPEAKER AND TROUBLE MAKER.
POTATO KUGEL?
MY *FAVORITE*!
"NOTHING I HAD BEEN TOLD ADEQUATELY EXPRESSED THE MOVING QUALITY OF HIS VOICE... PAUL WAS ALSO A LOVABLE PERSONALITY, ENTIRELY FREE FROM THE SELF-IMPORTANCE OF THE STAR."
BUT EVEN IN THIS RAREFIED WORLD, RACISM HAD NOT BEEN EXTINGUISHED. LIGHT-SKINNED ESLANDA MADE THEIR RESERVATIONS AND BOUGHT TICKETS.
BALLETS RUSSE de Monte Carlo
STARRING
TWO ORCHESTRA SEATS FOR TOMORROW NIGHT, PLEASE...
THERE WAS AN *AWKWARD INCIDENT* AT THE SAVOY GRILL...
SAVOY GRILL
I'M SORRY, SIR. OUR MANAGEMENT DOES NOT PERMIT NEGROES TO ENTER THE ROOMS ANY LONGER.
BUT I WAS INVITED TO MEET LORD BEAVERBROOK!
REPORTS IN THE ENGLISH NEWSPAPERS BLAMED U.S. TOURISTS FOR INCREASING RACIAL PREDJUDICE...
SHARON RUDAHL 2018

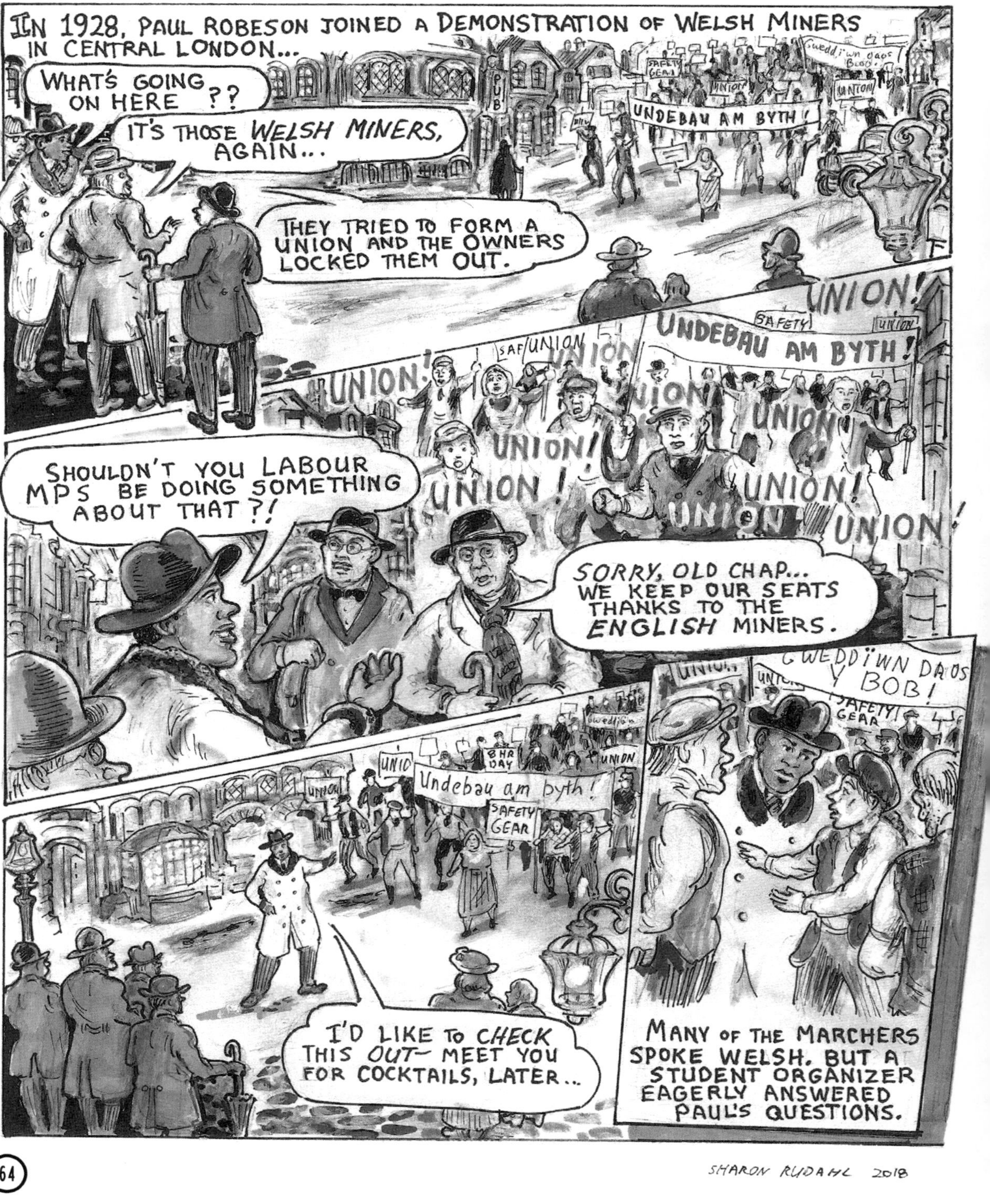

IN 1928, PAUL ROBESON JOINED A DEMONSTRATION OF WELSH MINERS IN CENTRAL LONDON...
WHAT'S GOING ON HERE ??
IT'S THOSE WELSH MINERS, AGAIN...
THEY TRIED TO FORM A UNION AND THE OWNERS LOCKED THEM OUT.
PUB
UNDEBAU AM BYTH!
UNION!
SAFETY
UNDEBAU AM BYTH!
SHOULDN'T YOU LABOUR MPS BE DOING SOMETHING ABOUT THAT ?!
SORRY, OLD CHAP... WE KEEP OUR SEATS THANKS TO THE ENGLISH MINERS.
Undebau am byth!
SAFETY GEAR
8HR DAY
I'D LIKE TO CHECK THIS OUT— MEET YOU FOR COCKTAILS, LATER...
GWEDDÏWN DAOS Y BOB!
SAFETY GEAR
MANY OF THE MARCHERS SPOKE WELSH. BUT A STUDENT ORGANIZER EAGERLY ANSWERED PAUL'S QUESTIONS.

SHARON RUDAHL 2018

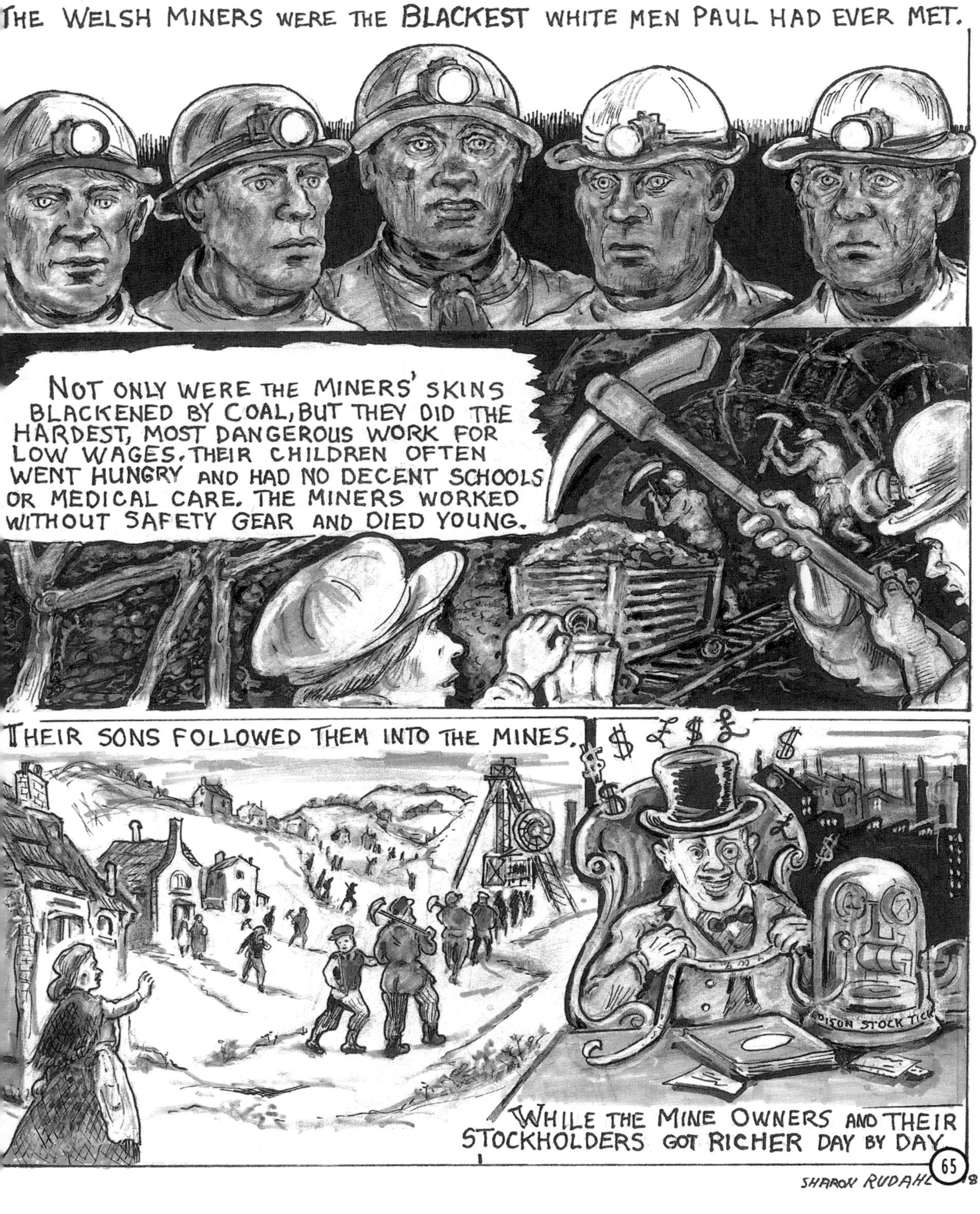
THE WELSH MINERS WERE THE BLACKEST WHITE MEN PAUL HAD EVER MET.
NOT ONLY WERE THE MINERS' SKINS BLACKENED BY COAL, BUT THEY DID THE HARDEST, MOST DANGEROUS WORK FOR LOW WAGES. THEIR CHILDREN OFTEN WENT HUNGRY AND HAD NO DECENT SCHOOLS OR MEDICAL CARE. THE MINERS WORKED WITHOUT SAFETY GEAR AND DIED YOUNG.
THEIR SONS FOLLOWED THEM INTO THE MINES.
DISON STOCK TICK
WHILE THE MINE OWNERS AND THEIR STOCKHOLDERS GOT RICHER DAY BY DAY.
SHARON RUDAHL '18

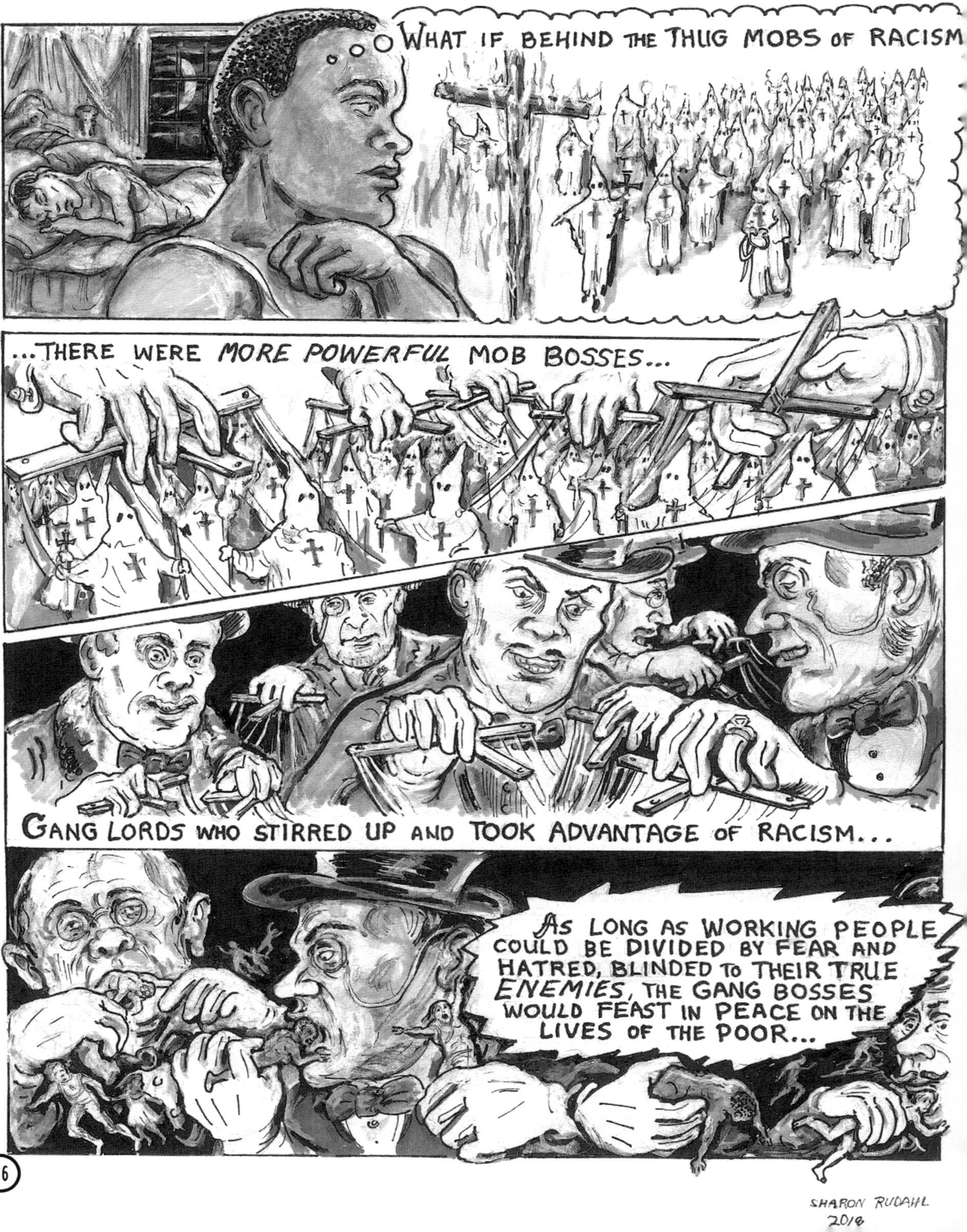

WHAT IF BEHIND THE THUG MOBS OF RACISM
...THERE WERE MORE POWERFUL MOB BOSSES...
GANG LORDS WHO STIRRED UP AND TOOK ADVANTAGE OF RACISM...
AS LONG AS WORKING PEOPLE COULD BE DIVIDED BY FEAR AND HATRED, BLINDED TO THEIR TRUE ENEMIES, THE GANG BOSSES WOULD FEAST IN PEACE ON THE LIVES OF THE POOR...
SHARON RUDAHL 2018

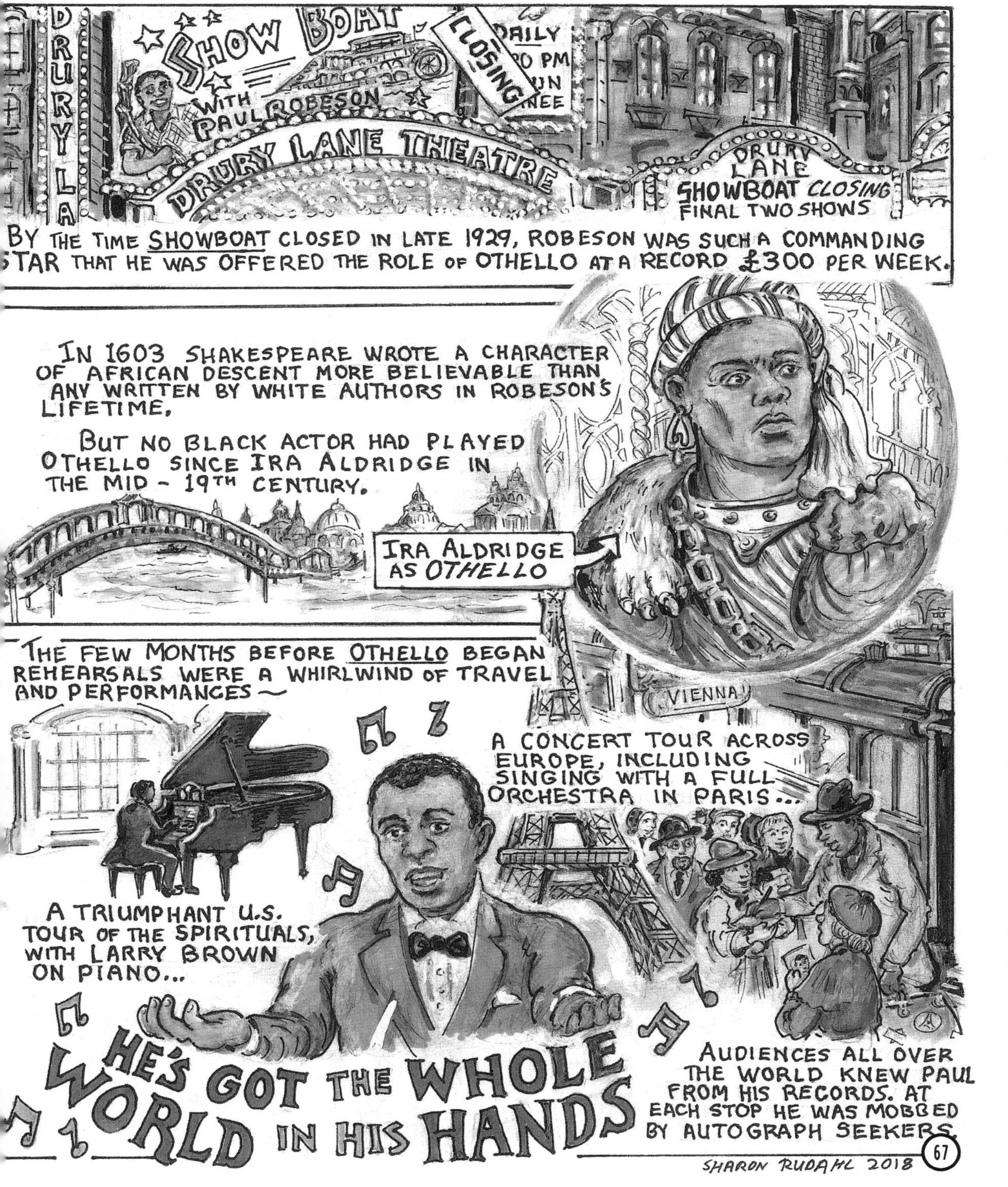

DRURY LA
SHOW BOAT
WITH PAUL ROBESON
CLOSING
DAILY
DRURY LANE THEATRE
DRURY LANE
SHOWBOAT CLOSING
FINAL TWO SHOWS
BY THE TIME SHOWBOAT CLOSED IN LATE 1929, ROBESON WAS SUCH A COMMANDING STAR THAT HE WAS OFFERED THE ROLE OF OTHELLO AT A RECORD £300 PER WEEK.
IN 1603 SHAKESPEARE WROTE A CHARACTER OF AFRICAN DESCENT MORE BELIEVABLE THAN ANY WRITTEN BY WHITE AUTHORS IN ROBESON'S LIFETIME.
BUT NO BLACK ACTOR HAD PLAYED OTHELLO SINCE IRA ALDRIDGE IN THE MID-19TH CENTURY.
IRA ALDRIDGE AS OTHELLO
THE FEW MONTHS BEFORE OTHELLO BEGAN REHEARSALS WERE A WHIRLWIND OF TRAVEL AND PERFORMANCES~
VIENNA
A CONCERT TOUR ACROSS EUROPE, INCLUDING SINGING WITH A FULL ORCHESTRA IN PARIS...
A TRIUMPHANT U.S. TOUR OF THE SPIRITUALS, WITH LARRY BROWN ON PIANO...
HE'S GOT THE WHOLE WORLD IN HIS HANDS
AUDIENCES ALL OVER THE WORLD KNEW PAUL FROM HIS RECORDS. AT EACH STOP HE WAS MOBBED BY AUTOGRAPH SEEKERS.
SHARON RUDAHL 2018

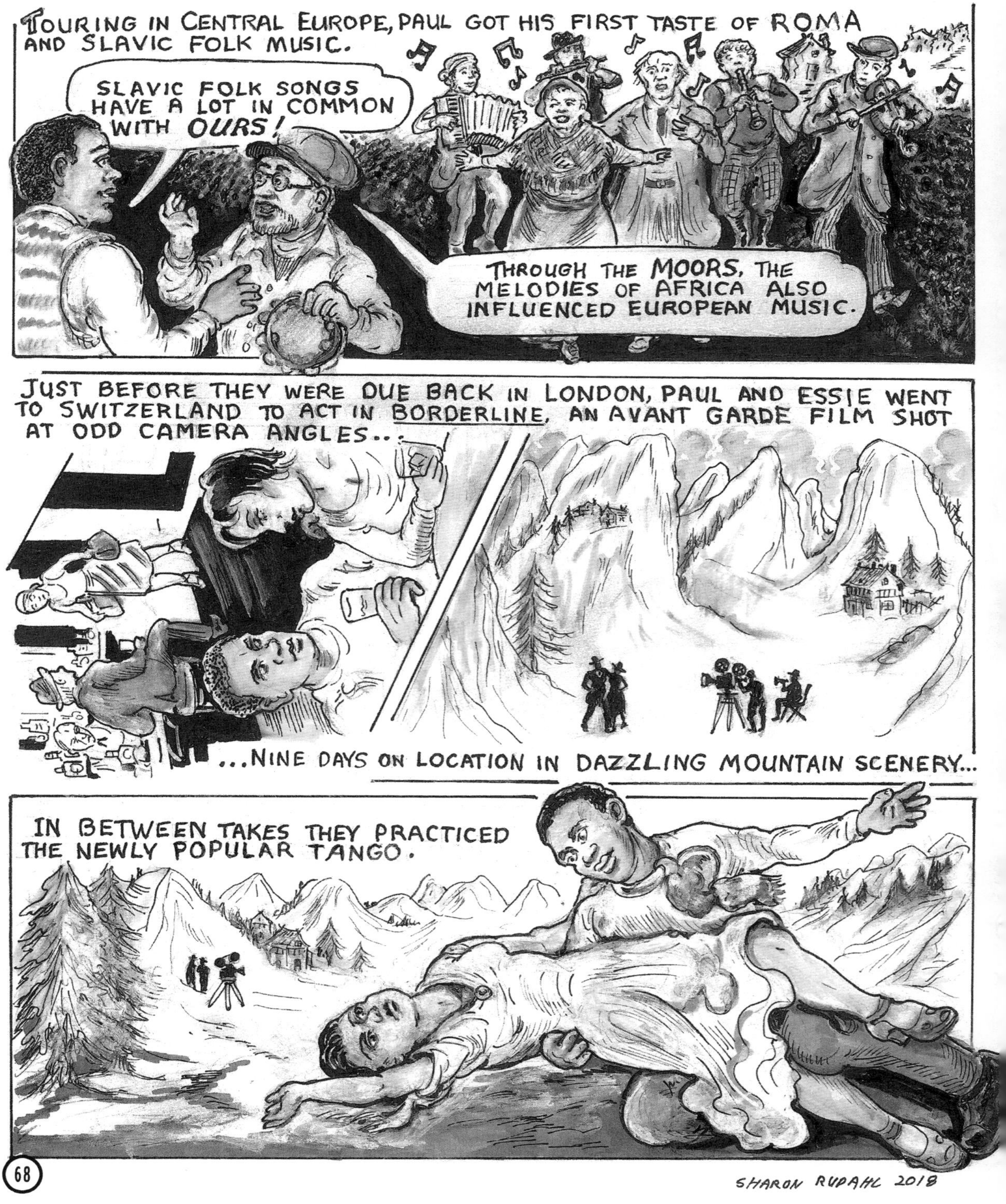
TOURING IN CENTRAL EUROPE, PAUL GOT HIS FIRST TASTE OF ROMA AND SLAVIC FOLK MUSIC.
SLAVIC FOLK SONGS HAVE A LOT IN COMMON WITH OURS!
THROUGH THE MOORS, THE MELODIES OF AFRICA ALSO INFLUENCED EUROPEAN MUSIC.
JUST BEFORE THEY WERE DUE BACK IN LONDON, PAUL AND ESSIE WENT TO SWITZERLAND TO ACT IN BORDERLINE, AN AVANT GARDE FILM SHOT AT ODD CAMERA ANGLES...
...NINE DAYS ON LOCATION IN DAZZLING MOUNTAIN SCENERY...
IN BETWEEN TAKES THEY PRACTICED THE NEWLY POPULAR TANGO.
SHARON RUDAHL 2018

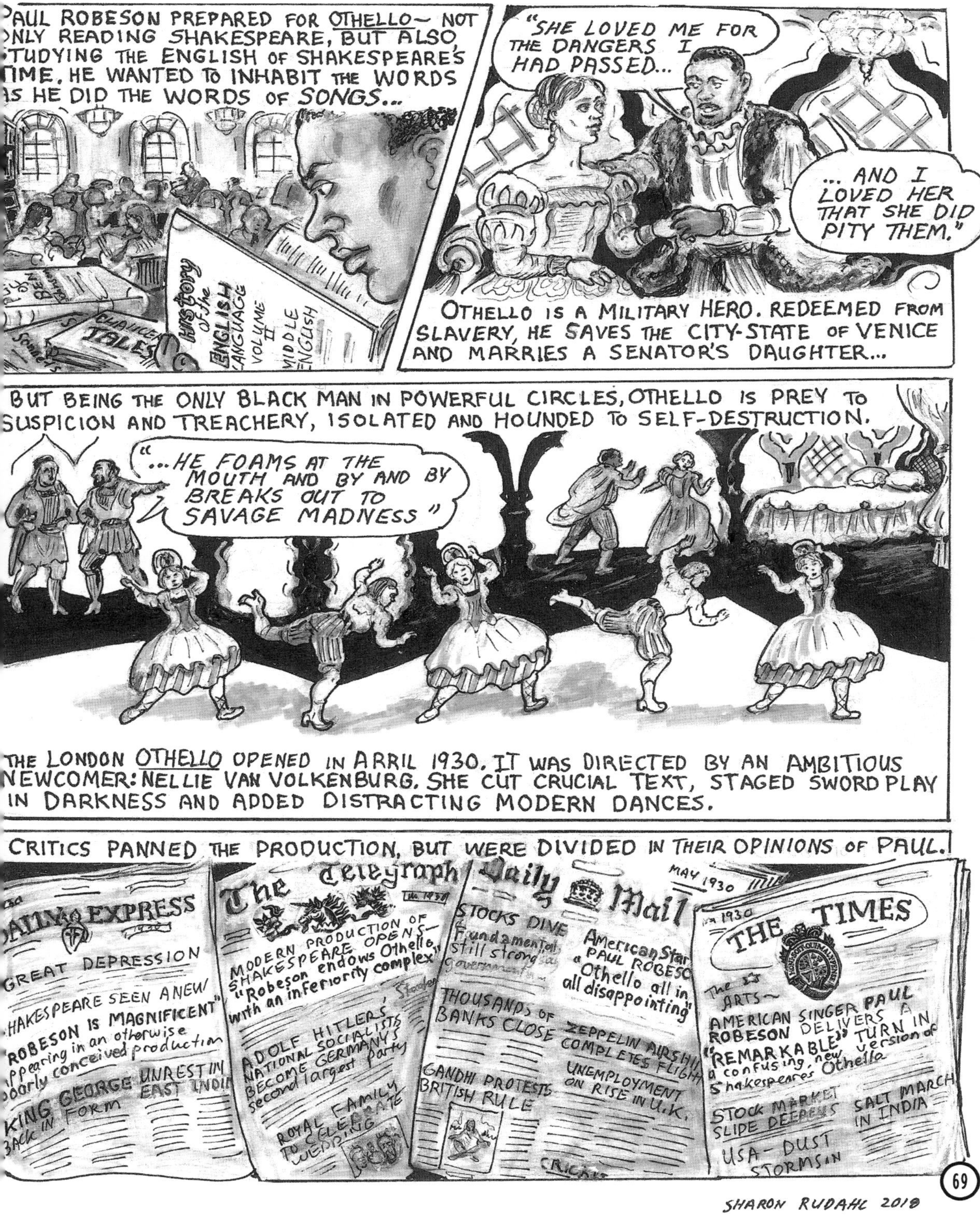

PAUL ROBESON PREPARED FOR OTHELLO— NOT ONLY READING SHAKESPEARE, BUT ALSO, STUDYING THE ENGLISH OF SHAKESPEARE'S TIME, HE WANTED TO INHABIT THE WORDS AS HE DID THE WORDS OF SONGS...
History of the ENGLISH LANGUAGE VOLUME II MIDDLE ENGLISH
CHAUCER TALES
"SHE LOVED ME FOR THE DANGERS I HAD PASSED...
... AND I LOVED HER THAT SHE DID PITY THEM."
OTHELLO IS A MILITARY HERO. REDEEMED FROM SLAVERY, HE SAVES THE CITY-STATE OF VENICE AND MARRIES A SENATOR'S DAUGHTER...
BUT BEING THE ONLY BLACK MAN IN POWERFUL CIRCLES, OTHELLO IS PREY TO SUSPICION AND TREACHERY, ISOLATED AND HOUNDED TO SELF-DESTRUCTION.
"...HE FOAMS AT THE MOUTH AND BY AND BY BREAKS OUT TO SAVAGE MADNESS"
THE LONDON OTHELLO OPENED IN ARRIL 1930. IT WAS DIRECTED BY AN AMBITIOUS NEWCOMER: NELLIE VAN VOLKENBURG. SHE CUT CRUCIAL TEXT, STAGED SWORD PLAY IN DARKNESS AND ADDED DISTRACTING MODERN DANCES.
CRITICS PANNED THE PRODUCTION, BUT WERE DIVIDED IN THEIR OPINIONS OF PAUL.
DAILY EXPRESS
GREAT DEPRESSION
SHAKESPEARE SEEN ANEW
ROBESON IS MAGNIFICENT"
appearing in an otherwise poorly conceived production
KING GEORGE BACK IN FORM
UNREST IN EAST INDIA
The Telegraph
MODERN PRODUCTION OF SHAKESPEARE OPENS— "Robeson endows Othello with an inferiority complex"
ADOLF HITLER'S NATIONAL SOCIALISTS BECOME GERMANY'S second largest party
ROYAL FAMILY TO CELEBRATE WEDDING
Daily Mail
MAY 1930
STOCKS DIVE
Fundamentals still strong
American Star PAUL ROBESON "Othello all in all disappointing"
THOUSANDS OF BANKS CLOSE
ZEPPELIN AIRSHIP COMPLETES FLIGHT
GANDHI PROTESTS BRITISH RULE
UNEMPLOYMENT ON RISE IN U.K.
THE TIMES
The ARTS—
AMERICAN SINGER PAUL ROBESON DELIVERS A "REMARKABLE" TURN IN a confusing, new version of Shakespeare's Othello
STOCK MARKET SLIDE DEEPENS
SALT MARCH IN INDIA
USA- DUST STORMS
SHARON RUDAHL 2018

AFTER A FEW MONTHS OF WEAK TICKET SALES, THE SHOW CLOSED, BUT ROBESON HAD GROWN IN THE ROLE, IMPROVING WITH EACH PERFORMANCE...

"OTHELLO HAS OPENED TO ME NEW AND WIDER FIELDS."

CONTRACTUAL SQUABBLES KEPT PAUL FROM ACCEPTING OFFERS TO PLAY OTHELLO IN OTHER PRODUCTIONS. AS WELL, PERSONAL TROUBLES BESET THE ROBESON FAMILY. PAUL JUNIOR SUFFERED A SERIES OF PAINFUL ILLNESSES.

ESSIE WROTE *PAUL ROBESON - NEGRO*, TIMED AS PUBLICITY FOR THE OPENING OF OTHELLO. IN AN ATTEMPT AT ANALYSIS, SHE HINTED THAT PAUL WAS SO DEVOTED TO HIS ART THAT HE WAS A LESS THAN ATTENTIVE FATHER AND HUSBAND.

PAUL ROBESON NEGRO

£1

by Eslanda Robeson

READ ABOUT THE SENSATIONAL NEW STAR ☆ The INSIDE STORY!

USUALLY *EASY-GOING*, PAUL WAS DEEPLY OFFENDED.

ESSIE INTERCEPTED A *LOVE LETTER* FROM PEGGY ASHCROFT, PAUL'S YOUNG DESDEMONA.

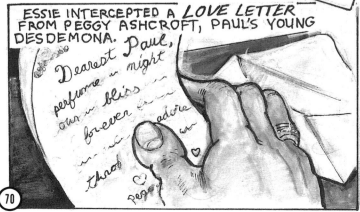

Dearest Paul, perfume ~ night our ~ bliss forever ~~ adore ~~ throb ~ Peggy

HOTEL
HASTINGS HOTEL

USUALLY *TOLERANT*, ESSIE SENT HIM PACKING.

70

SHARON RUDAHL 2018

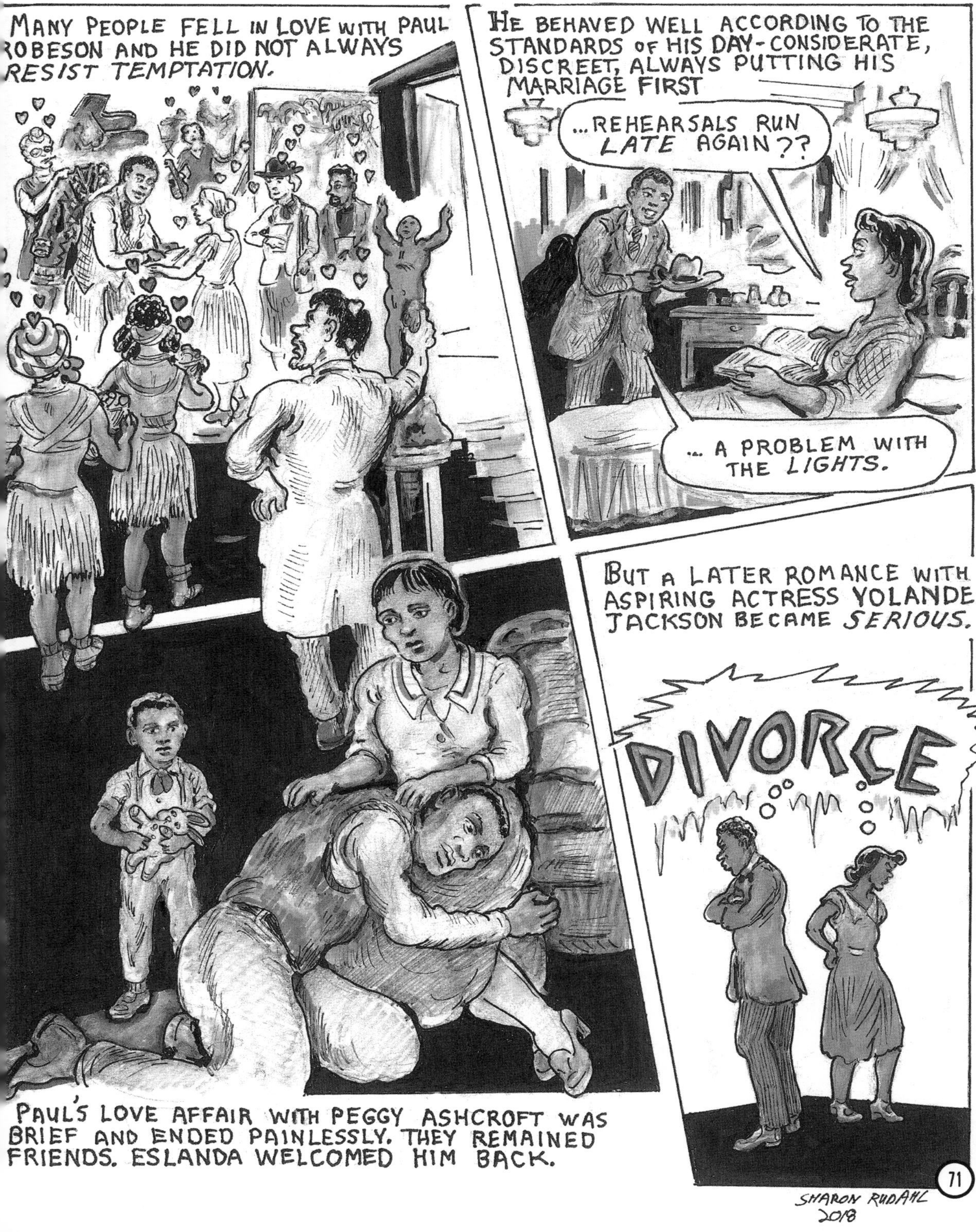
MANY PEOPLE FELL IN LOVE WITH PAUL ROBESON AND HE DID NOT ALWAYS RESIST TEMPTATION.
HE BEHAVED WELL ACCORDING TO THE STANDARDS OF HIS DAY - CONSIDERATE, DISCREET, ALWAYS PUTTING HIS MARRIAGE FIRST
...REHEARSALS RUN LATE AGAIN??
... A PROBLEM WITH THE LIGHTS.
PAUL'S LOVE AFFAIR WITH PEGGY ASHCROFT WAS BRIEF AND ENDED PAINLESSLY. THEY REMAINED FRIENDS. ESLANDA WELCOMED HIM BACK.
BUT A LATER ROMANCE WITH ASPIRING ACTRESS YOLANDE JACKSON BECAME SERIOUS.
DIVORCE
SHARON RUDAHL 2018

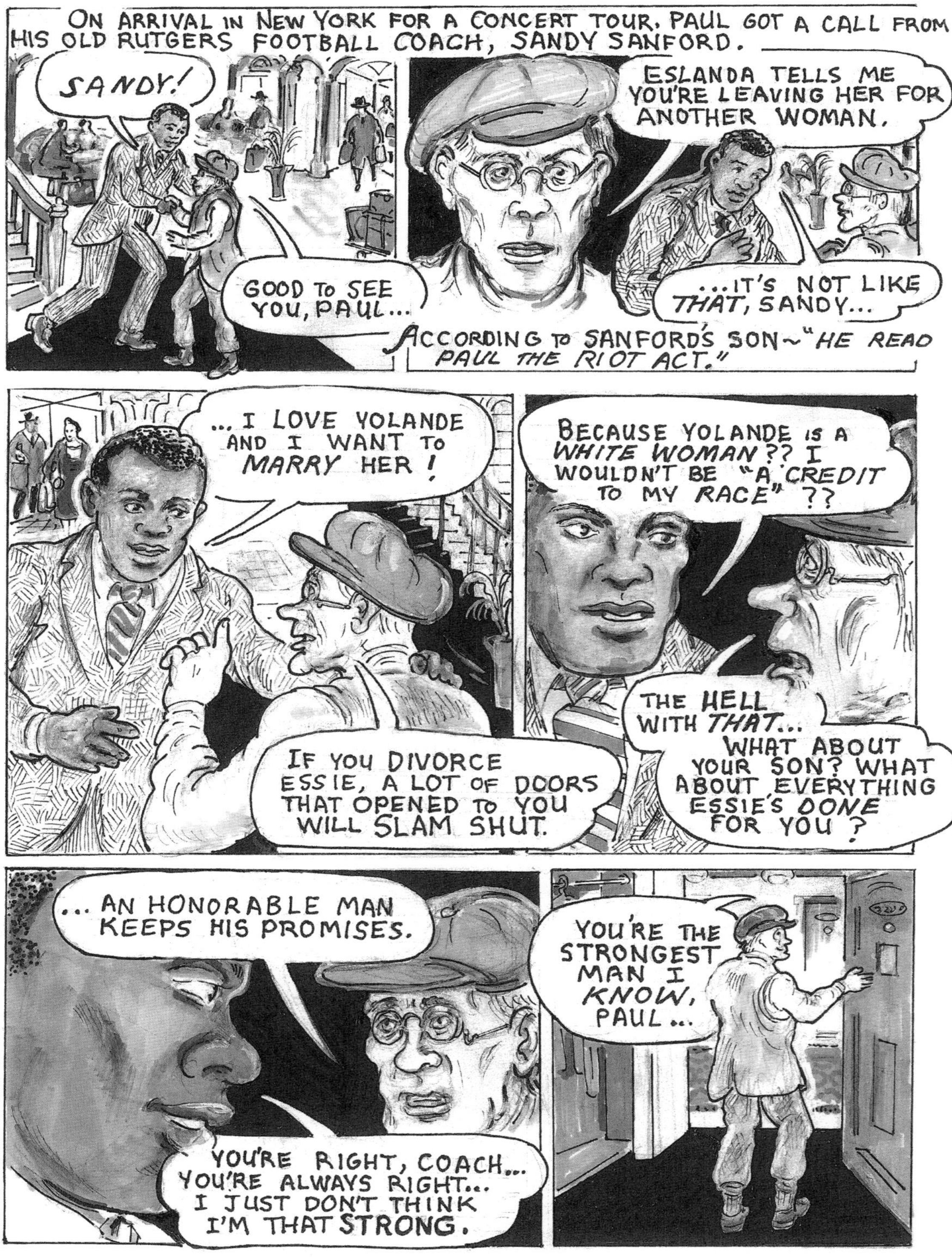
ON ARRIVAL IN NEW YORK FOR A CONCERT TOUR, PAUL GOT A CALL FROM HIS OLD RUTGERS FOOTBALL COACH, SANDY SANFORD.
SANDY!
GOOD TO SEE YOU, PAUL...
ESLANDA TELLS ME YOU'RE LEAVING HER FOR ANOTHER WOMAN.
...IT'S NOT LIKE THAT, SANDY...
ACCORDING TO SANFORD'S SON~"HE READ PAUL THE RIOT ACT."
...I LOVE YOLANDE AND I WANT TO MARRY HER!
IF YOU DIVORCE ESSIE, A LOT OF DOORS THAT OPENED TO YOU WILL SLAM SHUT.
BECAUSE YOLANDE IS A WHITE WOMAN?? I WOULDN'T BE "A CREDIT TO MY RACE"??
THE HELL WITH THAT... WHAT ABOUT YOUR SON? WHAT ABOUT EVERYTHING ESSIE'S DONE FOR YOU?
...AN HONORABLE MAN KEEPS HIS PROMISES.
YOU'RE RIGHT, COACH... YOU'RE ALWAYS RIGHT... I JUST DON'T THINK I'M THAT STRONG.
YOU'RE THE STRONGEST MAN I KNOW, PAUL...

SHARON RUDAHL
2018

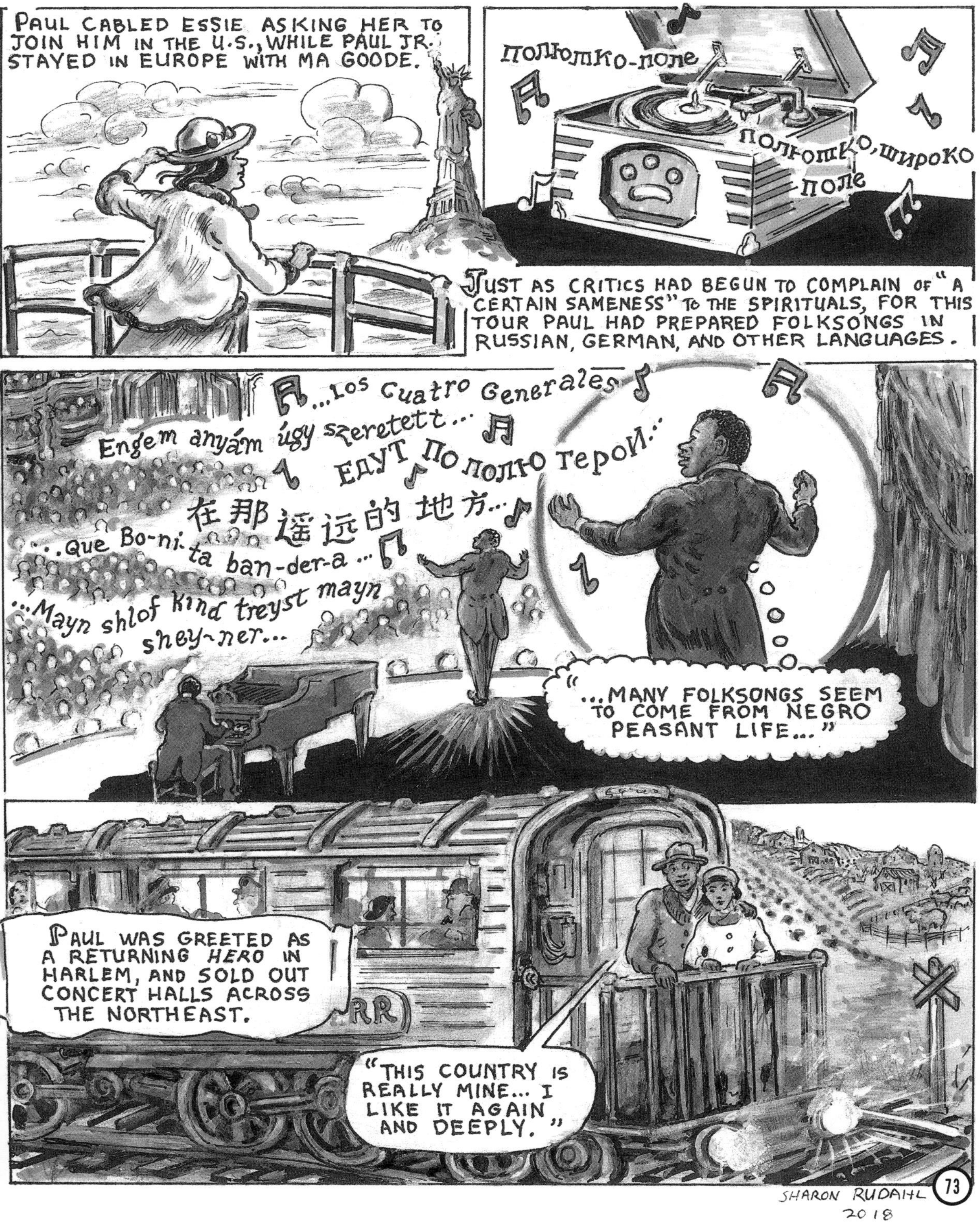
PAUL CABLED ESSIE ASKING HER TO JOIN HIM IN THE U.S., WHILE PAUL JR. STAYED IN EUROPE WITH MA GOODE.
полюшко-поле
полюшко, широко поле
JUST AS CRITICS HAD BEGUN TO COMPLAIN OF "A CERTAIN SAMENESS" TO THE SPIRITUALS, FOR THIS TOUR PAUL HAD PREPARED FOLKSONGS IN RUSSIAN, GERMAN, AND OTHER LANGUAGES.
...Los Cuatro Generales
Engem anyám úgy szeretett...
ЕДУТ по полю герои...
在那遥远的地方...
...que Bo-ni-ta ban-der-a...
...Mayn shlof kind treyst mayn shey-ner...
"...MANY FOLKSONGS SEEM TO COME FROM NEGRO PEASANT LIFE..."
PAUL WAS GREETED AS A RETURNING *HERO* IN HARLEM, AND SOLD OUT CONCERT HALLS ACROSS THE NORTHEAST.
RR
"THIS COUNTRY IS REALLY MINE... I LIKE IT AGAIN AND DEEPLY."

SHARON RUDAHL 2018

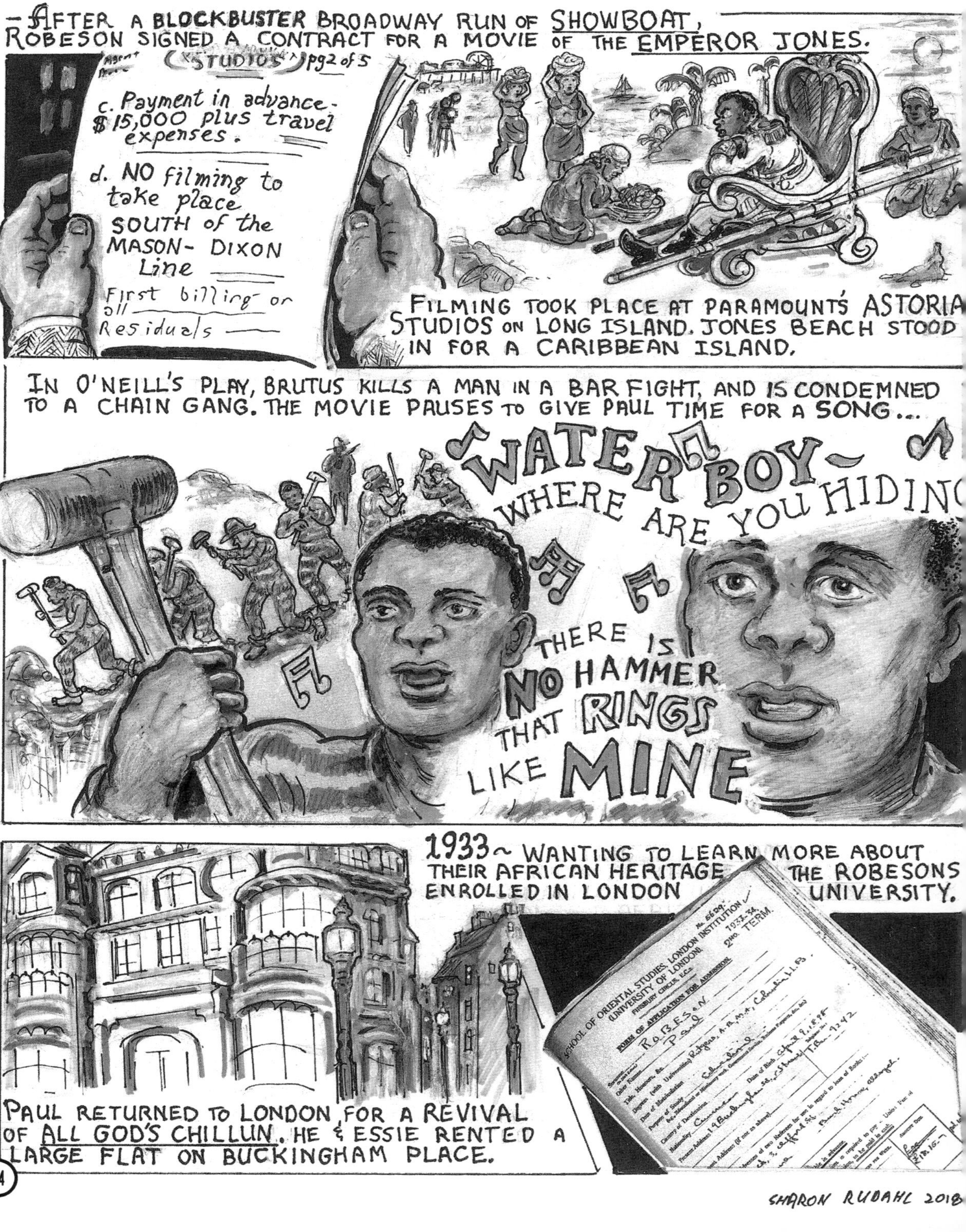

–AFTER A BLOCKBUSTER BROADWAY RUN OF SHOWBOAT, ROBESON SIGNED A CONTRACT FOR A MOVIE OF THE EMPEROR JONES.
"STUDIOS" pg2 of 5
c. Payment in advance - $15,000 plus travel expenses.
d. NO filming to take place SOUTH of the MASON-DIXON Line
First billing or all
Residuals
FILMING TOOK PLACE AT PARAMOUNT'S ASTORIA STUDIOS ON LONG ISLAND. JONES BEACH STOOD IN FOR A CARIBBEAN ISLAND.
IN O'NEILL'S PLAY, BRUTUS KILLS A MAN IN A BAR FIGHT, AND IS CONDEMNED TO A CHAIN GANG. THE MOVIE PAUSES TO GIVE PAUL TIME FOR A SONG...
~WATER BOY~
WHERE ARE YOU HIDING
THERE IS NO HAMMER THAT RINGS LIKE MINE
1933 ~ WANTING TO LEARN MORE ABOUT THEIR AFRICAN HERITAGE THE ROBESONS ENROLLED IN LONDON UNIVERSITY.
SCHOOL OF ORIENTAL STUDIES, LONDON INSTITUTION
(UNIVERSITY OF LONDON)
FINSBURY CIRCUS, E.C.2
No. 5629
1933-34
2ND TERM
FORM OF APPLICATION FOR ADMISSION
ROBESON
Paul
PAUL RETURNED TO LONDON FOR A REVIVAL OF ALL GOD'S CHILLUN. HE & ESSIE RENTED A LARGE FLAT ON BUCKINGHAM PLACE.
SHARON RUDAHL 2018

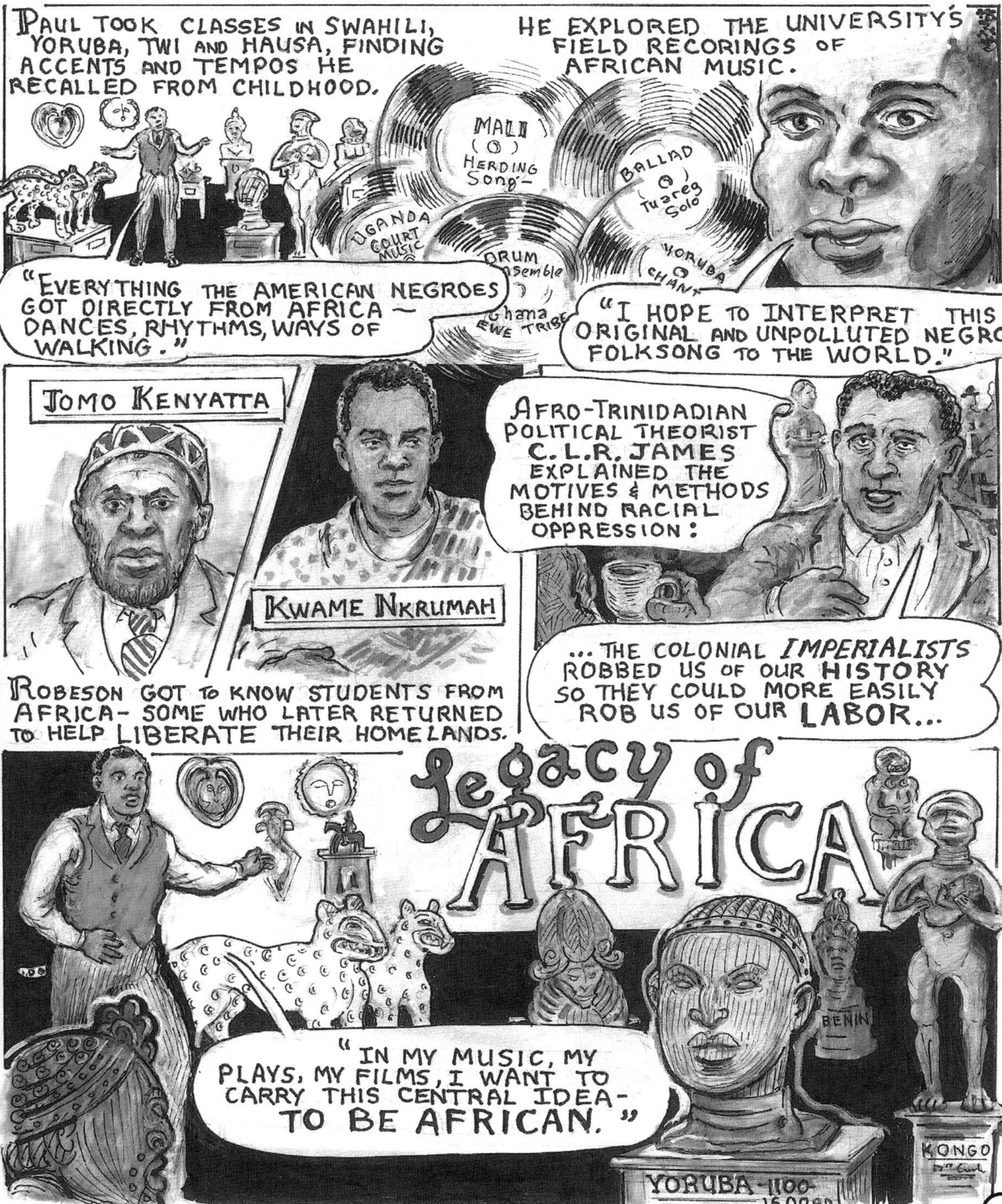
PAUL TOOK CLASSES IN SWAHILI, YORUBA, TWI AND HAUSA, FINDING ACCENTS AND TEMPOS HE RECALLED FROM CHILDHOOD.
HE EXPLORED THE UNIVERSITY'S FIELD RECORINGS OF AFRICAN MUSIC.
MALI HERDING Song-
BALLAD Tuareg Solo
UGANDA COURT MUSIC
DRUM Ensemble
YORUBA CHANT
Ghana EWE TRIBE
"EVERYTHING THE AMERICAN NEGROES GOT DIRECTLY FROM AFRICA — DANCES, RHYTHMS, WAYS OF WALKING."
"I HOPE TO INTERPRET THIS ORIGINAL AND UNPOLLUTED NEGRO FOLKSONG TO THE WORLD."
JOMO KENYATTA
KWAME NKRUMAH
ROBESON GOT TO KNOW STUDENTS FROM AFRICA- SOME WHO LATER RETURNED TO HELP LIBERATE THEIR HOMELANDS.
AFRO-TRINIDADIAN POLITICAL THEORIST C.L.R. JAMES EXPLAINED THE MOTIVES & METHODS BEHIND RACIAL OPPRESSION:
...THE COLONIAL IMPERIALISTS ROBBED US OF OUR HISTORY SO THEY COULD MORE EASILY ROB US OF OUR LABOR...
SHARON RUDAHL 2018
Legacy of AFRICA
BENIN
"IN MY MUSIC, MY PLAYS, MY FILMS, I WANT TO CARRY THIS CENTRAL IDEA- TO BE AFRICAN."
KONGO
YORUBA 1100-1500 AD

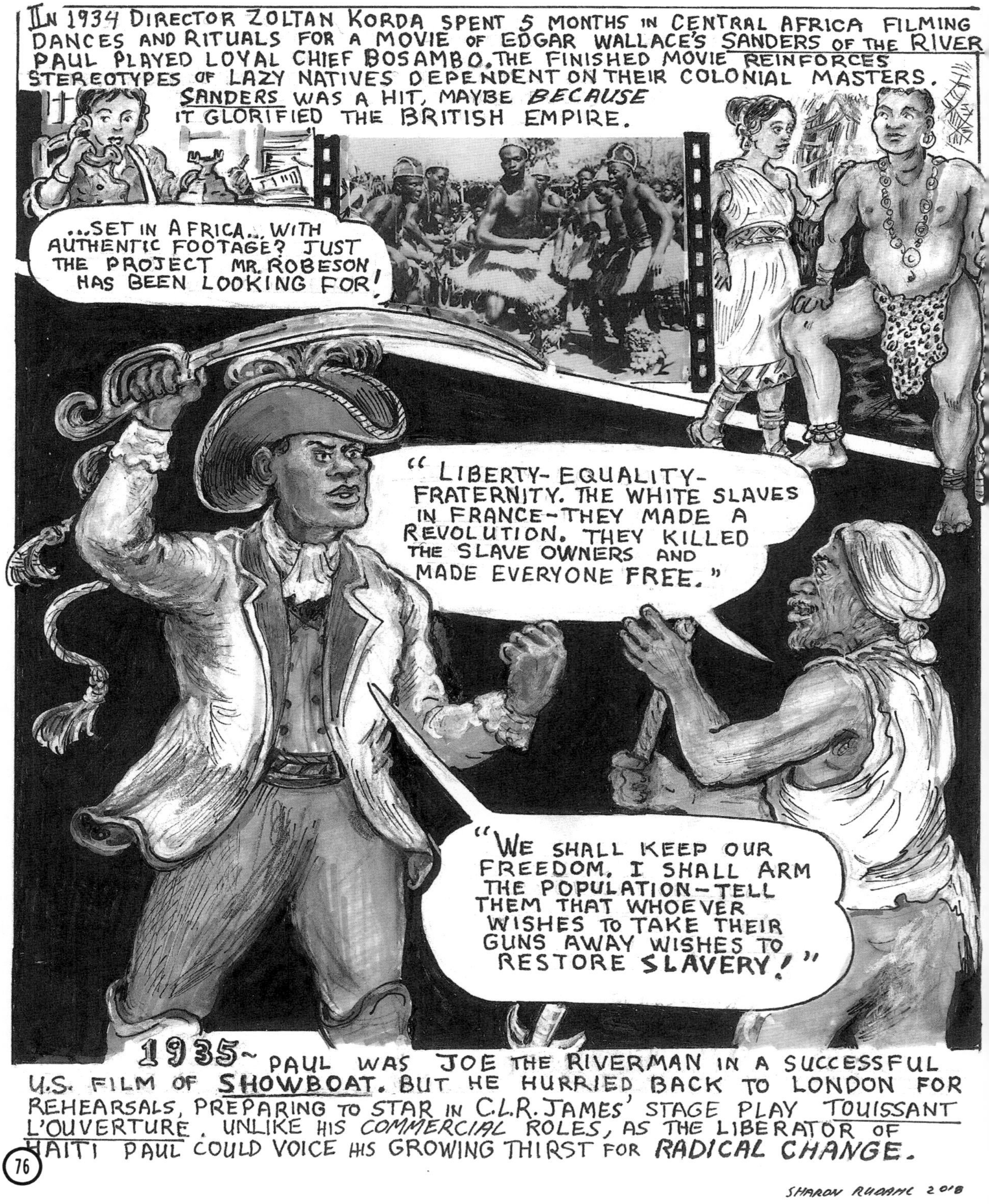
IN 1934 DIRECTOR ZOLTAN KORDA SPENT 5 MONTHS IN CENTRAL AFRICA FILMING DANCES AND RITUALS FOR A MOVIE OF EDGAR WALLACE'S SANDERS OF THE RIVER. PAUL PLAYED LOYAL CHIEF BOSAMBO. THE FINISHED MOVIE REINFORCES STEREOTYPES OF LAZY NATIVES DEPENDENT ON THEIR COLONIAL MASTERS.
SANDERS WAS A HIT, MAYBE BECAUSE IT GLORIFIED THE BRITISH EMPIRE.
...SET IN AFRICA... WITH AUTHENTIC FOOTAGE? JUST THE PROJECT MR. ROBESON HAS BEEN LOOKING FOR!
"LIBERTY-EQUALITY-FRATERNITY. THE WHITE SLAVES IN FRANCE-THEY MADE A REVOLUTION. THEY KILLED THE SLAVE OWNERS AND MADE EVERYONE FREE."
"WE SHALL KEEP OUR FREEDOM. I SHALL ARM THE POPULATION-TELL THEM THAT WHOEVER WISHES TO TAKE THEIR GUNS AWAY WISHES TO RESTORE SLAVERY!"
1935~ PAUL WAS JOE THE RIVERMAN IN A SUCCESSFUL U.S. FILM OF SHOWBOAT. BUT HE HURRIED BACK TO LONDON FOR REHEARSALS, PREPARING TO STAR IN C.L.R. JAMES' STAGE PLAY TOUISSANT L'OUVERTURE. UNLIKE HIS COMMERCIAL ROLES, AS THE LIBERATOR OF HAITI PAUL COULD VOICE HIS GROWING THIRST FOR RADICAL CHANGE.
SHARON RUDAHL 2018

CHAPTER IV

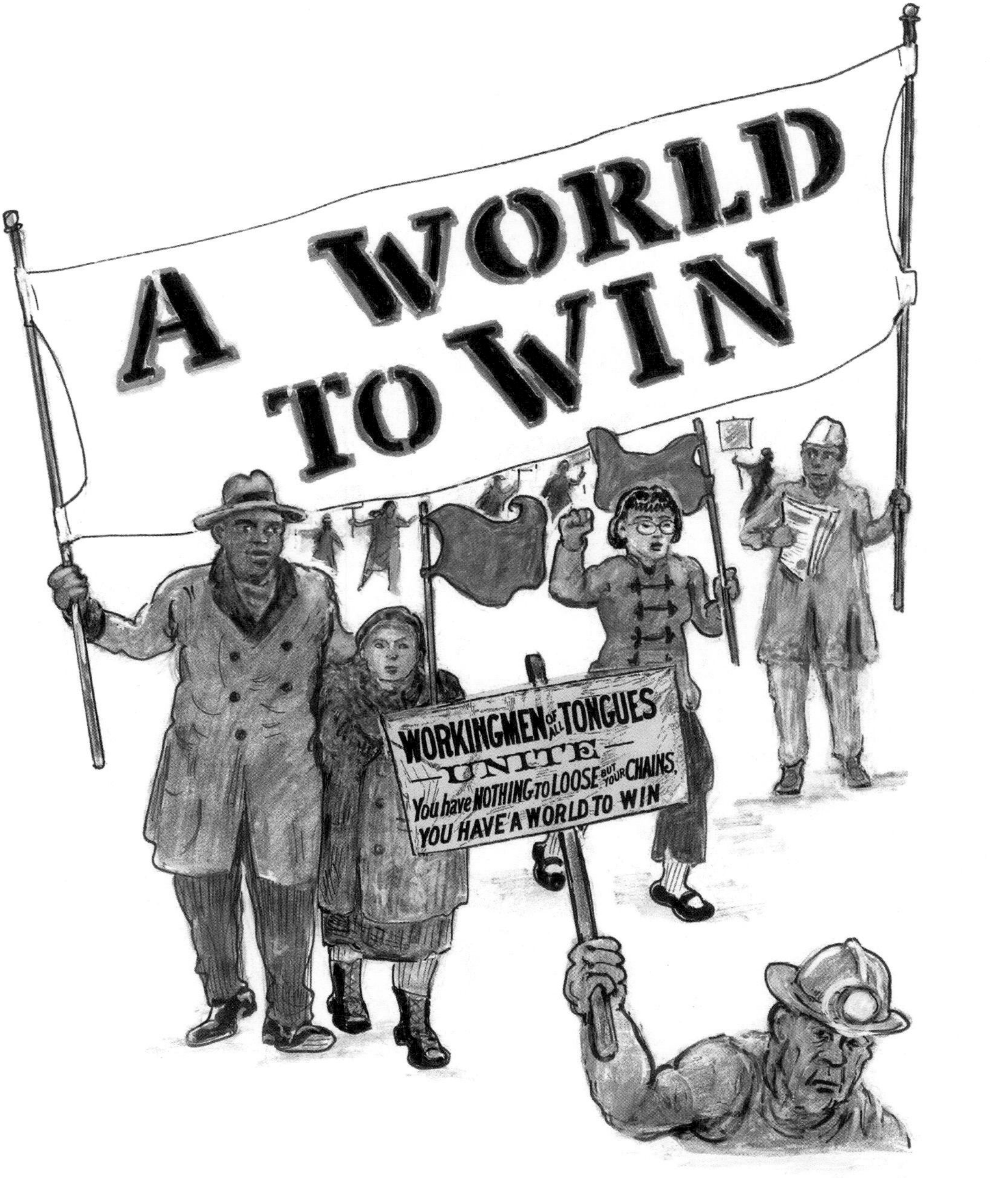
A WORLD
TO WIN
WORKINGMEN OF ALL TONGUES
UNITE
You have NOTHING TO LOOSE BUT YOUR CHAINS,
YOU HAVE A WORLD TO WIN
SHARON RUDAHL 2019

After the 1929 stock market crash, a great depression darkened much of the world. Germany's economy had been crushed by payments demanded at the end of World War I. Rabble-rousers advanced on soaring hunger, homelessness and anger. They promised jobs, pride, and revenge. In Italy their party took the name of an ancient Roman symbol of power:

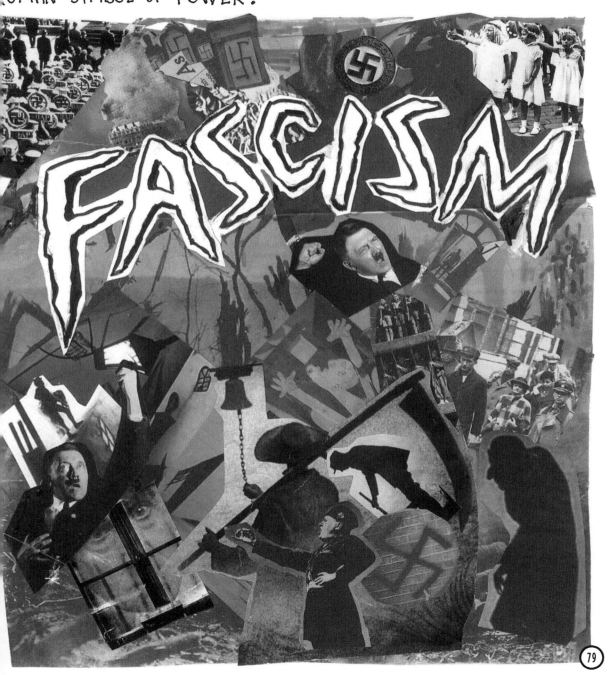

FASCISM

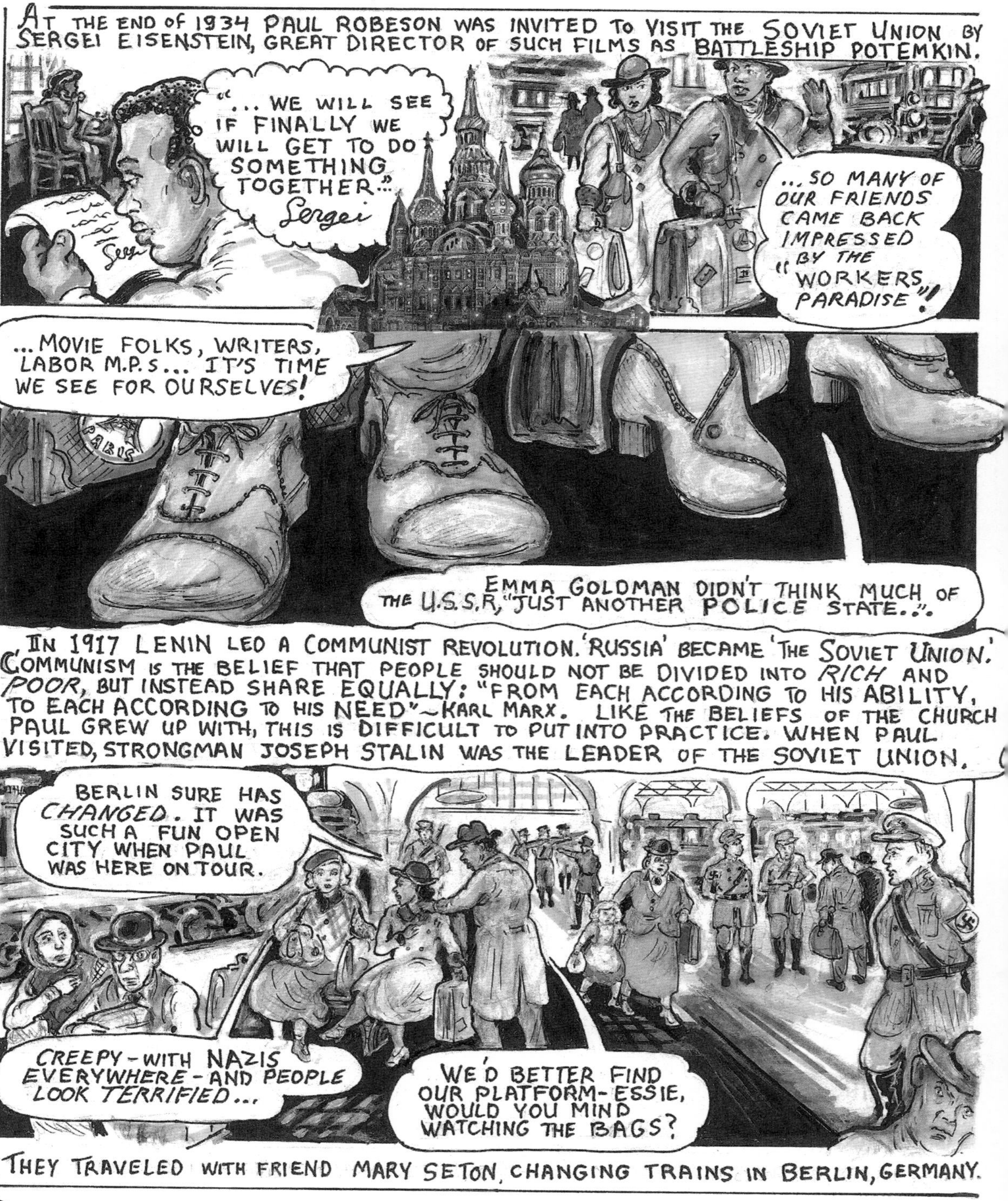

AT THE END OF 1934 PAUL ROBESON WAS INVITED TO VISIT THE SOVIET UNION BY SERGEI EISENSTEIN, GREAT DIRECTOR OF SUCH FILMS AS BATTLESHIP POTEMKIN.
"... WE WILL SEE IF FINALLY WE WILL GET TO DO SOMETHING TOGETHER..." Sergei
... SO MANY OF OUR FRIENDS CAME BACK IMPRESSED BY THE "WORKERS PARADISE"!
... MOVIE FOLKS, WRITERS, LABOR M.P.S ... IT'S TIME WE SEE FOR OURSELVES!
PARIS
EMMA GOLDMAN DIDN'T THINK MUCH OF THE U.S.S.R, "JUST ANOTHER POLICE STATE...".
IN 1917 LENIN LED A COMMUNIST REVOLUTION. 'RUSSIA' BECAME 'THE SOVIET UNION.' COMMUNISM IS THE BELIEF THAT PEOPLE SHOULD NOT BE DIVIDED INTO RICH AND POOR, BUT INSTEAD SHARE EQUALLY: "FROM EACH ACCORDING TO HIS ABILITY, TO EACH ACCORDING TO HIS NEED" ~ KARL MARX. LIKE THE BELIEFS OF THE CHURCH PAUL GREW UP WITH, THIS IS DIFFICULT TO PUT INTO PRACTICE. WHEN PAUL VISITED, STRONGMAN JOSEPH STALIN WAS THE LEADER OF THE SOVIET UNION.
BERLIN SURE HAS CHANGED. IT WAS SUCH A FUN OPEN CITY WHEN PAUL WAS HERE ON TOUR.
CREEPY - WITH NAZIS EVERYWHERE - AND PEOPLE LOOK TERRIFIED...
WE'D BETTER FIND OUR PLATFORM - ESSIE, WOULD YOU MIND WATCHING THE BAGS?
THEY TRAVELED WITH FRIEND MARY SETON, CHANGING TRAINS IN BERLIN, GERMANY.

SHARON RUDAHL 2018

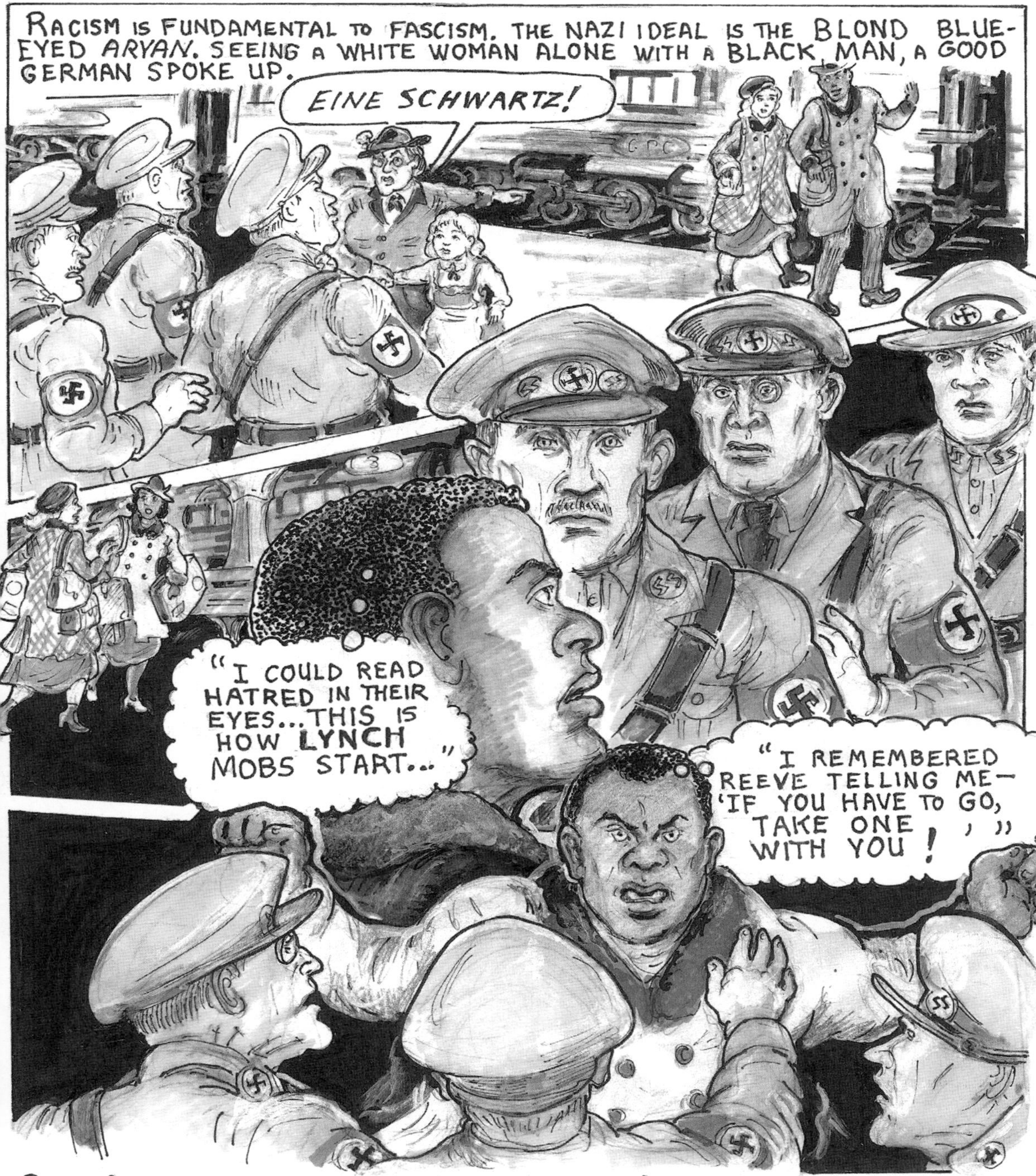
RACISM IS FUNDAMENTAL TO FASCISM. THE NAZI IDEAL IS THE BLOND BLUE-EYED ARYAN. SEEING A WHITE WOMAN ALONE WITH A BLACK MAN, A GOOD GERMAN SPOKE UP.
EINE SCHWARTZ!
"I COULD READ HATRED IN THEIR EYES...THIS IS HOW LYNCH MOBS START..."
"I REMEMBERED REEVE TELLING ME— 'IF YOU HAVE TO GO, TAKE ONE WITH YOU!'"

PAUL ROBESON SPREAD HIS ARMS WIDE AND ADVANCED TOWARD THE NAZIS.

SHARON RUDAHL

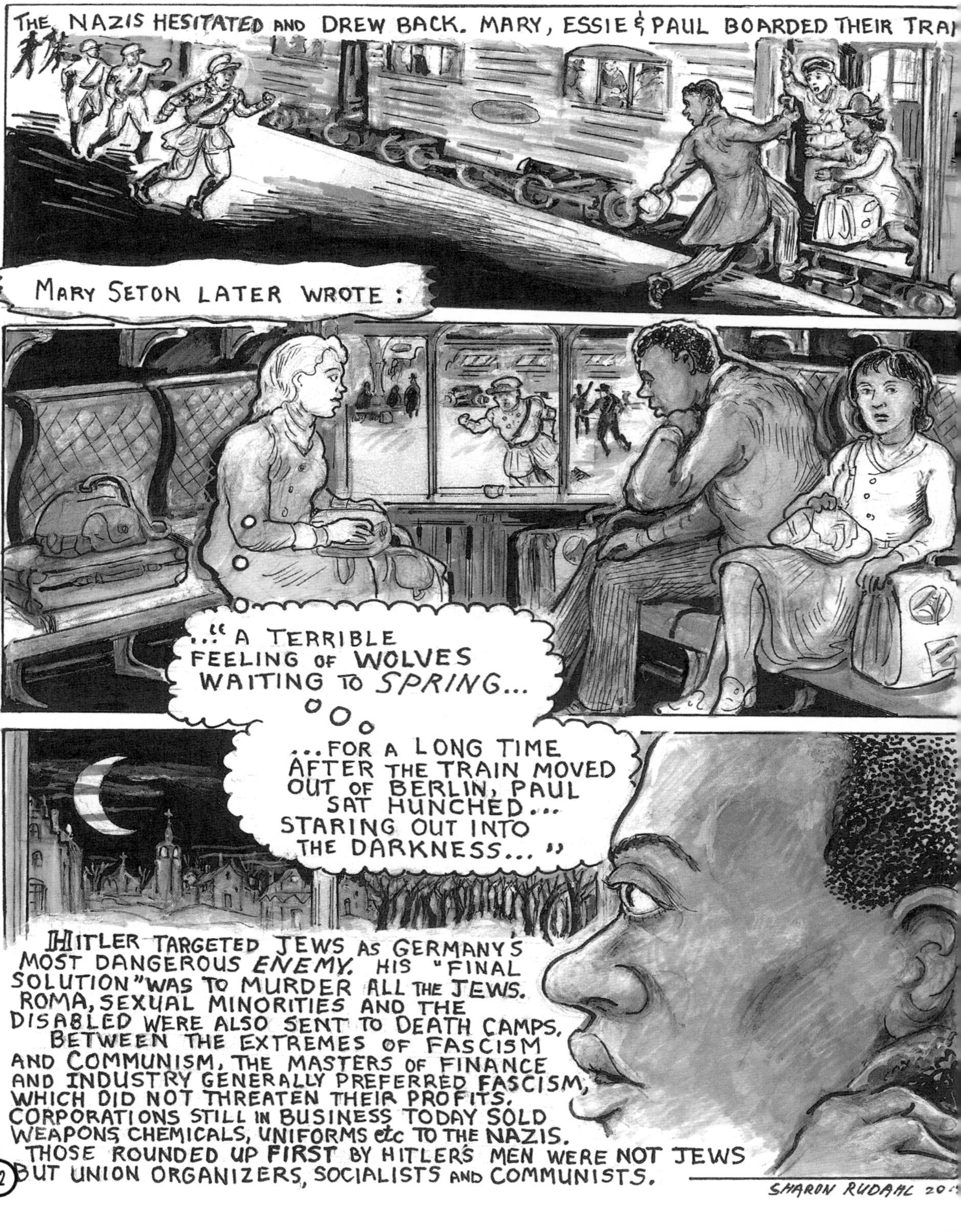
THE NAZIS HESITATED AND DREW BACK. MARY, ESSIE & PAUL BOARDED THEIR TRAI
MARY SETON LATER WROTE:
..."A TERRIBLE FEELING OF WOLVES WAITING TO SPRING...
...FOR A LONG TIME AFTER THE TRAIN MOVED OUT OF BERLIN, PAUL SAT HUNCHED... STARING OUT INTO THE DARKNESS..."
HITLER TARGETED JEWS AS GERMANY'S MOST DANGEROUS ENEMY. HIS "FINAL SOLUTION" WAS TO MURDER ALL THE JEWS. ROMA, SEXUAL MINORITIES AND THE DISABLED WERE ALSO SENT TO DEATH CAMPS. BETWEEN THE EXTREMES OF FASCISM AND COMMUNISM, THE MASTERS OF FINANCE AND INDUSTRY GENERALLY PREFERRED FASCISM, WHICH DID NOT THREATEN THEIR PROFITS. CORPORATIONS STILL IN BUSINESS TODAY SOLD WEAPONS, CHEMICALS, UNIFORMS etc TO THE NAZIS. THOSE ROUNDED UP FIRST BY HITLER'S MEN WERE NOT JEWS BUT UNION ORGANIZERS, SOCIALISTS AND COMMUNISTS.
SHARON RUDAHL

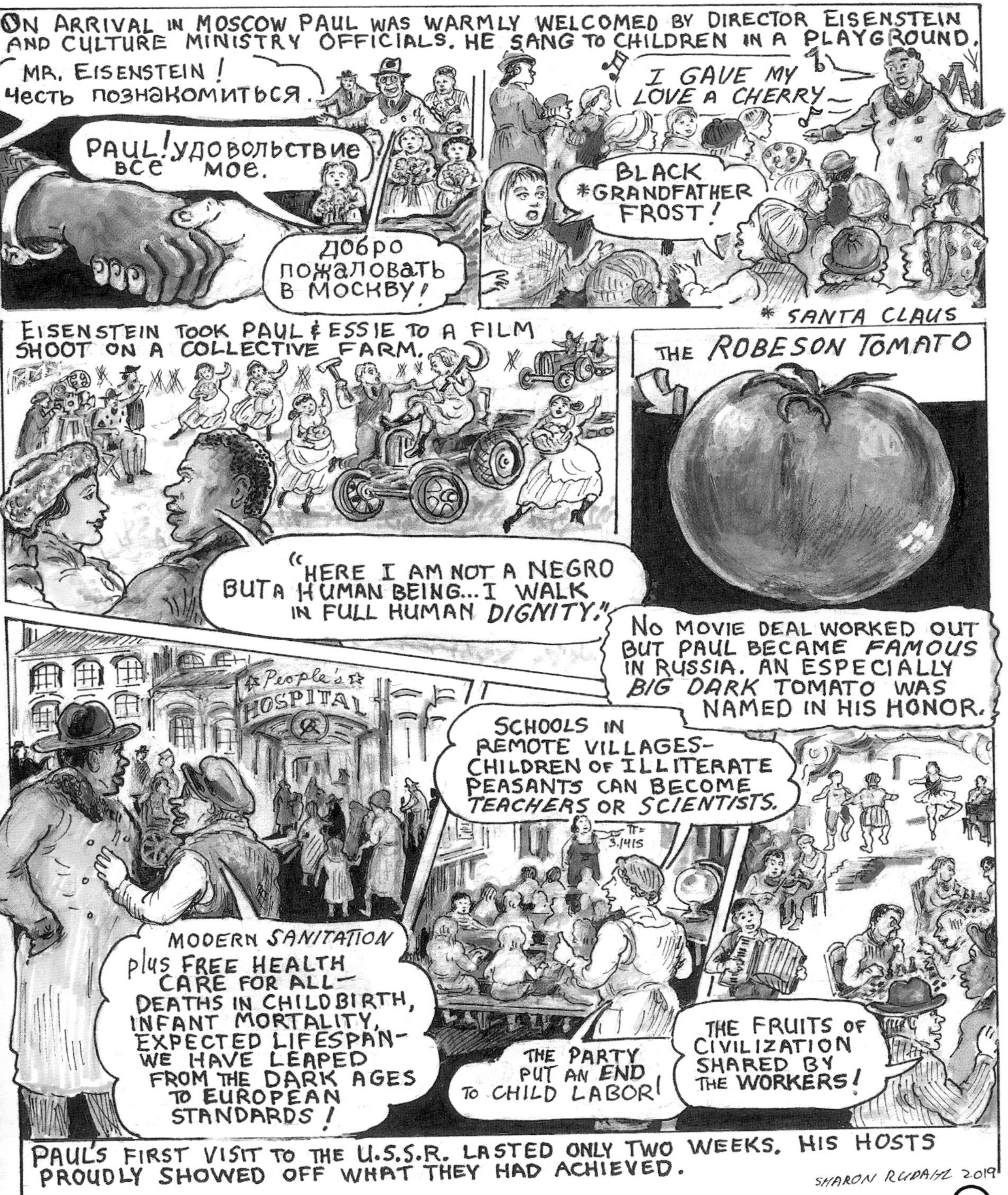
ON ARRIVAL IN MOSCOW PAUL WAS WARMLY WELCOMED BY DIRECTOR EISENSTEIN AND CULTURE MINISTRY OFFICIALS. HE SANG TO CHILDREN IN A PLAYGROUND.
MR. EISENSTEIN! Честь познакомиться.
PAUL! Удовольствие все мое.
Добро пожаловать в Москву!
I GAVE MY LOVE A CHERRY
BLACK *GRANDFATHER FROST!
* SANTA CLAUS
EISENSTEIN TOOK PAUL & ESSIE TO A FILM SHOOT ON A COLLECTIVE FARM.
"HERE I AM NOT A NEGRO BUT A HUMAN BEING... I WALK IN FULL HUMAN DIGNITY."
THE ROBESON TOMATO
NO MOVIE DEAL WORKED OUT BUT PAUL BECAME FAMOUS IN RUSSIA. AN ESPECIALLY BIG DARK TOMATO WAS NAMED IN HIS HONOR.
People's HOSPITAL
SCHOOLS IN REMOTE VILLAGES- CHILDREN OF ILLITERATE PEASANTS CAN BECOME TEACHERS OR SCIENTISTS.
π= 3.1415
MODERN SANITATION plus FREE HEALTH CARE FOR ALL- DEATHS IN CHILDBIRTH, INFANT MORTALITY, EXPECTED LIFESPAN- WE HAVE LEAPED FROM THE DARK AGES TO EUROPEAN STANDARDS!
THE PARTY PUT AN END TO CHILD LABOR!
THE FRUITS OF CIVILIZATION SHARED BY THE WORKERS!
PAUL'S FIRST VISIT TO THE U.S.S.R. LASTED ONLY TWO WEEKS. HIS HOSTS PROUDLY SHOWED OFF WHAT THEY HAD ACHIEVED.
SHARON RUDAHL 2019

BUT HONORED GUESTS ARE NOT INVITED INTO *EVERY* ROOM...

SORRY, NOT OPEN TO VISITORS.

CENSORSHIP AND THOUGHT CONTROL

SECRET POLICE PURGES AND SHOW TRIALS

FORCED COLLECTIVE FARMING —FAMINE—

POLITICAL PRISONERS — LABOR CAMPS

Workers Councils DICTATORSHIP

IN THE EARLY HOPEFUL DAYS AFTER THE 1917 REVOLUTION, EFFORTS WERE MADE TO WELCOME THE RELIGIOUS AND RACIAL MINORITIES FROM THE FRINGES OF THE CZARS' EMPIRE: JEWS, MOSLEMS, CENTRAL ASIANS, SIBERIANS. BUT BIGOTRY PERSISTED.

PEOPLE OF AFRICAN DESCENT WERE NOT A TRADITIONAL TARGET OF RACISM. RUSSIA'S BELOVED NATIONAL POET, ALEXANDER PUSHKIN, WAS THE GRANDSON OF AN AFRICAN WHO ROSE TO HIGH POSITION IN THE COURT OF PETER THE GREAT.

ALEXANDER PUSHKIN 1799 – 1837

"I WISH OUR SON COULD EXPERIENCE LIFE WITHOUT *RACISM*..."

BEFORE RETURNING TO ENGLAND THE ROBESONS ARRANGED FOR PAUL JR. TO ATTEND A SOVIET MODEL SCHOOL.

WITH MA GOODE ALONG TO MAKE A HOME FOR HIM, PAUL JR. COMPLETED TWO TERMS AT THE RUSSIAN SCHOOL. HIS CLASSMATES INCLUDED STALIN'S DAUGHTER AND THE SON OF FOREIGN MINISTER MOLOTOV.

MY DAD'S THE BEST SINGER IN THE WHOLE WORLD!

MY DAD CAN MAKE *BOMBS* OUT OF SODA BOTTLES!

SHARON RUDAHL 2019

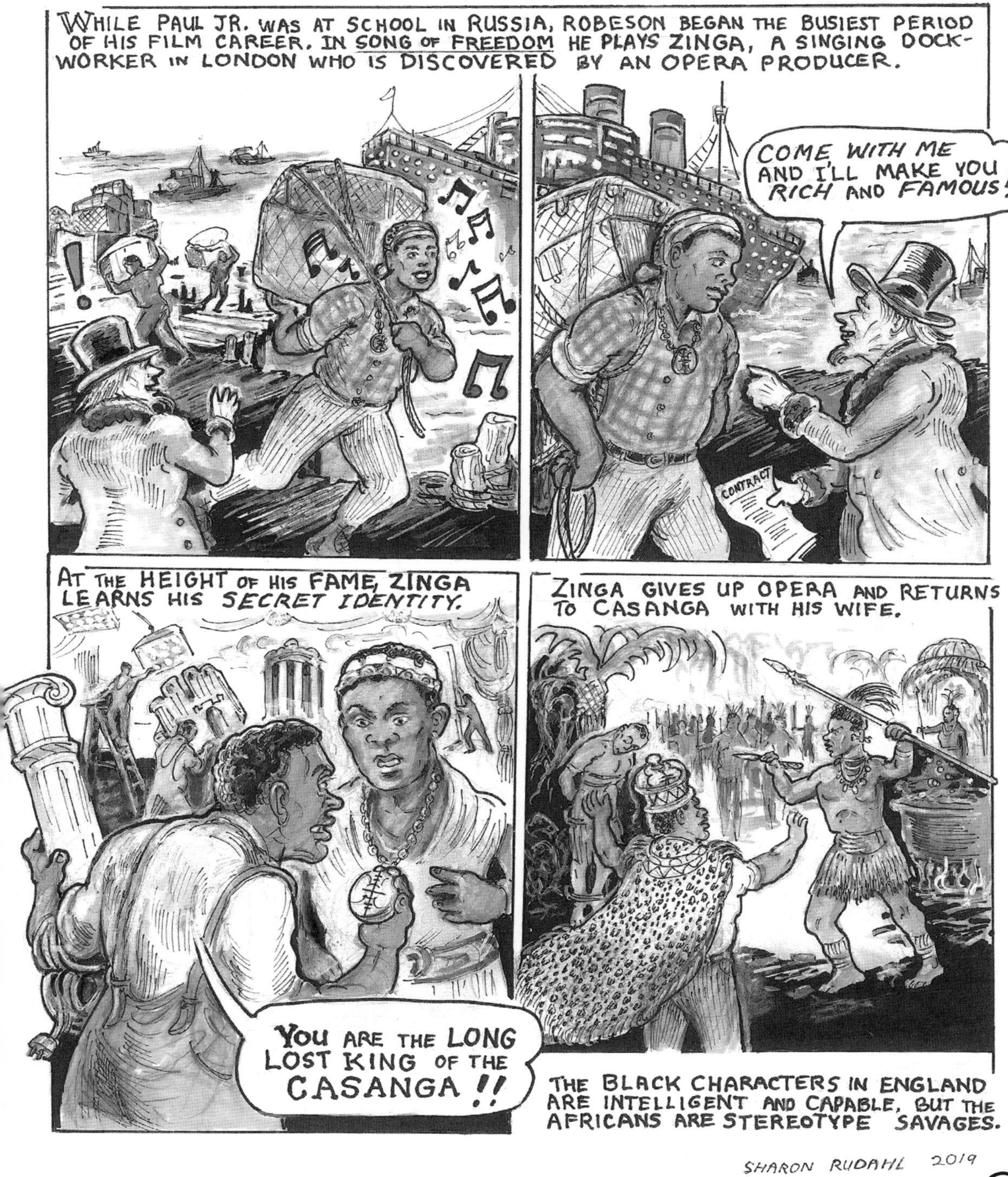
WHILE PAUL JR. WAS AT SCHOOL IN RUSSIA, ROBESON BEGAN THE BUSIEST PERIOD OF HIS FILM CAREER. IN SONG OF FREEDOM HE PLAYS ZINGA, A SINGING DOCK-WORKER IN LONDON WHO IS DISCOVERED BY AN OPERA PRODUCER.
!
COME WITH ME AND I'LL MAKE YOU RICH AND FAMOUS!
CONTRACT
AT THE HEIGHT OF HIS FAME, ZINGA LEARNS HIS SECRET IDENTITY.
YOU ARE THE LONG LOST KING OF THE CASANGA!!
ZINGA GIVES UP OPERA AND RETURNS TO CASANGA WITH HIS WIFE.
THE BLACK CHARACTERS IN ENGLAND ARE INTELLIGENT AND CAPABLE, BUT THE AFRICANS ARE STEREOTYPE SAVAGES.
SHARON RUDAHL 2019

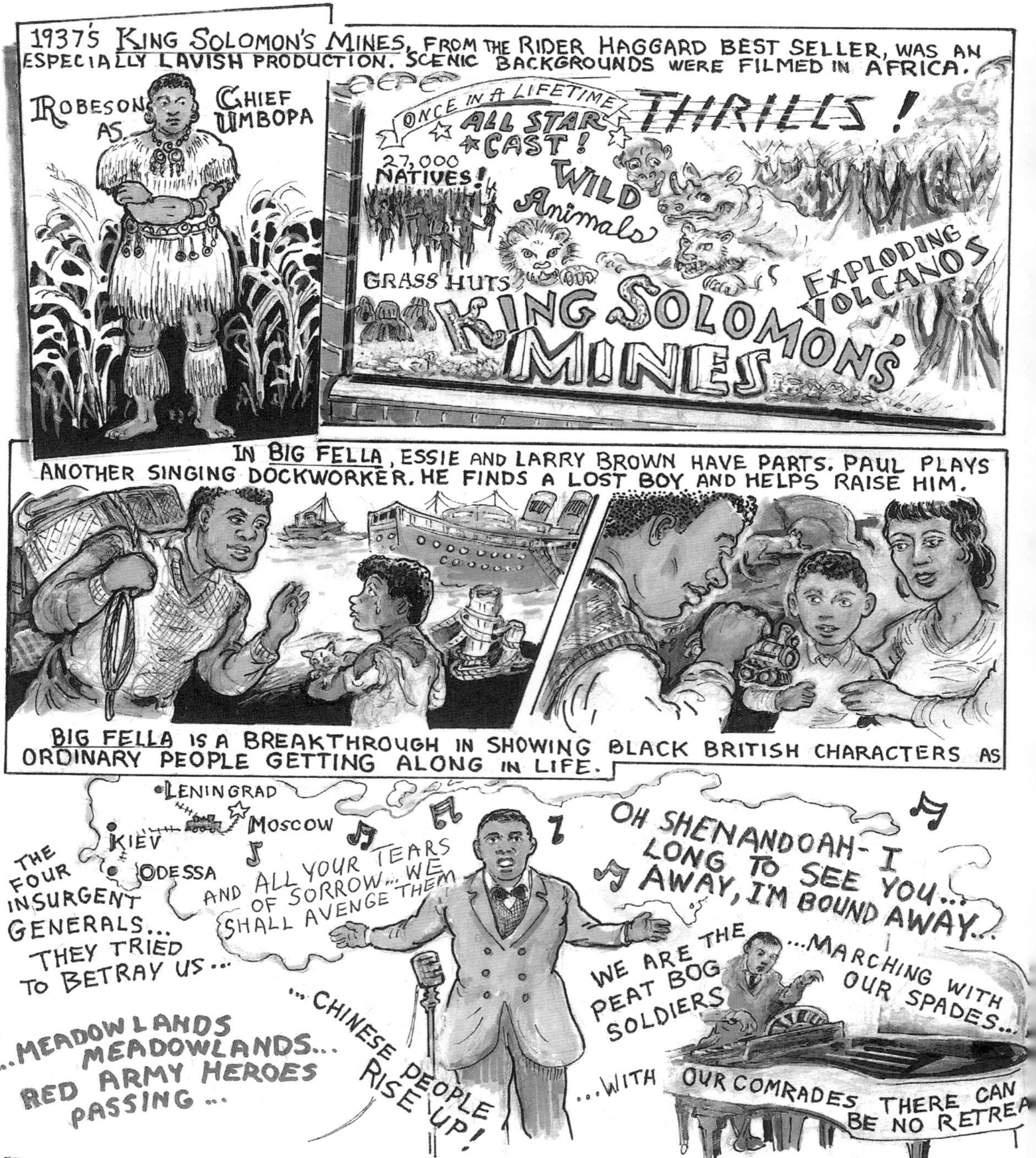
1937'S KING SOLOMON'S MINES, FROM THE RIDER HAGGARD BEST SELLER, WAS AN ESPECIALLY LAVISH PRODUCTION. SCENIC BACKGROUNDS WERE FILMED IN AFRICA.
ROBESON AS CHIEF UMBOPA
ONCE IN A LIFETIME
ALL STAR CAST!
THRILLS!
27,000 NATIVES!
WILD Animals
GRASS HUTS
EXPLODING VOLCANOS
KING SOLOMON'S MINES
IN BIG FELLA, ESSIE AND LARRY BROWN HAVE PARTS. PAUL PLAYS ANOTHER SINGING DOCKWORKER. HE FINDS A LOST BOY AND HELPS RAISE HIM.
BIG FELLA IS A BREAKTHROUGH IN SHOWING BLACK BRITISH CHARACTERS AS ORDINARY PEOPLE GETTING ALONG IN LIFE.
LENINGRAD
MOSCOW
KIEV
ODESSA
THE FOUR INSURGENT GENERALS... THEY TRIED TO BETRAY US...
AND ALL YOUR TEARS OF SORROW... WE SHALL AVENGE THEM
OH SHENANDOAH- I LONG TO SEE YOU... AWAY, I'M BOUND AWAY...
WE ARE THE PEAT BOG SOLDIERS
...MARCHING WITH OUR SPADES...
...MEADOWLANDS MEADOWLANDS... RED ARMY HEROES PASSING...
...CHINESE PEOPLE RISE UP!
...WITH OUR COMRADES THERE CAN BE NO RETREA
BETWEEN WORK ON KING SOLOMON'S MINES AND GOING ON LOCATION IN EGYPT FOR THE MOVIE JERICHO, PAUL ROBESON WENT ON A MONTHLONG CONCERT TOUR IN THE SOVIET UNION, PERFORMING FOLK AND PROTEST SONGS FROM MANY LANDS.
SHARON RUDAHL 2019

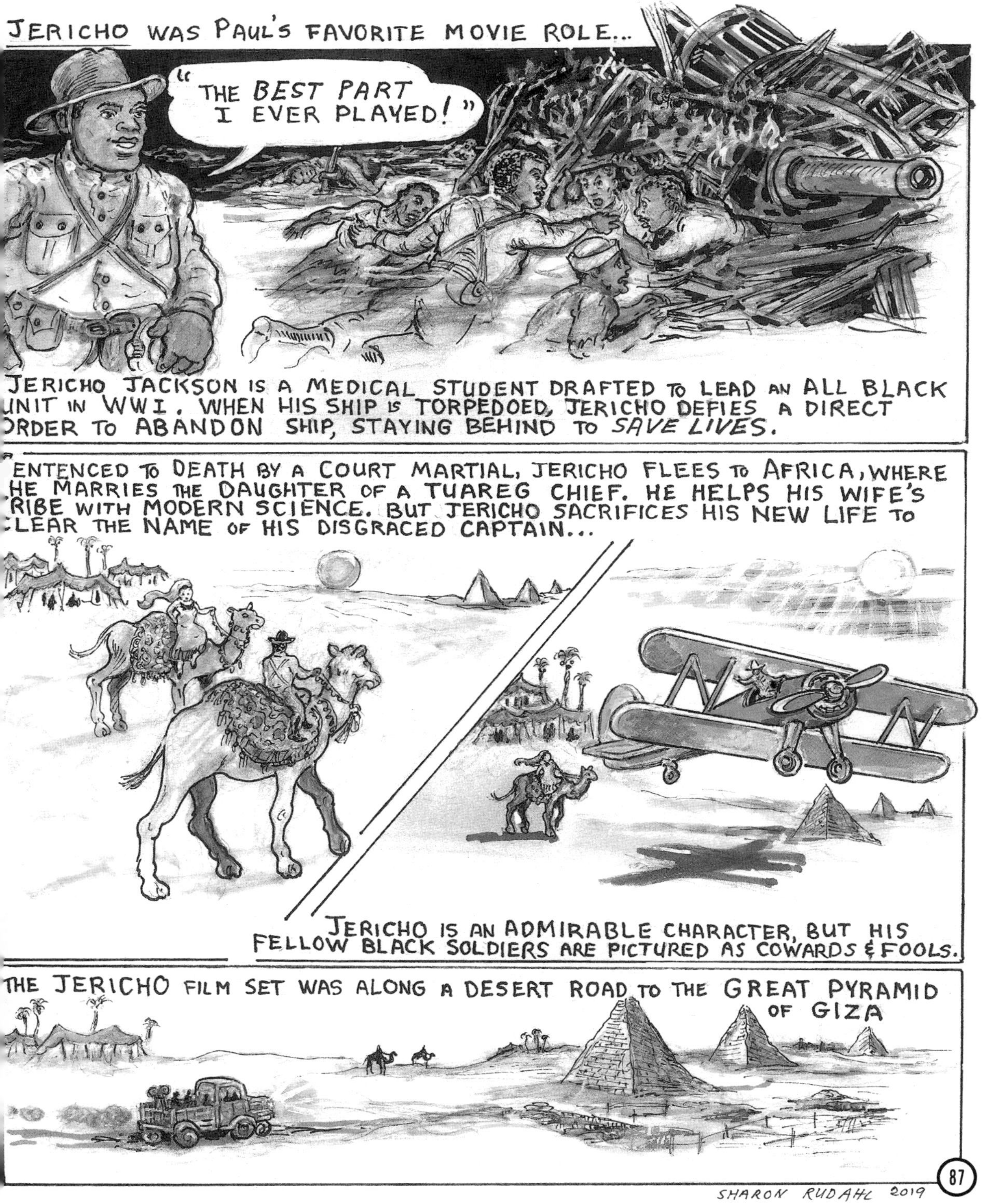
JERICHO WAS PAUL'S FAVORITE MOVIE ROLE...
"THE BEST PART I EVER PLAYED!"
JERICHO JACKSON IS A MEDICAL STUDENT DRAFTED TO LEAD AN ALL BLACK UNIT IN WWI. WHEN HIS SHIP IS TORPEDOED, JERICHO DEFIES A DIRECT ORDER TO ABANDON SHIP, STAYING BEHIND TO SAVE LIVES.
ENTENCED TO DEATH BY A COURT MARTIAL, JERICHO FLEES TO AFRICA, WHERE HE MARRIES THE DAUGHTER OF A TUAREG CHIEF. HE HELPS HIS WIFE'S RIBE WITH MODERN SCIENCE. BUT JERICHO SACRIFICES HIS NEW LIFE TO LEAR THE NAME OF HIS DISGRACED CAPTAIN...
JERICHO IS AN ADMIRABLE CHARACTER, BUT HIS FELLOW BLACK SOLDIERS ARE PICTURED AS COWARDS & FOOLS.
THE JERICHO FILM SET WAS ALONG A DESERT ROAD TO THE GREAT PYRAMID OF GIZA
SHARON RUDAHL 2019

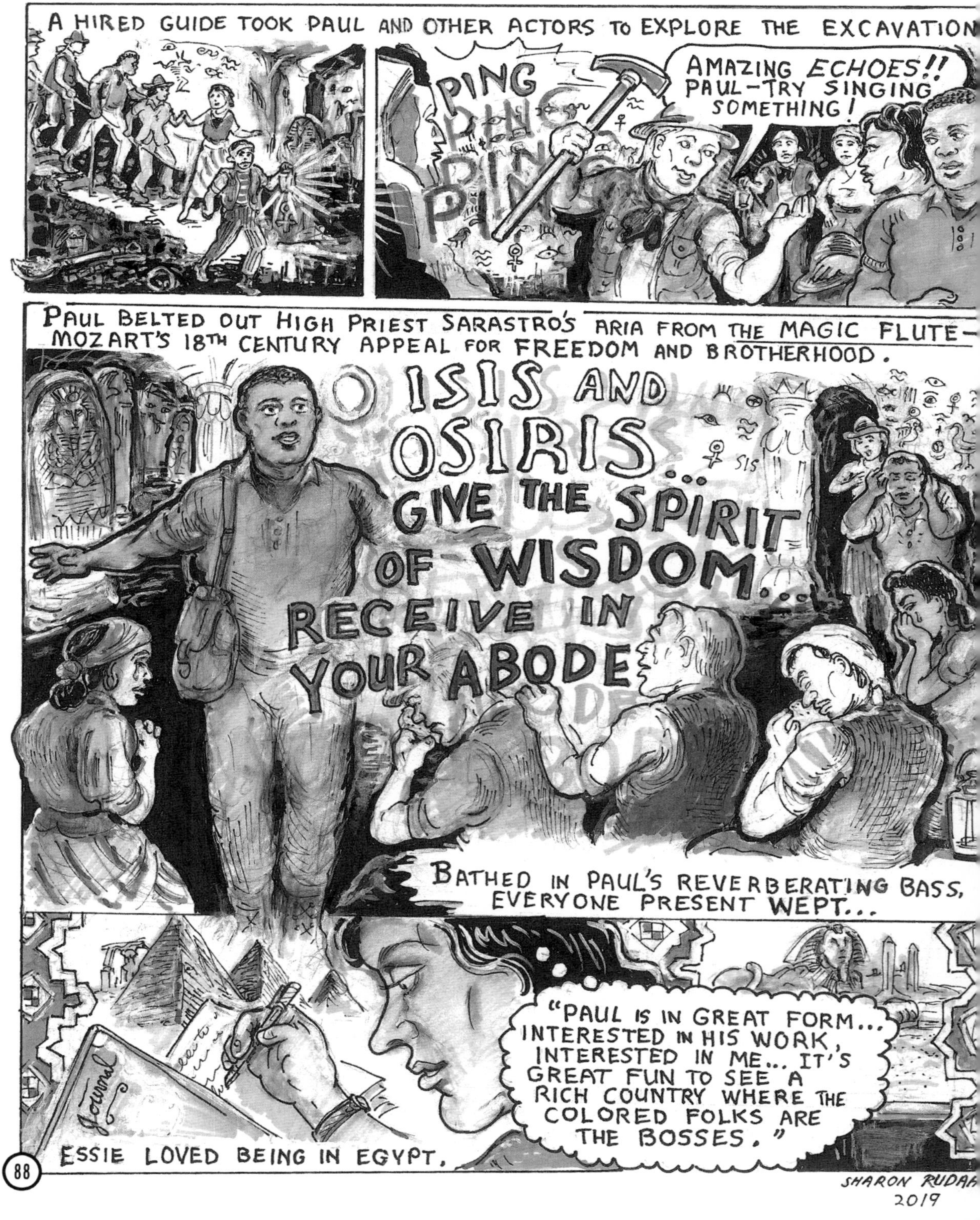
A HIRED GUIDE TOOK PAUL AND OTHER ACTORS TO EXPLORE THE EXCAVATION
PING PING PING PING
AMAZING ECHOES!! PAUL–TRY SINGING SOMETHING!
PAUL BELTED OUT HIGH PRIEST SARASTRO'S ARIA FROM THE MAGIC FLUTE– MOZART'S 18TH CENTURY APPEAL FOR FREEDOM AND BROTHERHOOD.
O ISIS AND OSIRIS... GIVE THE SPIRIT OF WISDOM... RECEIVE IN YOUR ABODE
BATHED IN PAUL'S REVERBERATING BASS, EVERYONE PRESENT WEPT...
Journal
"PAUL IS IN GREAT FORM... INTERESTED IN HIS WORK, INTERESTED IN ME... IT'S GREAT FUN TO SEE A RICH COUNTRY WHERE THE COLORED FOLKS ARE THE BOSSES."
ESSIE LOVED BEING IN EGYPT.
SHARON RUDAH
2019

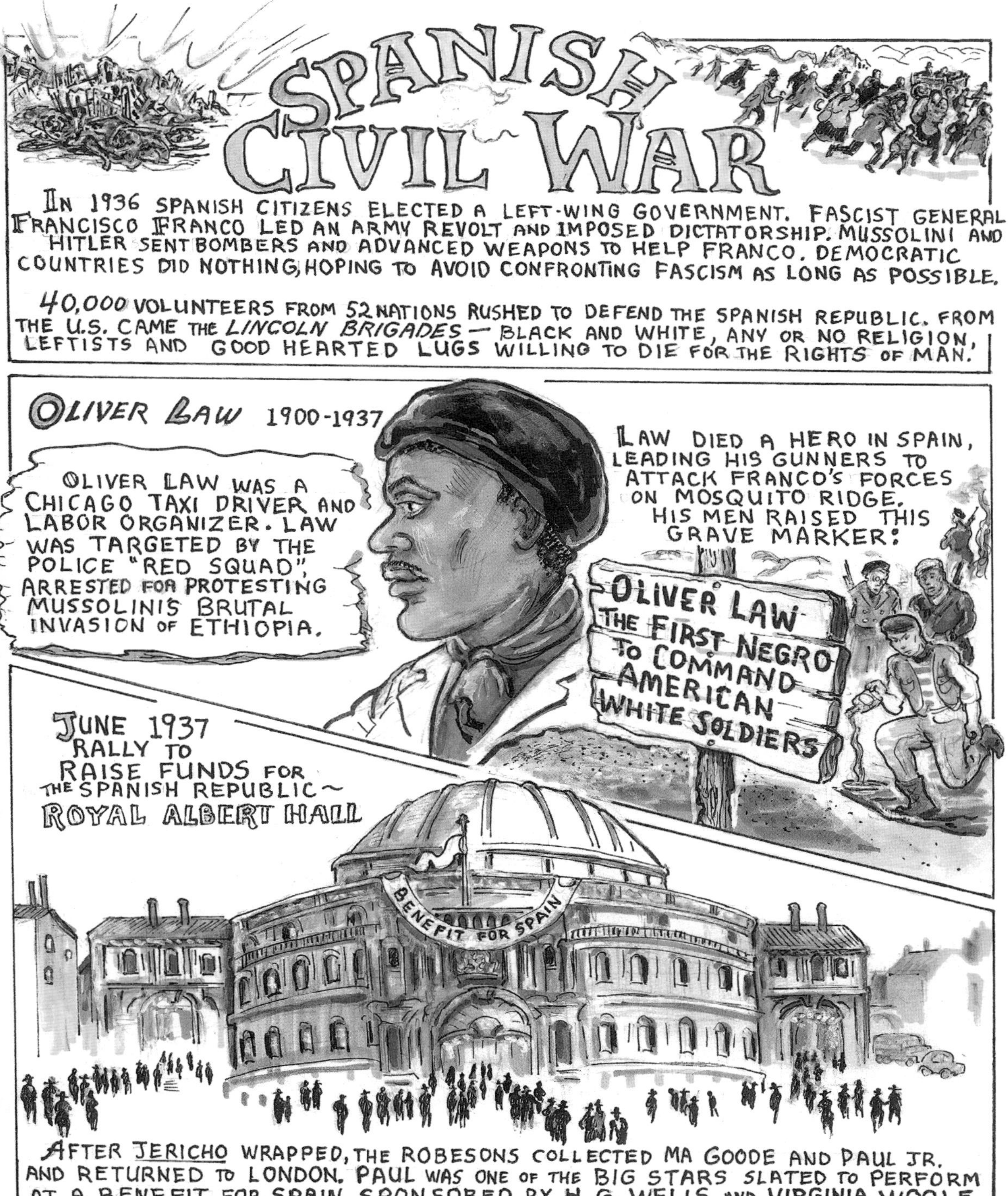
SPANISH CIVIL WAR
IN 1936 SPANISH CITIZENS ELECTED A LEFT-WING GOVERNMENT. FASCIST GENERAL FRANCISCO FRANCO LED AN ARMY REVOLT AND IMPOSED DICTATORSHIP. MUSSOLINI AND HITLER SENT BOMBERS AND ADVANCED WEAPONS TO HELP FRANCO. DEMOCRATIC COUNTRIES DID NOTHING, HOPING TO AVOID CONFRONTING FASCISM AS LONG AS POSSIBLE.
40,000 VOLUNTEERS FROM 52 NATIONS RUSHED TO DEFEND THE SPANISH REPUBLIC. FROM THE U.S. CAME THE LINCOLN BRIGADES — BLACK AND WHITE, ANY OR NO RELIGION, LEFTISTS AND GOOD HEARTED LUGS WILLING TO DIE FOR THE RIGHTS OF MAN.'
OLIVER LAW 1900-1937
OLIVER LAW WAS A CHICAGO TAXI DRIVER AND LABOR ORGANIZER. LAW WAS TARGETED BY THE POLICE "RED SQUAD", ARRESTED FOR PROTESTING MUSSOLINI'S BRUTAL INVASION OF ETHIOPIA.
LAW DIED A HERO IN SPAIN, LEADING HIS GUNNERS TO ATTACK FRANCO'S FORCES ON MOSQUITO RIDGE. HIS MEN RAISED THIS GRAVE MARKER:
OLIVER LAW THE FIRST NEGRO TO COMMAND AMERICAN WHITE SOLDIERS
JUNE 1937 RALLY TO RAISE FUNDS FOR THE SPANISH REPUBLIC ~ ROYAL ALBERT HALL
BENEFIT FOR SPAIN
AFTER JERICHO WRAPPED, THE ROBESONS COLLECTED MA GOODE AND PAUL JR. AND RETURNED TO LONDON. PAUL WAS ONE OF THE BIG STARS SLATED TO PERFORM AT A BENEFIT FOR SPAIN SPONSORED BY H.G. WELLS AND VIRGINIA WOOLF.
SHARON RUDAHL 2019

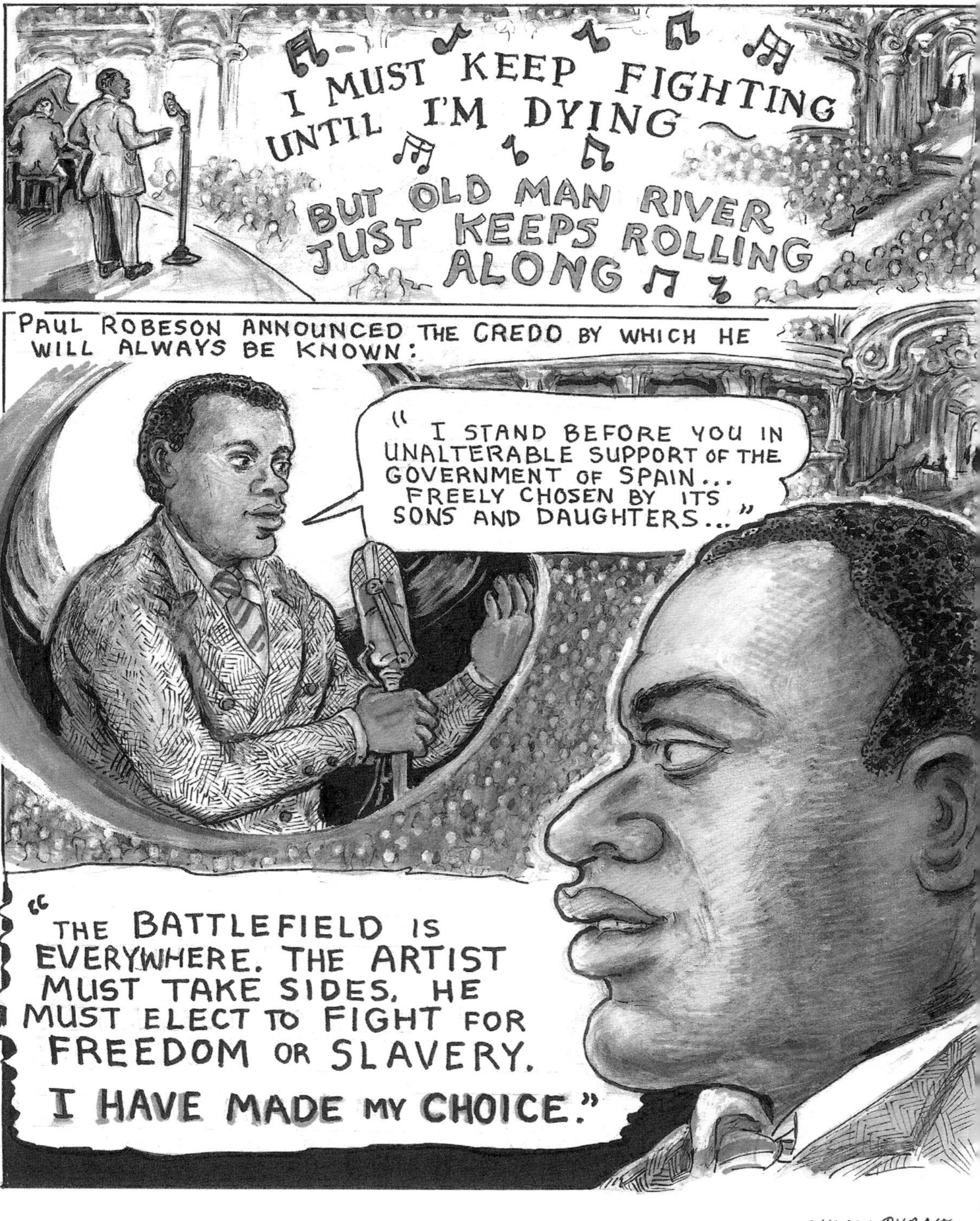
I MUST KEEP FIGHTING UNTIL I'M DYING
BUT OLD MAN RIVER JUST KEEPS ROLLING ALONG
PAUL ROBESON ANNOUNCED THE CREDO BY WHICH HE WILL ALWAYS BE KNOWN:
"I STAND BEFORE YOU IN UNALTERABLE SUPPORT OF THE GOVERNMENT OF SPAIN... FREELY CHOSEN BY ITS SONS AND DAUGHTERS..."
"THE BATTLEFIELD IS EVERYWHERE. THE ARTIST MUST TAKE SIDES. HE MUST ELECT TO FIGHT FOR FREEDOM OR SLAVERY.
I HAVE MADE MY CHOICE."

SHARON RUDAHL 2019

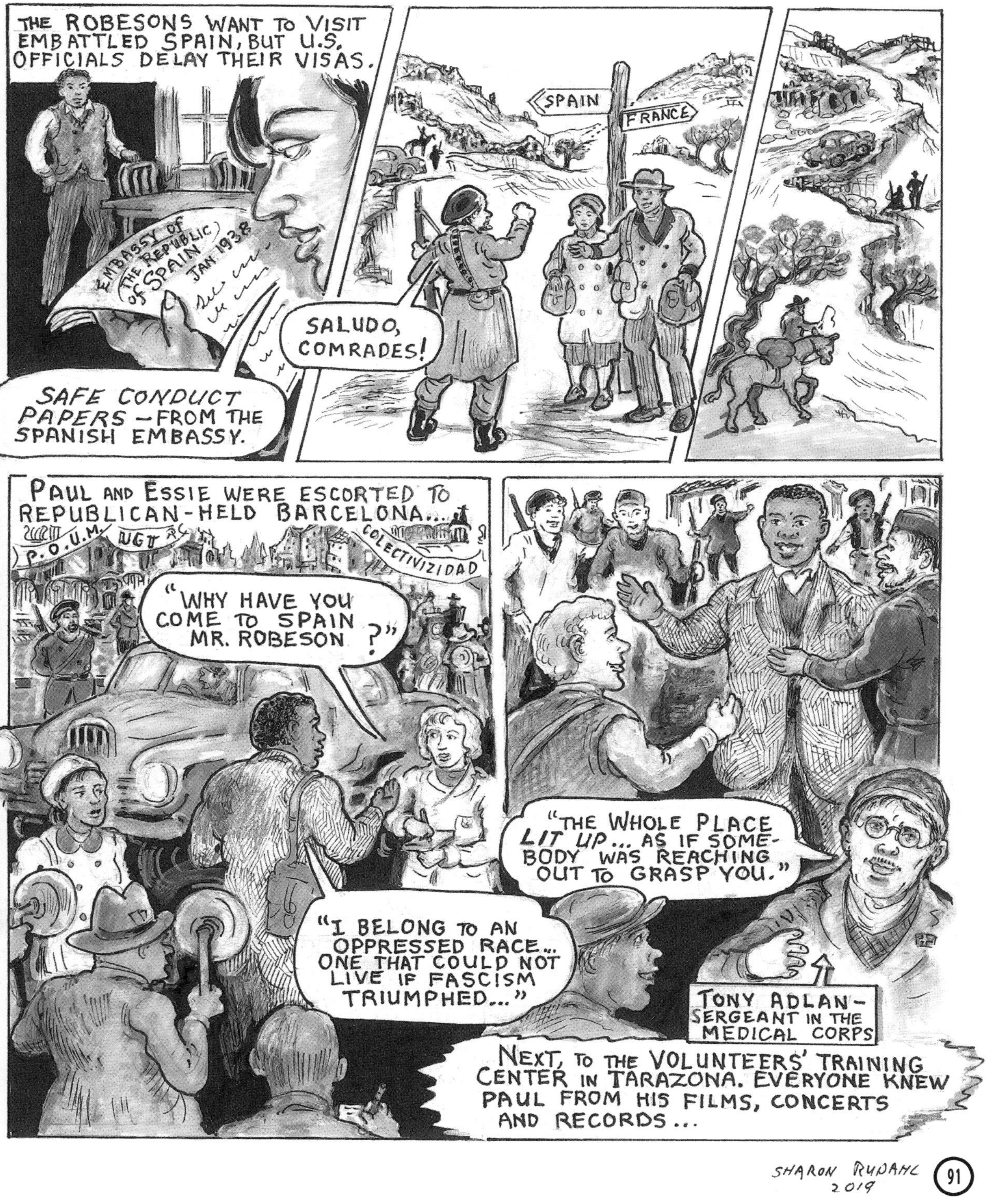
THE ROBESONS WANT TO VISIT EMBATTLED SPAIN, BUT U.S. OFFICIALS DELAY THEIR VISAS.
EMBASSY OF THE REPUBLIC OF SPAIN JAN. 1938
SAFE CONDUCT PAPERS — FROM THE SPANISH EMBASSY.
SPAIN
FRANCE
SALUDO, COMRADES!
PAUL AND ESSIE WERE ESCORTED TO REPUBLICAN-HELD BARCELONA...
P.O.U.M.
UGT
COLECTIVIZIDAD
"WHY HAVE YOU COME TO SPAIN MR. ROBESON?"
"I BELONG TO AN OPPRESSED RACE... ONE THAT COULD NOT LIVE IF FASCISM TRIUMPHED..."
"THE WHOLE PLACE LIT UP... AS IF SOMEBODY WAS REACHING OUT TO GRASP YOU."
TONY ADLAN — SERGEANT IN THE MEDICAL CORPS
NEXT, TO THE VOLUNTEERS' TRAINING CENTER IN TARAZONA. EVERYONE KNEW PAUL FROM HIS FILMS, CONCERTS AND RECORDS...
SHARON RUDAHL 2019

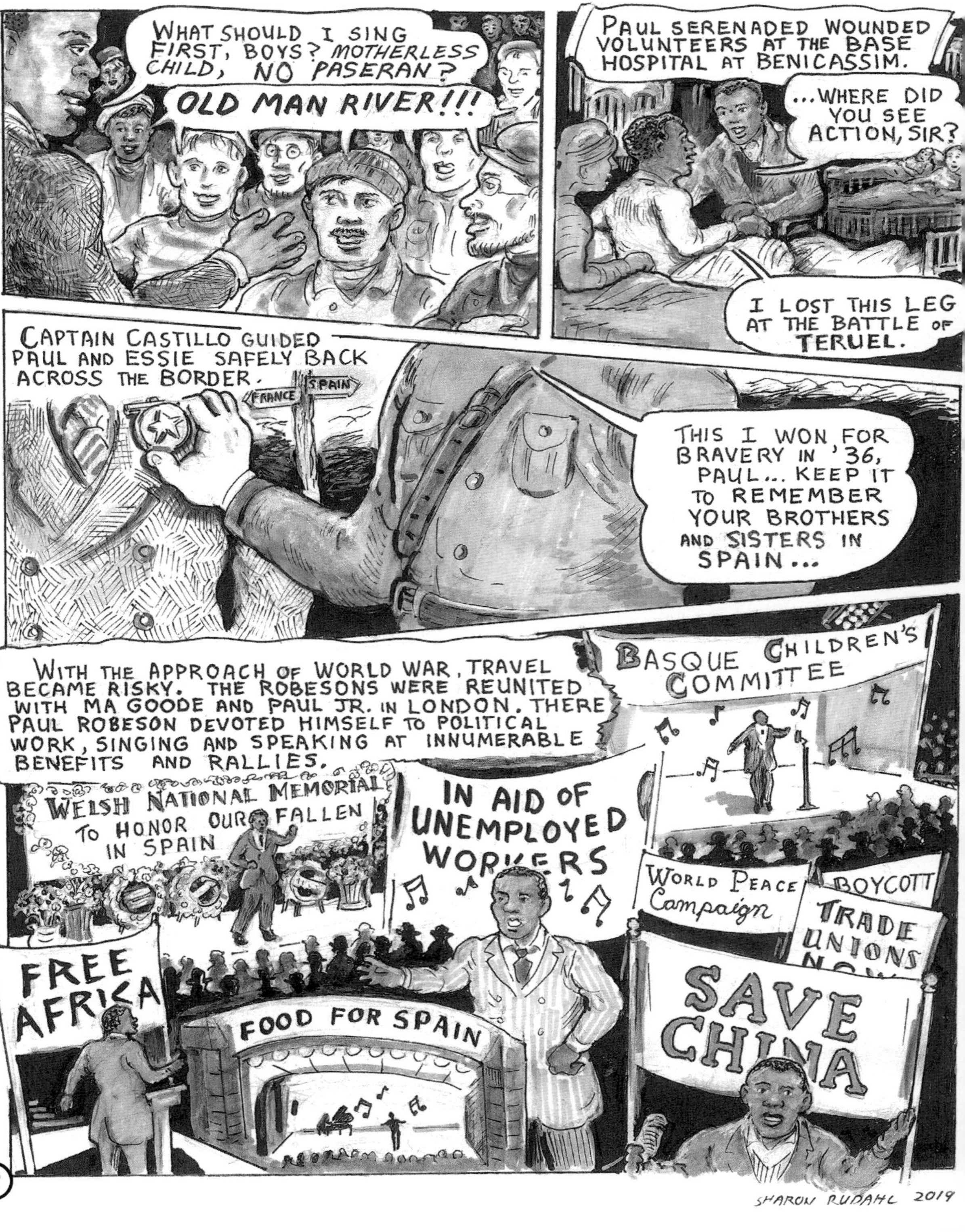

WHAT SHOULD I SING FIRST, BOYS? MOTHERLESS CHILD, NO PASERAN?
OLD MAN RIVER!!!
PAUL SERENADED WOUNDED VOLUNTEERS AT THE BASE HOSPITAL AT BENICASSIM.
...WHERE DID YOU SEE ACTION, SIR?
I LOST THIS LEG AT THE BATTLE OF TERUEL.
CAPTAIN CASTILLO GUIDED PAUL AND ESSIE SAFELY BACK ACROSS THE BORDER.
FRANCE
SPAIN
THIS I WON FOR BRAVERY IN '36, PAUL... KEEP IT TO REMEMBER YOUR BROTHERS AND SISTERS IN SPAIN...
WITH THE APPROACH OF WORLD WAR, TRAVEL BECAME RISKY. THE ROBESONS WERE REUNITED WITH MA GOODE AND PAUL JR. IN LONDON. THERE PAUL ROBESON DEVOTED HIMSELF TO POLITICAL WORK, SINGING AND SPEAKING AT INNUMERABLE BENEFITS AND RALLIES.
BASQUE CHILDREN'S COMMITTEE
WELSH NATIONAL MEMORIAL TO HONOR OUR FALLEN IN SPAIN
IN AID OF UNEMPLOYED WORKERS
WORLD PEACE Campaign
BOYCOTT
TRADE UNIONS
FREE AFRICA
FOOD FOR SPAIN
SAVE CHINA
SHARON RUDAHL 2019

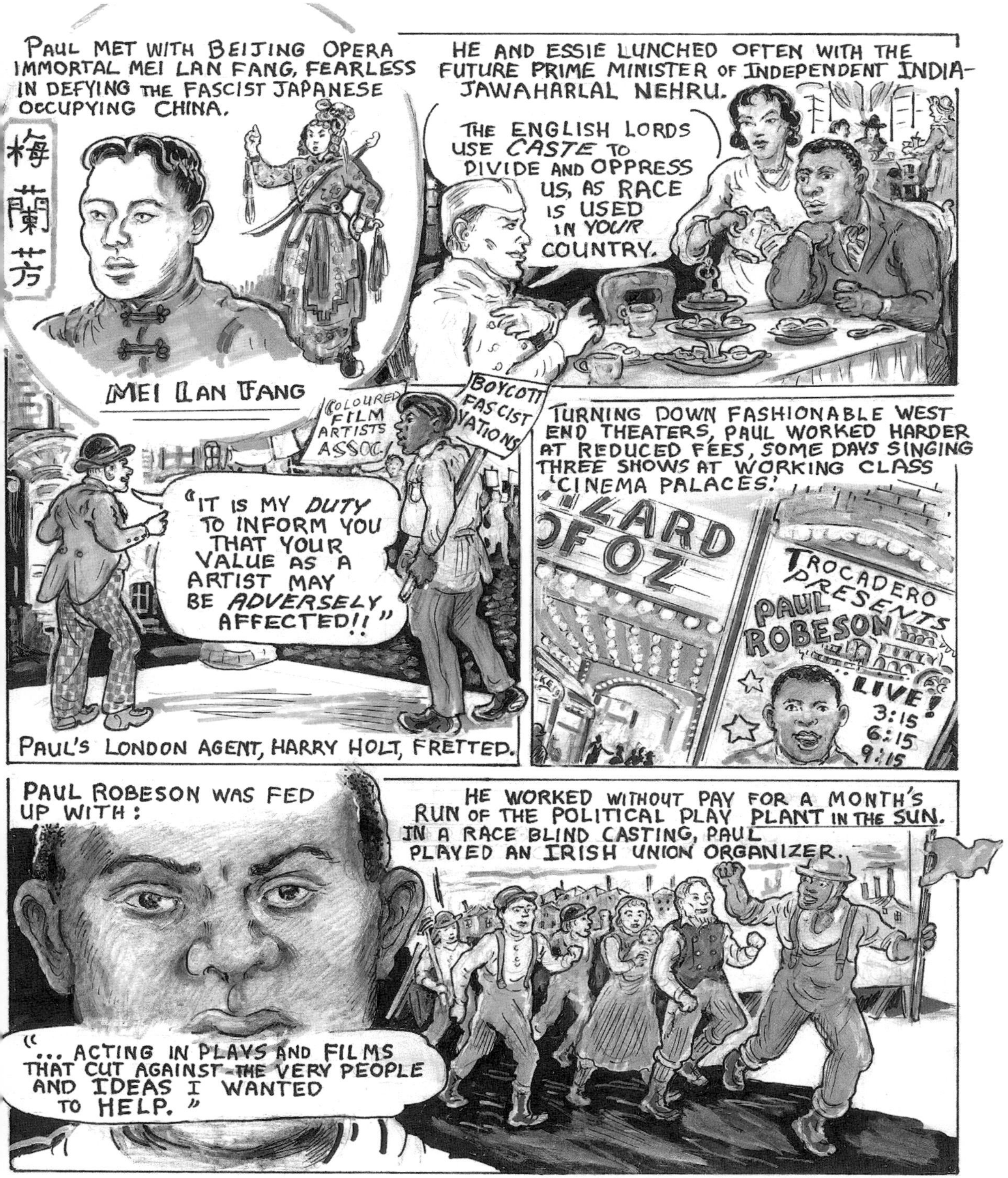
PAUL MET WITH BEIJING OPERA IMMORTAL MEI LAN FANG, FEARLESS IN DEFYING THE FASCIST JAPANESE OCCUPYING CHINA.
梅蘭芳
MEI LAN FANG
HE AND ESSIE LUNCHED OFTEN WITH THE FUTURE PRIME MINISTER OF INDEPENDENT INDIA- JAWAHARLAL NEHRU.
THE ENGLISH LORDS USE CASTE TO DIVIDE AND OPPRESS US, AS RACE IS USED IN YOUR COUNTRY.
COLOURED FILM ARTISTS ASSOC.
BOYCOTT FASCIST NATIONS
"IT IS MY DUTY TO INFORM YOU THAT YOUR VALUE AS A ARTIST MAY BE ADVERSELY AFFECTED!!"
PAUL'S LONDON AGENT, HARRY HOLT, FRETTED.
TURNING DOWN FASHIONABLE WEST END THEATERS, PAUL WORKED HARDER AT REDUCED FEES, SOME DAYS SINGING THREE SHOWS AT WORKING CLASS 'CINEMA PALACES.'
ZARD OF OZ
TROCADERO PRESENTS PAUL ROBESON LIVE! 3:15 6:15 9:15
PAUL ROBESON WAS FED UP WITH:
"... ACTING IN PLAYS AND FILMS THAT CUT AGAINST THE VERY PEOPLE AND IDEAS I WANTED TO HELP."
HE WORKED WITHOUT PAY FOR A MONTH'S RUN OF THE POLITICAL PLAY PLANT IN THE SUN. IN A RACE BLIND CASTING, PAUL PLAYED AN IRISH UNION ORGANIZER.
SHARON RUDAHL 20

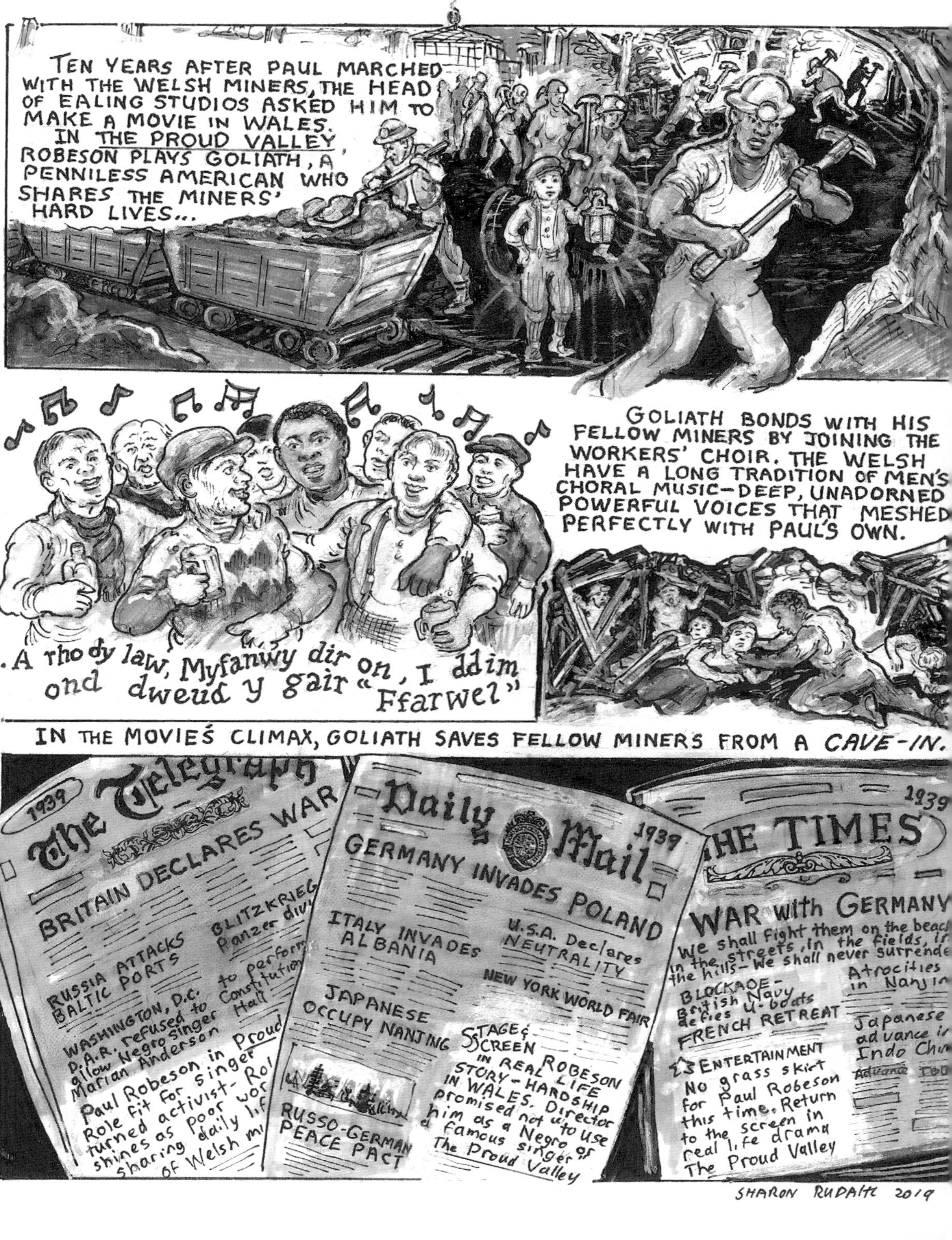
TEN YEARS AFTER PAUL MARCHED WITH THE WELSH MINERS, THE HEAD OF EALING STUDIOS ASKED HIM TO MAKE A MOVIE IN WALES.
IN THE PROUD VALLEY, ROBESON PLAYS GOLIATH, A PENNILESS AMERICAN WHO SHARES THE MINERS' HARD LIVES...
GOLIATH BONDS WITH HIS FELLOW MINERS BY JOINING THE WORKERS' CHOIR. THE WELSH HAVE A LONG TRADITION OF MEN'S CHORAL MUSIC—DEEP, UNADORNED POWERFUL VOICES THAT MESHED PERFECTLY WITH PAUL'S OWN.
...A rhody law, Myfanwy dirion, I ddim ond dweud y gair "Ffarwel"
IN THE MOVIE'S CLIMAX, GOLIATH SAVES FELLOW MINERS FROM A CAVE-IN.
1939
The Telegraph
BRITAIN DECLARES WAR
BLITZKRIEG
Panzer divi
RUSSIA ATTACKS BALTIC PORTS
WASHINGTON, D.C. D.A.R. refused to allow Negro singer Marian Anderson to perform Constitution Hall
Paul Robeson in Proud Role fit for singer turned activist- Rol shines as poor wor sharing daily lif of Welsh mi
Daily Mail 1939
GERMANY INVADES POLAND
ITALY INVADES ALBANIA
U.S.A. Declares NEUTRALITY
NEW YORK WORLD FAIR
JAPANESE OCCUPY NANJING
STAGE & SCREEN
ROBESON IN REAL LIFE STORY - HARDSHIP IN WALES. Director promised not to use him as a Negro or a famous singer" The Proud Valley
RUSSO-GERMAN PEACE PACT
1939
THE TIMES
WAR with GERMANY
We shall fight them on the beach in the streets, in the fields, in the hills - We shall never surrende
BLOCKADE - British Navy defies U-boats
FRENCH RETREAT
Atrocities in Nanjin
Japanese advance in Indo Chin
ENTERTAINMENT
No grass skirt for Paul Robeson this time. Return to the screen in real life drama The Proud Valley
SHARON RUDAHL 2019

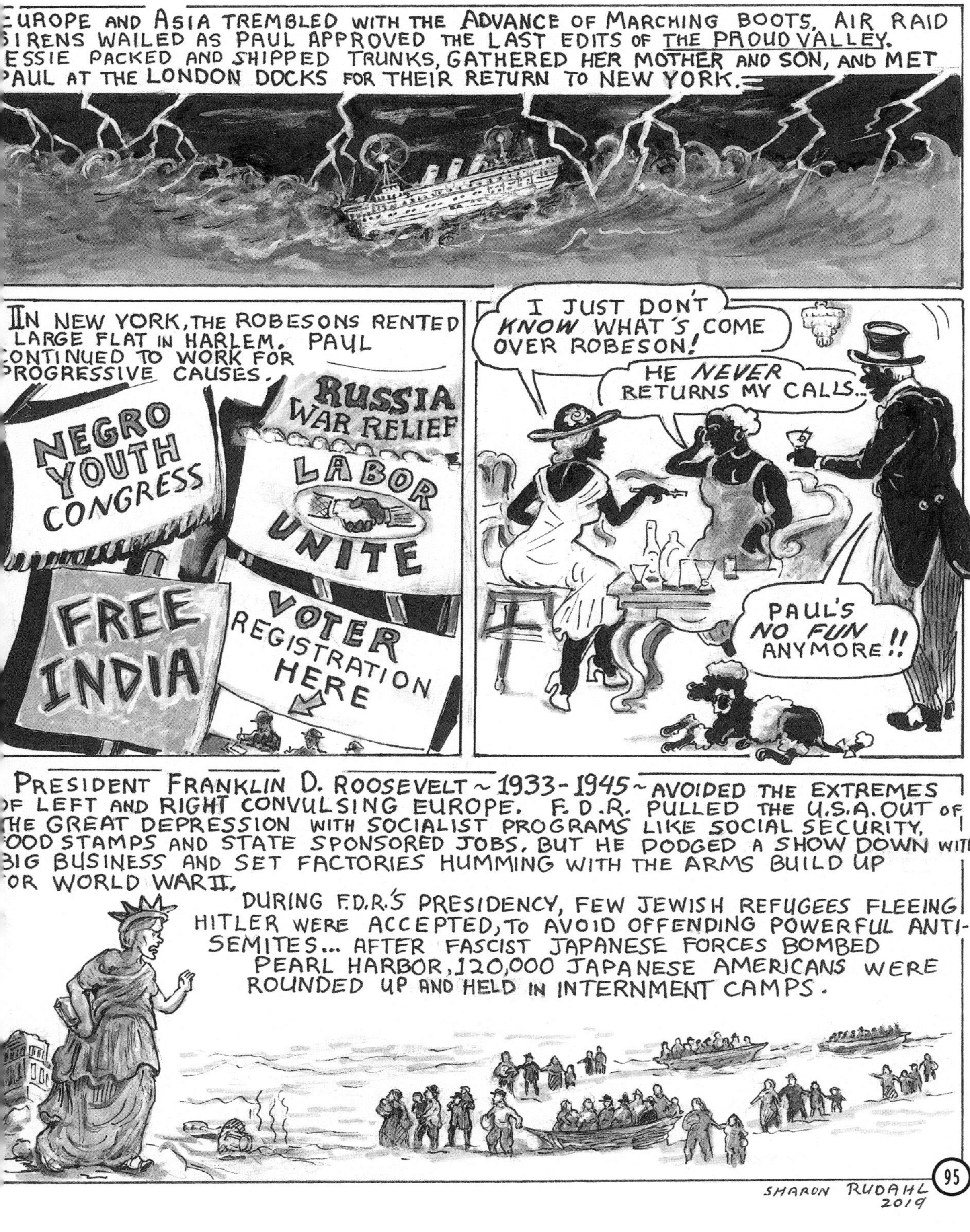
EUROPE AND ASIA TREMBLED WITH THE ADVANCE OF MARCHING BOOTS. AIR RAID SIRENS WAILED AS PAUL APPROVED THE LAST EDITS OF THE PROUD VALLEY. ESSIE PACKED AND SHIPPED TRUNKS, GATHERED HER MOTHER AND SON, AND MET PAUL AT THE LONDON DOCKS FOR THEIR RETURN TO NEW YORK.
IN NEW YORK, THE ROBESONS RENTED LARGE FLAT IN HARLEM. PAUL CONTINUED TO WORK FOR PROGRESSIVE CAUSES.
NEGRO YOUTH CONGRESS
RUSSIA WAR RELIEF
LABOR UNITE
FREE INDIA
VOTER REGISTRATION HERE
I JUST DON'T KNOW WHAT'S COME OVER ROBESON!
HE NEVER RETURNS MY CALLS...
PAUL'S NO FUN ANYMORE!!
PRESIDENT FRANKLIN D. ROOSEVELT ~ 1933-1945 ~ AVOIDED THE EXTREMES OF LEFT AND RIGHT CONVULSING EUROPE. F.D.R. PULLED THE U.S.A. OUT OF THE GREAT DEPRESSION WITH SOCIALIST PROGRAMS LIKE SOCIAL SECURITY, FOOD STAMPS AND STATE SPONSORED JOBS. BUT HE DODGED A SHOW DOWN WITH BIG BUSINESS AND SET FACTORIES HUMMING WITH THE ARMS BUILD UP FOR WORLD WAR II.
DURING F.D.R.'S PRESIDENCY, FEW JEWISH REFUGEES FLEEING HITLER WERE ACCEPTED, TO AVOID OFFENDING POWERFUL ANTI-SEMITES... AFTER FASCIST JAPANESE FORCES BOMBED PEARL HARBOR, 120,000 JAPANESE AMERICANS WERE ROUNDED UP AND HELD IN INTERNMENT CAMPS.
SHARON RUDAHL 2019

In the late 1930s and early '40s anti-fascist Americans of all factions united in a Popular Front. Even mass magazines praised our brave Russian allies. Folk music and crafts were prized as expressions of common people. The government 'Works Progress Administration' paid artists to paint murals of heroic workers, stage progressive plays and create photo essays about Appalachian poverty. November 1939 – a few weeks after returning to the U.S., Robeson was asked to sing on a national radio broadcast, a brand new song written for a WPA theater project by John Latouch and Earl Robinson.

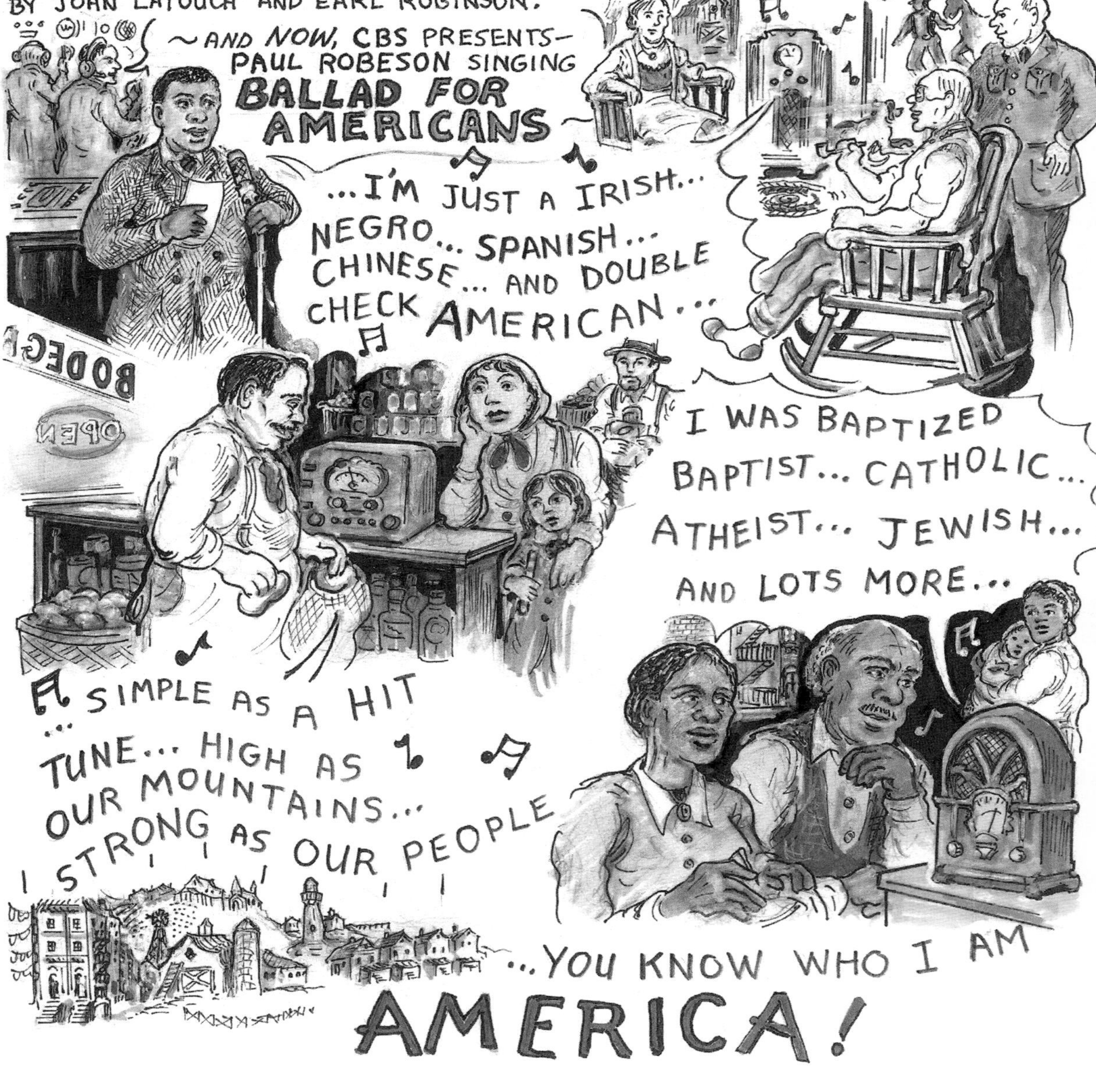
~AND NOW, CBS PRESENTS– PAUL ROBESON SINGING
BALLAD FOR AMERICANS
...I'M JUST A IRISH... NEGRO... SPANISH... CHINESE... AND DOUBLE CHECK AMERICAN...
I WAS BAPTIZED BAPTIST... CATHOLIC... ATHEIST... JEWISH... AND LOTS MORE...
SIMPLE AS A HIT TUNE... HIGH AS OUR MOUNTAINS... STRONG AS OUR PEOPLE
...YOU KNOW WHO I AM
AMERICA!

SHARON RUDAHL 2019

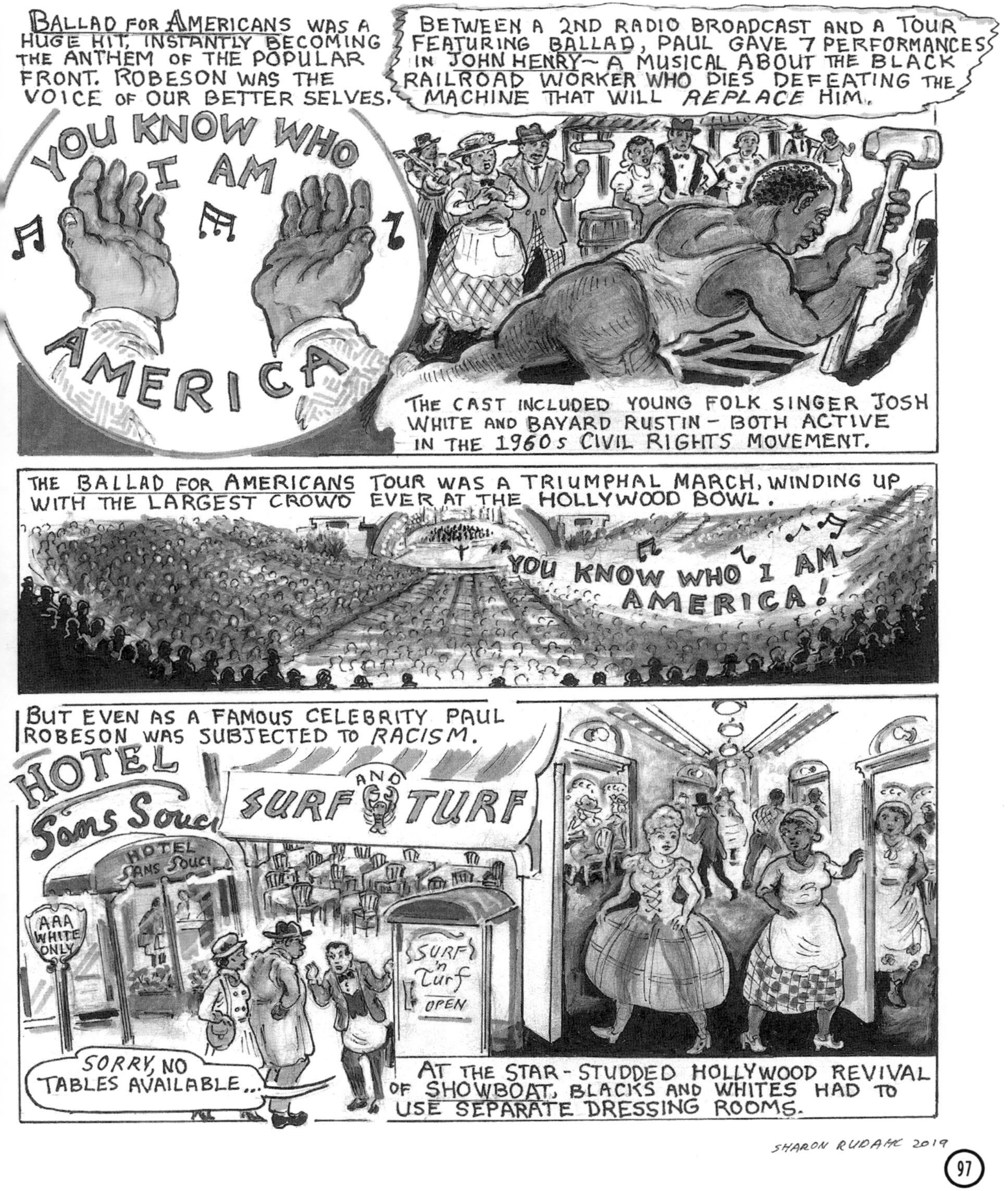

BALLAD FOR AMERICANS WAS A HUGE HIT, INSTANTLY BECOMING THE ANTHEM OF THE POPULAR FRONT. ROBESON WAS THE VOICE OF OUR BETTER SELVES.
BETWEEN A 2ND RADIO BROADCAST AND A TOUR FEATURING BALLAD, PAUL GAVE 7 PERFORMANCES IN JOHN HENRY ~ A MUSICAL ABOUT THE BLACK RAILROAD WORKER WHO DIES DEFEATING THE MACHINE THAT WILL REPLACE HIM.
YOU KNOW WHO I AM AMERICA
THE CAST INCLUDED YOUNG FOLK SINGER JOSH WHITE AND BAYARD RUSTIN - BOTH ACTIVE IN THE 1960s CIVIL RIGHTS MOVEMENT.
THE BALLAD FOR AMERICANS TOUR WAS A TRIUMPHAL MARCH, WINDING UP WITH THE LARGEST CROWD EVER AT THE HOLLYWOOD BOWL.
YOU KNOW WHO I AM AMERICA!
BUT EVEN AS A FAMOUS CELEBRITY PAUL ROBESON WAS SUBJECTED TO RACISM.
HOTEL Sans Souci
HOTEL SANS SOUCI
SURF AND TURF
AAA WHITE ONLY
SURF 'n Turf OPEN
SORRY, NO TABLES AVAILABLE...
AT THE STAR-STUDDED HOLLYWOOD REVIVAL OF SHOWBOAT, BLACKS AND WHITES HAD TO USE SEPARATE DRESSING ROOMS.
SHARON RUDAHL 2019

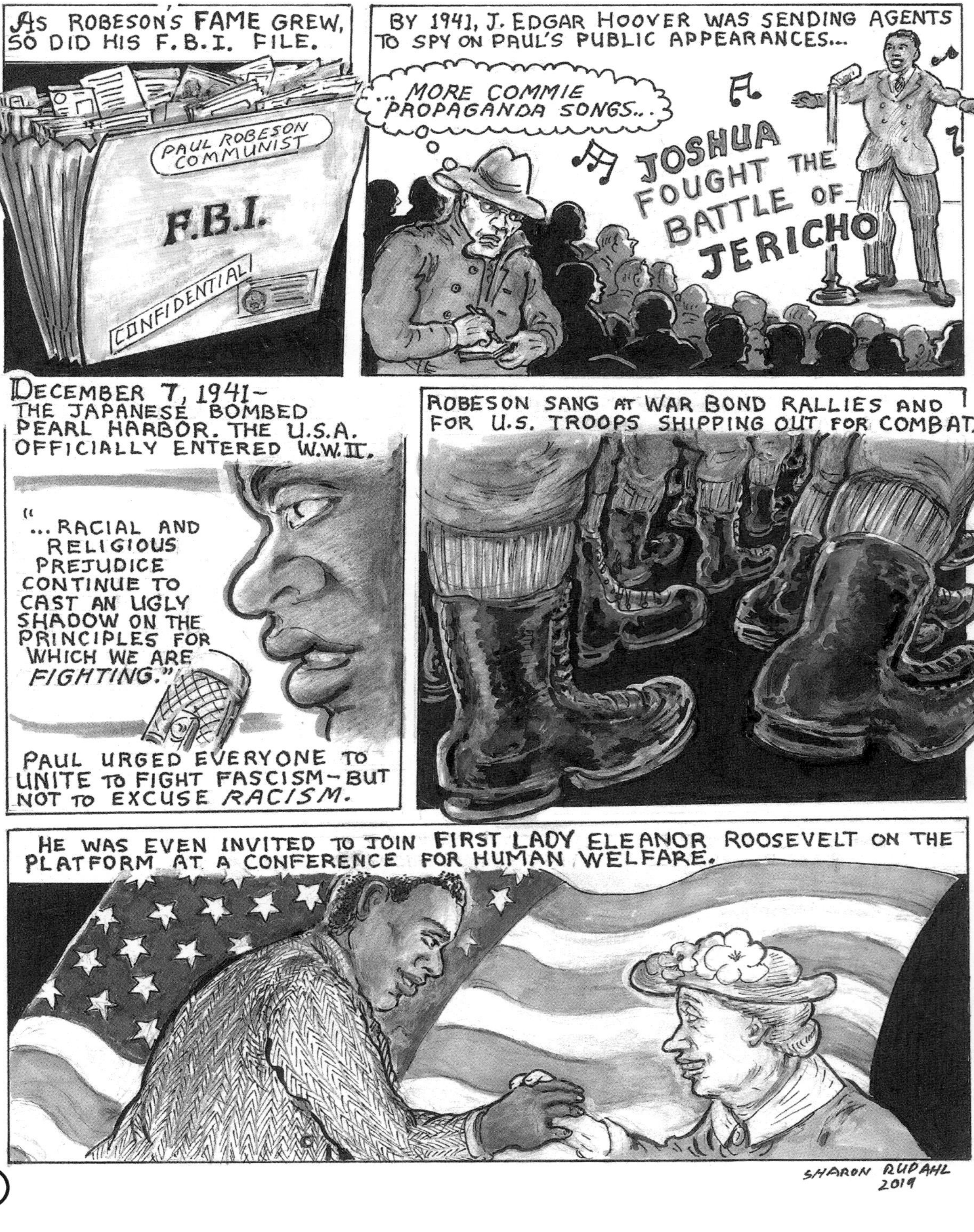

AS ROBESON'S FAME GREW, SO DID HIS F.B.I. FILE.
PAUL ROBESON COMMUNIST
F.B.I.
CONFIDENTIAL
BY 1941, J. EDGAR HOOVER WAS SENDING AGENTS TO SPY ON PAUL'S PUBLIC APPEARANCES...
...MORE COMMIE PROPAGANDA SONGS...
JOSHUA FOUGHT THE BATTLE OF JERICHO
DECEMBER 7, 1941– THE JAPANESE BOMBED PEARL HARBOR. THE U.S.A. OFFICIALLY ENTERED W.W.II.
"...RACIAL AND RELIGIOUS PREJUDICE CONTINUE TO CAST AN UGLY SHADOW ON THE PRINCIPLES FOR WHICH WE ARE FIGHTING."
PAUL URGED EVERYONE TO UNITE TO FIGHT FASCISM–BUT NOT TO EXCUSE RACISM.
ROBESON SANG AT WAR BOND RALLIES AND FOR U.S. TROOPS SHIPPING OUT FOR COMBAT.
HE WAS EVEN INVITED TO JOIN FIRST LADY ELEANOR ROOSEVELT ON THE PLATFORM AT A CONFERENCE FOR HUMAN WELFARE.
SHARON RUDAHL 2019

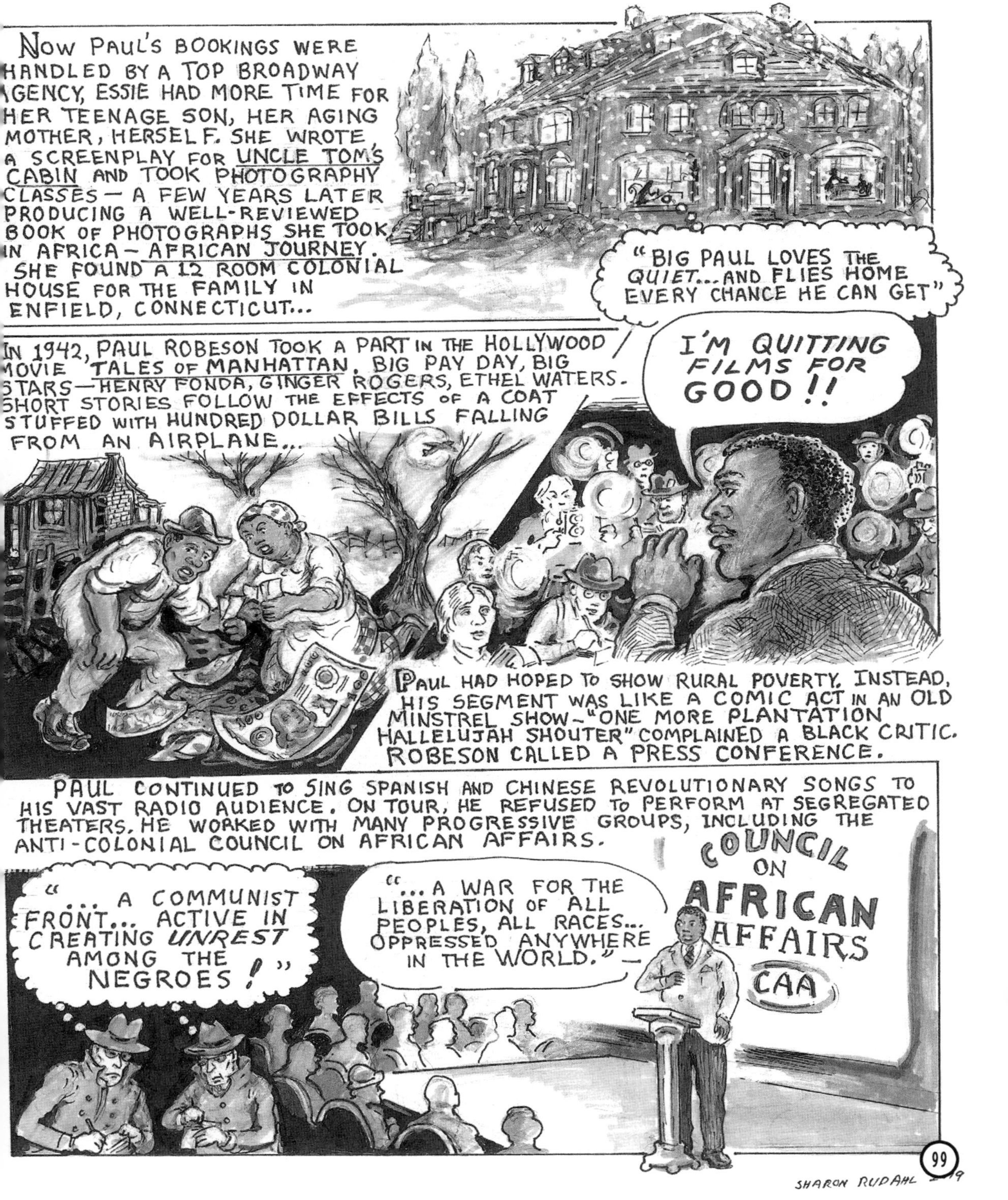

NOW PAUL'S BOOKINGS WERE HANDLED BY A TOP BROADWAY AGENCY, ESSIE HAD MORE TIME FOR HER TEENAGE SON, HER AGING MOTHER, HERSELF. SHE WROTE A SCREENPLAY FOR UNCLE TOM'S CABIN AND TOOK PHOTOGRAPHY CLASSES — A FEW YEARS LATER PRODUCING A WELL-REVIEWED BOOK OF PHOTOGRAPHS SHE TOOK IN AFRICA — AFRICAN JOURNEY. SHE FOUND A 12 ROOM COLONIAL HOUSE FOR THE FAMILY IN ENFIELD, CONNECTICUT...
"BIG PAUL LOVES THE QUIET... AND FLIES HOME EVERY CHANCE HE CAN GET"
IN 1942, PAUL ROBESON TOOK A PART IN THE HOLLYWOOD MOVIE TALES OF MANHATTAN. BIG PAY DAY, BIG STARS — HENRY FONDA, GINGER ROGERS, ETHEL WATERS. SHORT STORIES FOLLOW THE EFFECTS OF A COAT STUFFED WITH HUNDRED DOLLAR BILLS FALLING FROM AN AIRPLANE...
I'M QUITTING FILMS FOR GOOD!!
PAUL HAD HOPED TO SHOW RURAL POVERTY. INSTEAD, HIS SEGMENT WAS LIKE A COMIC ACT IN AN OLD MINSTREL SHOW — "ONE MORE PLANTATION HALLELUJAH SHOUTER" COMPLAINED A BLACK CRITIC. ROBESON CALLED A PRESS CONFERENCE.
PAUL CONTINUED TO SING SPANISH AND CHINESE REVOLUTIONARY SONGS TO HIS VAST RADIO AUDIENCE. ON TOUR, HE REFUSED TO PERFORM AT SEGREGATED THEATERS. HE WORKED WITH MANY PROGRESSIVE GROUPS, INCLUDING THE ANTI-COLONIAL COUNCIL ON AFRICAN AFFAIRS.
"... A COMMUNIST FRONT... ACTIVE IN CREATING UNREST AMONG THE NEGROES!"
"... A WAR FOR THE LIBERATION OF ALL PEOPLES, ALL RACES... OPPRESSED ANYWHERE IN THE WORLD." —
COUNCIL ON AFRICAN AFFAIRS
CAA
SHARON RUDAHL

IN 1943, AFTER A U.S. CONCERT TOUR WITH LARRY BROWN, PAUL ROBESON MADE HISTORY AS THE 1ST BLACK OTHELLO ON BROADWAY. UTA HAGEN WAS DESDEMONA AND JOSE FERRER PLAYED TREACHEROUS IAGO. AT AGE 45, TO EMBODY THE WAR HERO, PAUL *LOST WEIGHT* AND GREW A *BEARD*. FOR OPENING NIGHT HIS SISTER MARIAN CAME FROM PHILADELPHIA, BROTHER BEN FROM HIS CHURCH IN HARLEM

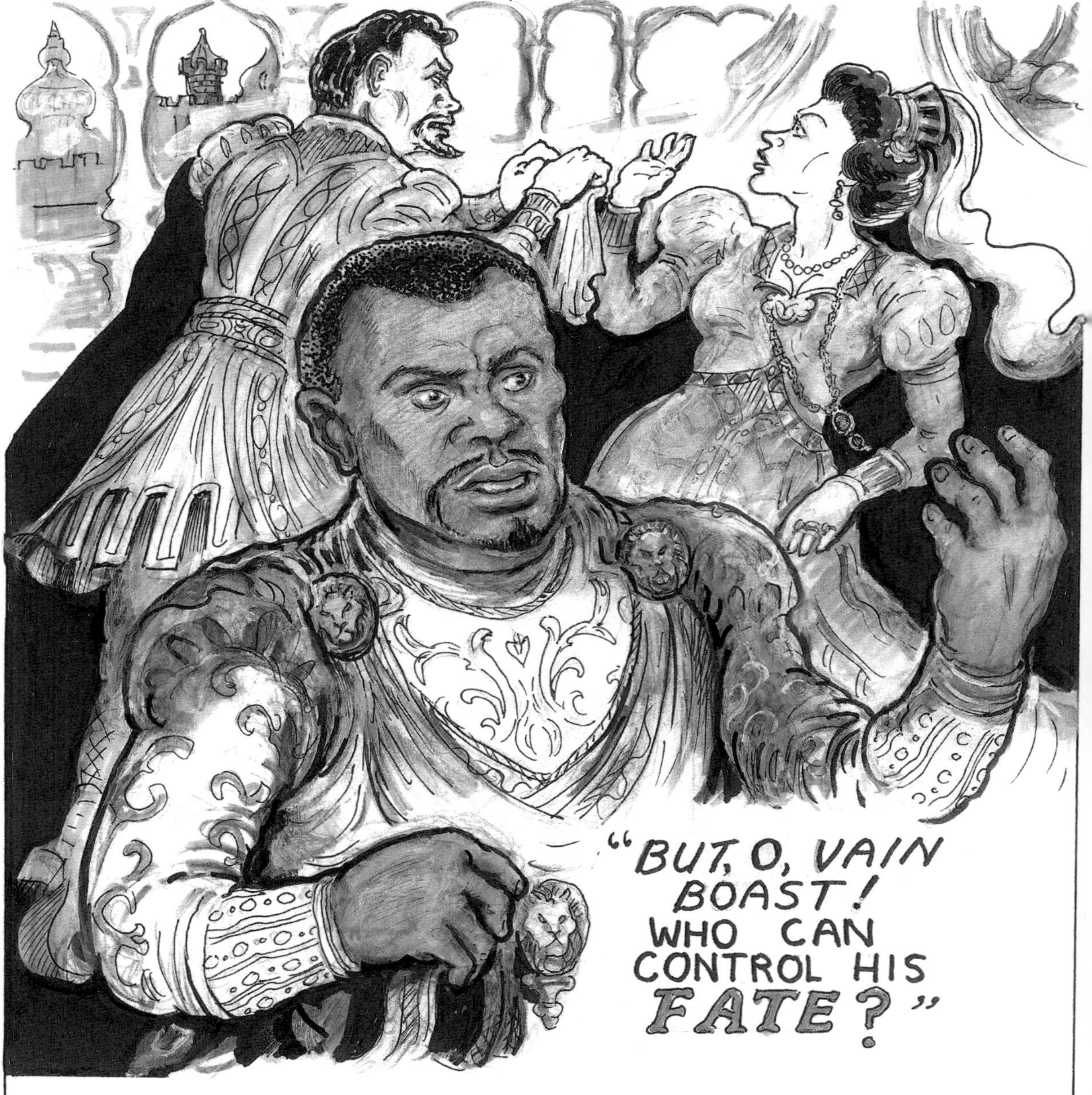
"BUT, O, VAIN BOAST! WHO CAN CONTROL HIS FATE?"

WHAT ROBESON MAY HAVE LACKED IN TRAINED TECHNIQUE OR MODERN METHOD, HE SUPPLIED WITH CONVICTION AND HEART. THE AUDIENCE ROSE AS *ONE* TO AWARD PAUL A TWENTY MINUTE STANDING OVATION...

SHARON RUDAHL 2019

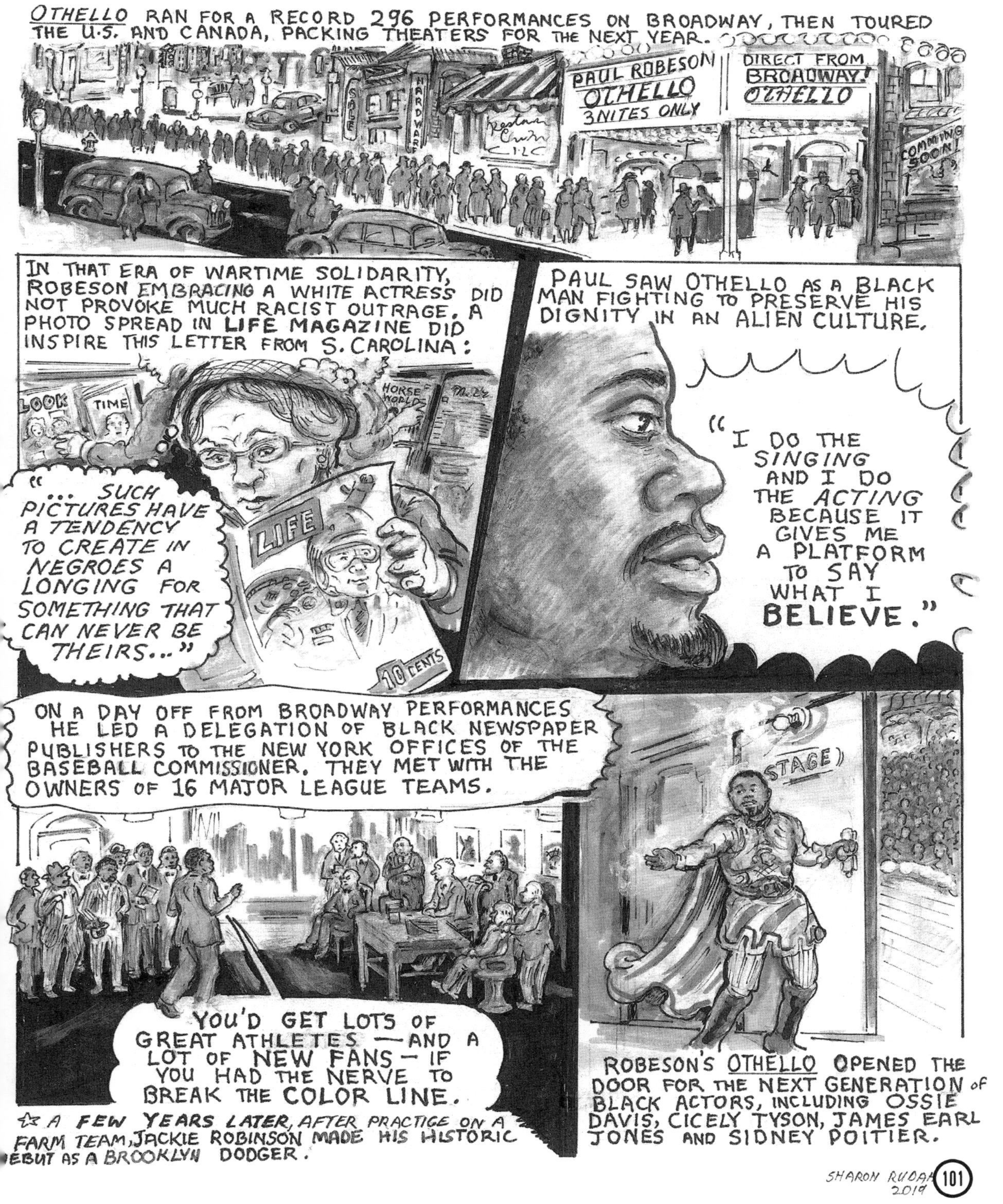
OTHELLO RAN FOR A RECORD 296 PERFORMANCES ON BROADWAY, THEN TOURED THE U.S. AND CANADA, PACKING THEATERS FOR THE NEXT YEAR.
PAUL ROBESON OTHELLO 3 NITES ONLY
DIRECT FROM BROADWAY! OTHELLO
SALE
HARDWARE
COMMING SOON!
IN THAT ERA OF WARTIME SOLIDARITY, ROBESON EMBRACING A WHITE ACTRESS DID NOT PROVOKE MUCH RACIST OUTRAGE. A PHOTO SPREAD IN LIFE MAGAZINE DID INSPIRE THIS LETTER FROM S. CAROLINA:
LOOK
TIME
HORSE WORLD
"... SUCH PICTURES HAVE A TENDENCY TO CREATE IN NEGROES A LONGING FOR SOMETHING THAT CAN NEVER BE THEIRS..."
LIFE
10 CENTS
PAUL SAW OTHELLO AS A BLACK MAN FIGHTING TO PRESERVE HIS DIGNITY IN AN ALIEN CULTURE.
"I DO THE SINGING AND I DO THE ACTING BECAUSE IT GIVES ME A PLATFORM TO SAY WHAT I BELIEVE."
ON A DAY OFF FROM BROADWAY PERFORMANCES HE LED A DELEGATION OF BLACK NEWSPAPER PUBLISHERS TO THE NEW YORK OFFICES OF THE BASEBALL COMMISSIONER. THEY MET WITH THE OWNERS OF 16 MAJOR LEAGUE TEAMS.
YOU'D GET LOTS OF GREAT ATHLETES — AND A LOT OF NEW FANS — IF YOU HAD THE NERVE TO BREAK THE COLOR LINE.
☆ A FEW YEARS LATER, AFTER PRACTICE ON A FARM TEAM, JACKIE ROBINSON MADE HIS HISTORIC DEBUT AS A BROOKLYN DODGER.
STAGE
ROBESON'S OTHELLO OPENED THE DOOR FOR THE NEXT GENERATION OF BLACK ACTORS, INCLUDING OSSIE DAVIS, CICELY TYSON, JAMES EARL JONES AND SIDNEY POITIER.
SHARON RUDAHL 2019

IN SPRING 1945, A WEEK AFTER HITLER'S SUICIDE, GERMANY SURRENDERED. IN AUGUST AFTER THE U.S. DROPPED ATOM BOMBS ON HIROSHIMA AND NAGASAKI, JAPAN CONCEDED DEFEAT. FOR THE U.S. "COMMUNISM" REPLACED "FASCISM" AS THE FATE WORSE THAN DEATH. OUT OF THE HORROR AND ASHES OF WORLD WAR II, THE VICTORS PROMISED— MORE HORROR AND **ASHES!**

U.S. AND U.S.S.R. AGENTS SCRAMBLED TO NAB THE BEST NAZI ROCKET SCIENTISTS. THE SOVIETS MOVED INTO LIBERATED EASTERN EUROPE, WHILE THE U.S. MARSHALL PLAN REVIVED BUSINESSES THAT HAD SERVED HITLER'S THIRD REICH.

☐ GOOD = U.S. ALLIES

▨ BAD = *FASCIST* *COMMUNIST*

▨ POCKETS OF ANTI-FASCISTS

SPINGARN

NATIONAL ASSOCIATION FOR THE ADVANCEMENT OF COLORED PEOPLE

NAACP
FOUNDED
1909

PAUL ROBESON
—1945—

PAUL'S TERM AS OTHELLO ENDED AS WWII WAS ENDING. HE WAS AT THE PEAK OF SUCCESS—A SOURCE OF PRIDE TO BLACK AND A USEFUL TOKEN OF TOLERANCE FOR WHITE SOCIETY. HE RECEIVED AN HONORARY DOCTORATE FROM MOREHOUSE COLLEGE, AND THE NAACP'S MOST PRESTIGIOUS *SPINGARN MEDAL*

BUT AT THE APEX OF HIS STARDOM, PAUL ROBESON'S DOWNFALL WAS ALREADY BEING PREPARED.

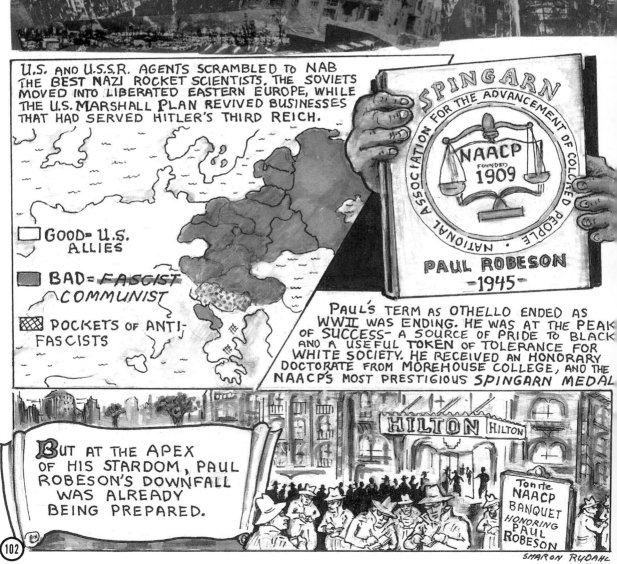

HILTON   Hilton

Tonite
NAACP
BANQUET
HONORING
PAUL
ROBESON

102

SHARON RUDAHL
2019

CHAPTER V
BLOODIED BUT UNBOWED

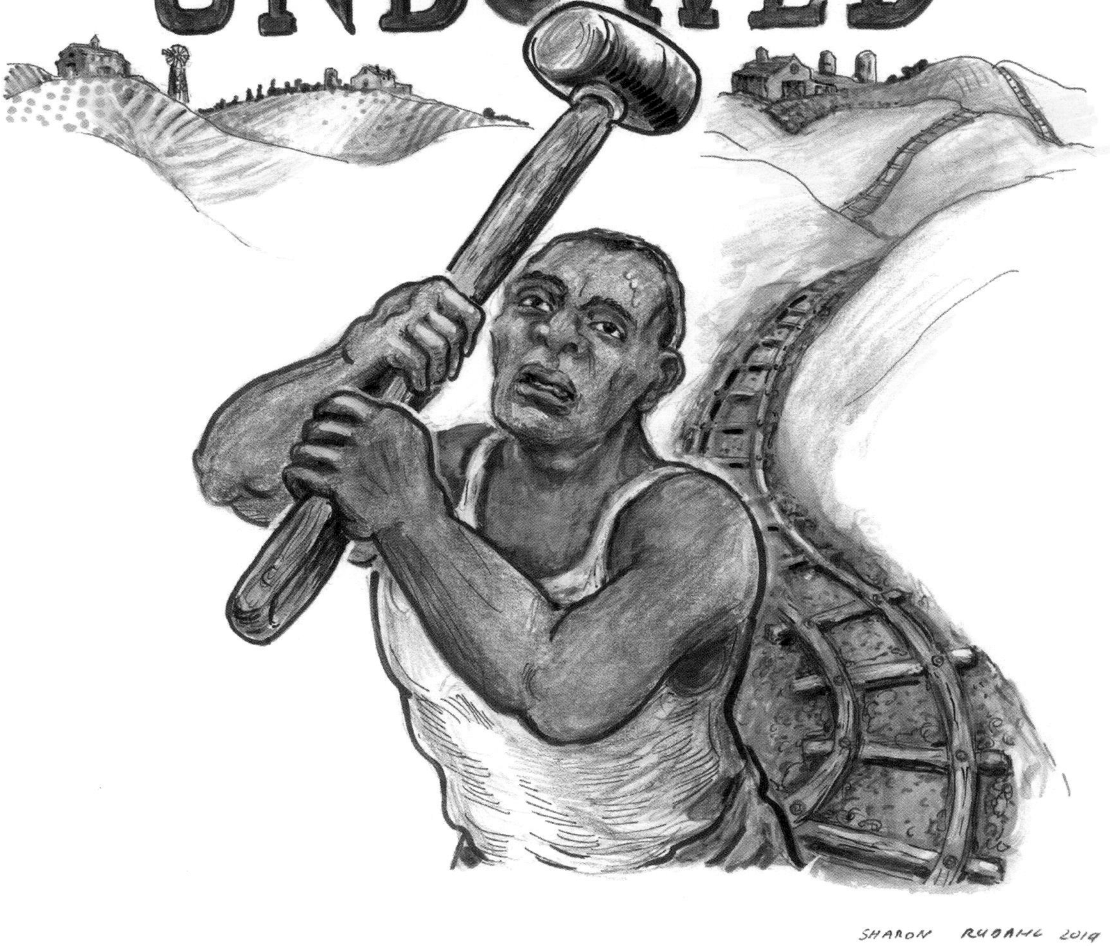
SHARON RUDAHL 2019

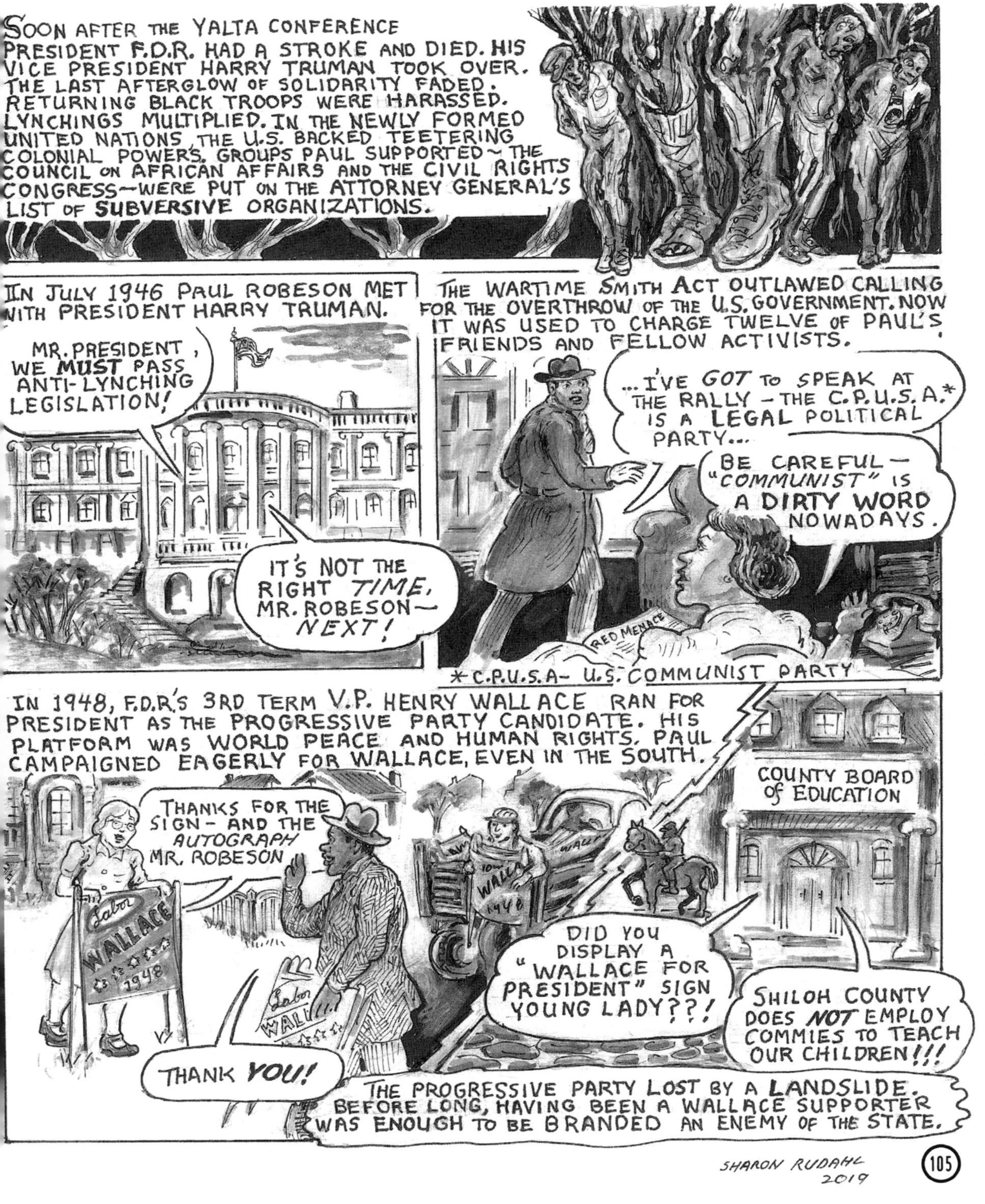
SOON AFTER THE YALTA CONFERENCE PRESIDENT F.D.R. HAD A STROKE AND DIED. HIS VICE PRESIDENT HARRY TRUMAN TOOK OVER. THE LAST AFTERGLOW OF SOLIDARITY FADED. RETURNING BLACK TROOPS WERE HARASSED. LYNCHINGS MULTIPLIED. IN THE NEWLY FORMED UNITED NATIONS, THE U.S. BACKED TEETERING COLONIAL POWERS. GROUPS PAUL SUPPORTED ~ THE COUNCIL ON AFRICAN AFFAIRS AND THE CIVIL RIGHTS CONGRESS—WERE PUT ON THE ATTORNEY GENERAL'S LIST OF SUBVERSIVE ORGANIZATIONS.
IN JULY 1946 PAUL ROBESON MET WITH PRESIDENT HARRY TRUMAN.
MR. PRESIDENT, WE MUST PASS ANTI-LYNCHING LEGISLATION!
IT'S NOT THE RIGHT TIME, MR. ROBESON— NEXT!
THE WARTIME SMITH ACT OUTLAWED CALLING FOR THE OVERTHROW OF THE U.S. GOVERNMENT. NOW IT WAS USED TO CHARGE TWELVE OF PAUL'S FRIENDS AND FELLOW ACTIVISTS.
...I'VE GOT TO SPEAK AT THE RALLY - THE C.P.U.S.A.* IS A LEGAL POLITICAL PARTY...
BE CAREFUL— "COMMUNIST" IS A DIRTY WORD NOWADAYS.
RED MENACE
* C.P.U.S.A- U.S. COMMUNIST PARTY
IN 1948, F.D.R.'S 3RD TERM V.P. HENRY WALLACE RAN FOR PRESIDENT AS THE PROGRESSIVE PARTY CANDIDATE. HIS PLATFORM WAS WORLD PEACE AND HUMAN RIGHTS. PAUL CAMPAIGNED EAGERLY FOR WALLACE, EVEN IN THE SOUTH.
THANKS FOR THE SIGN- AND THE AUTOGRAPH MR. ROBESON
Labor WALLACE 1948
THANK YOU!
COUNTY BOARD of EDUCATION
DID YOU DISPLAY A "WALLACE FOR PRESIDENT" SIGN YOUNG LADY??!
SHILOH COUNTY DOES NOT EMPLOY COMMIES TO TEACH OUR CHILDREN!!!
THE PROGRESSIVE PARTY LOST BY A LANDSLIDE. BEFORE LONG, HAVING BEEN A WALLACE SUPPORTER WAS ENOUGH TO BE BRANDED AN ENEMY OF THE STATE.
SHARON RUDAHL 2019

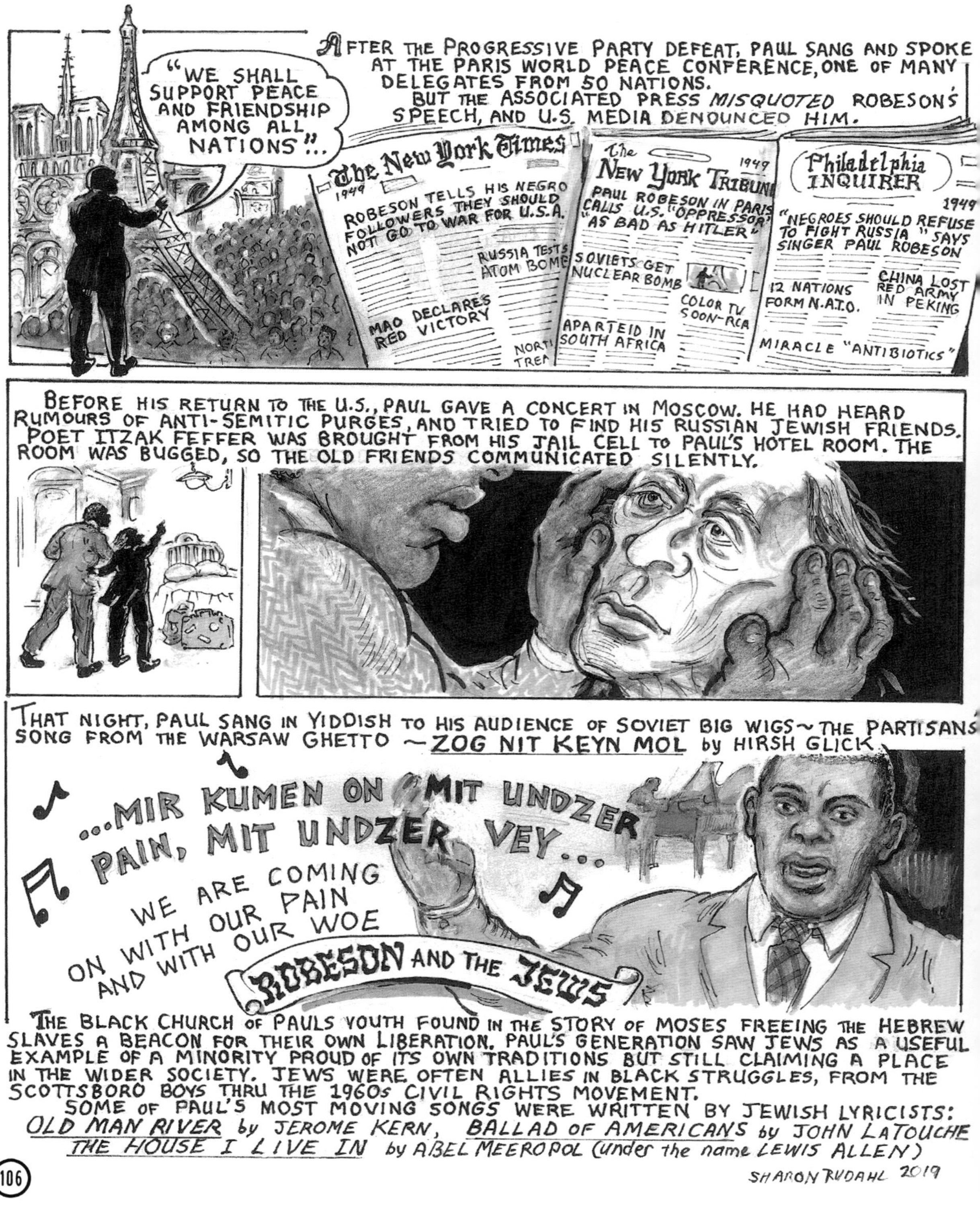
AFTER THE PROGRESSIVE PARTY DEFEAT, PAUL SANG AND SPOKE AT THE PARIS WORLD PEACE CONFERENCE, ONE OF MANY DELEGATES FROM 50 NATIONS.
BUT THE ASSOCIATED PRESS *MISQUOTED* ROBESON'S SPEECH, AND U.S. MEDIA DENOUNCED HIM.
"WE SHALL SUPPORT PEACE AND FRIENDSHIP AMONG ALL NATIONS"...
The New York Times 1949
ROBESON TELLS HIS NEGRO FOLLOWERS THEY SHOULD NOT GO TO WAR FOR U.S.A.
RUSSIA TESTS ATOM BOMB
MAO DECLARES RED VICTORY
The New York Tribune 1949
PAUL ROBESON IN PARIS CALLS U.S. "OPPRESSOR" "AS BAD AS HITLER"
SOVIETS GET NUCLEAR BOMB
COLOR TV SOON–RCA
APARTEID IN SOUTH AFRICA
Philadelphia INQUIRER 1949
"NEGROES SHOULD REFUSE TO FIGHT RUSSIA" SAYS SINGER PAUL ROBESON
CHINA LOST RED ARMY IN PEKING
12 NATIONS FORM N.A.T.O.
MIRACLE "ANTIBIOTICS"
BEFORE HIS RETURN TO THE U.S., PAUL GAVE A CONCERT IN MOSCOW. HE HAD HEARD RUMOURS OF ANTI-SEMITIC PURGES, AND TRIED TO FIND HIS RUSSIAN JEWISH FRIENDS. POET ITZAK FEFFER WAS BROUGHT FROM HIS JAIL CELL TO PAUL'S HOTEL ROOM. THE ROOM WAS BUGGED, SO THE OLD FRIENDS COMMUNICATED SILENTLY.
THAT NIGHT, PAUL SANG IN YIDDISH TO HIS AUDIENCE OF SOVIET BIG WIGS ~ THE PARTISANS' SONG FROM THE WARSAW GHETTO ~ ZOG NIT KEYN MOL by HIRSH GLICK
...MIR KUMEN ON MIT UNDZER PAIN, MIT UNDZER VEY...
WE ARE COMING ON WITH OUR PAIN AND WITH OUR WOE
ROBESON AND THE JEWS
THE BLACK CHURCH OF PAULS YOUTH FOUND IN THE STORY OF MOSES FREEING THE HEBREW SLAVES A BEACON FOR THEIR OWN LIBERATION. PAUL'S GENERATION SAW JEWS AS A USEFUL EXAMPLE OF A MINORITY PROUD OF ITS OWN TRADITIONS BUT STILL CLAIMING A PLACE IN THE WIDER SOCIETY. JEWS WERE OFTEN ALLIES IN BLACK STRUGGLES, FROM THE SCOTTSBORO BOYS THRU THE 1960s CIVIL RIGHTS MOVEMENT.
SOME OF PAUL'S MOST MOVING SONGS WERE WRITTEN BY JEWISH LYRICISTS: OLD MAN RIVER by JEROME KERN, BALLAD OF AMERICANS by JOHN LATOUCHE THE HOUSE I LIVE IN by ABEL MEEROPOL (under the name LEWIS ALLEN)
SHARON RUDAHL 2019

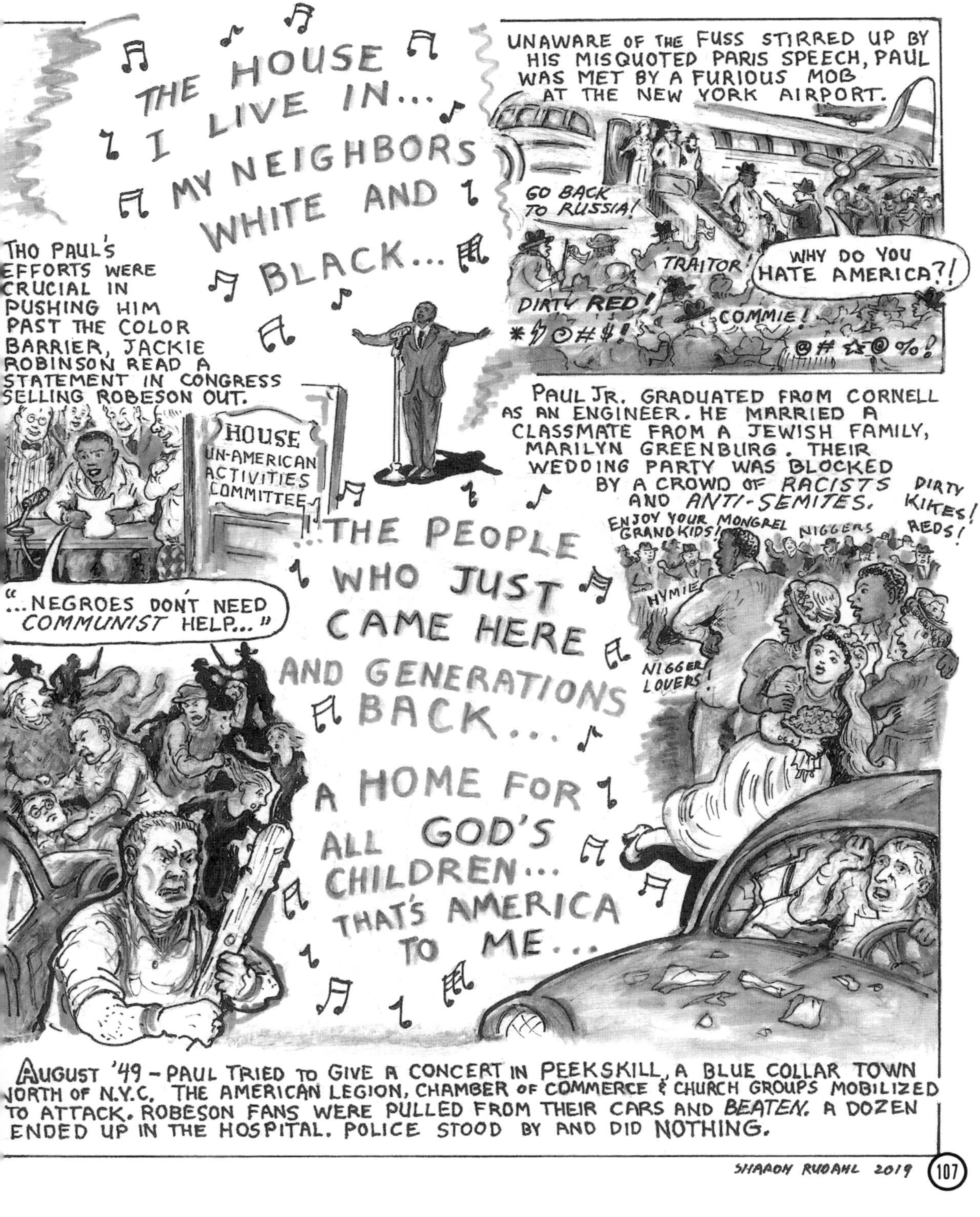
THE HOUSE I LIVE IN... MY NEIGHBORS WHITE AND BLACK...
UNAWARE OF THE FUSS STIRRED UP BY HIS MISQUOTED PARIS SPEECH, PAUL WAS MET BY A FURIOUS MOB AT THE NEW YORK AIRPORT.
GO BACK TO RUSSIA!
TRAITOR!
WHY DO YOU HATE AMERICA?!
DIRTY RED!
COMMIE!
*#@#$!
@#☆@%!
THO PAUL'S EFFORTS WERE CRUCIAL IN PUSHING HIM PAST THE COLOR BARRIER, JACKIE ROBINSON READ A STATEMENT IN CONGRESS SELLING ROBESON OUT.
HOUSE UN-AMERICAN ACTIVITIES COMMITTEE
"...NEGROES DON'T NEED COMMUNIST HELP..."
PAUL JR. GRADUATED FROM CORNELL AS AN ENGINEER. HE MARRIED A CLASSMATE FROM A JEWISH FAMILY, MARILYN GREENBURG. THEIR WEDDING PARTY WAS BLOCKED BY A CROWD OF RACISTS AND ANTI-SEMITES.
ENJOY YOUR MONGREL GRANDKIDS!
NIGGERS
DIRTY KIKES!
REDS!
HYMIE
NIGGER LOVERS!
...THE PEOPLE WHO JUST CAME HERE AND GENERATIONS BACK... A HOME FOR ALL GOD'S CHILDREN... THAT'S AMERICA TO ME...
AUGUST '49 – PAUL TRIED TO GIVE A CONCERT IN PEEKSKILL, A BLUE COLLAR TOWN NORTH OF N.Y.C. THE AMERICAN LEGION, CHAMBER OF COMMERCE & CHURCH GROUPS MOBILIZED TO ATTACK. ROBESON FANS WERE PULLED FROM THEIR CARS AND BEATEN. A DOZEN ENDED UP IN THE HOSPITAL. POLICE STOOD BY AND DID NOTHING.
SHARON RUDAHL 2019

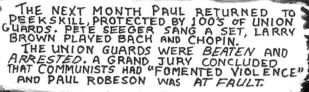

THE NEXT MONTH PAUL RETURNED TO PEEKSKILL, PROTECTED BY 100'S OF UNION GUARDS. PETE SEEGER SANG A SET, LARRY BROWN PLAYED BACH AND CHOPIN.

THE UNION GUARDS WERE *BEATEN* AND *ARRESTED*. A GRAND JURY CONCLUDED THAT COMMUNISTS HAD "FOMENTED VIOLENCE" AND PAUL ROBESON WAS *AT FAULT*.

IN 1950 SENATOR JOE McCARTHY ACCUSED THE STATE DEPARTMENT OF BEING FULL OF "*KNOWN COMMUNISTS*." NO ONE WAS SAFE FROM FALSE CHARGES.

PSTUDIOS

SASHA'S DELI PATRIOTIC BOYCOTT

SASHA'S DELI

BLACK LIST

ASSOCIATION OF UNIVERSITIES LOYALTY OATH NOT NOW, NOR EVER BEEN A MEMBER OF T...

Dearest... Because I could no longer provide for our family...

ELEANOR ROOSEVELT CANCELED PAUL ROBESON'S SCHEDULED PERFORMANCE ON HER RADIO PROGRAM.

ROBESON ATTEMPTED A NATIONAL TOUR. THEATERS REFUSED TO BOOK HIM. BUT UNION HALLS AND BLACK CHURCHES OPENED THEIR DOORS...

ΑΦΑ WELCOMES BROTHER PAUL ROBESON 2:30 – 5:00

ROBESON WAS STILL A BIG STAR OVERSEAS AND HE HOPED FOR SOME MUCH NEEDED INCOME FROM A EUROPEAN TOUR...

AIRLINES

ARRIVALS DEPART

I'M SORRY SIR... THERE SEEMS TO BE A HOLD ON YOUR PASSPORT.

IN CALIFORNIA, GOSSIP WRITER LOUELLA PARSONS FANNED FEARS OF RIOTS. BUT PAUL'S FRATERNITY ALPHA PHI ALPHA HELD A LUNCHEON IN HIS HONOR.

SHARON RUDAHL 2019

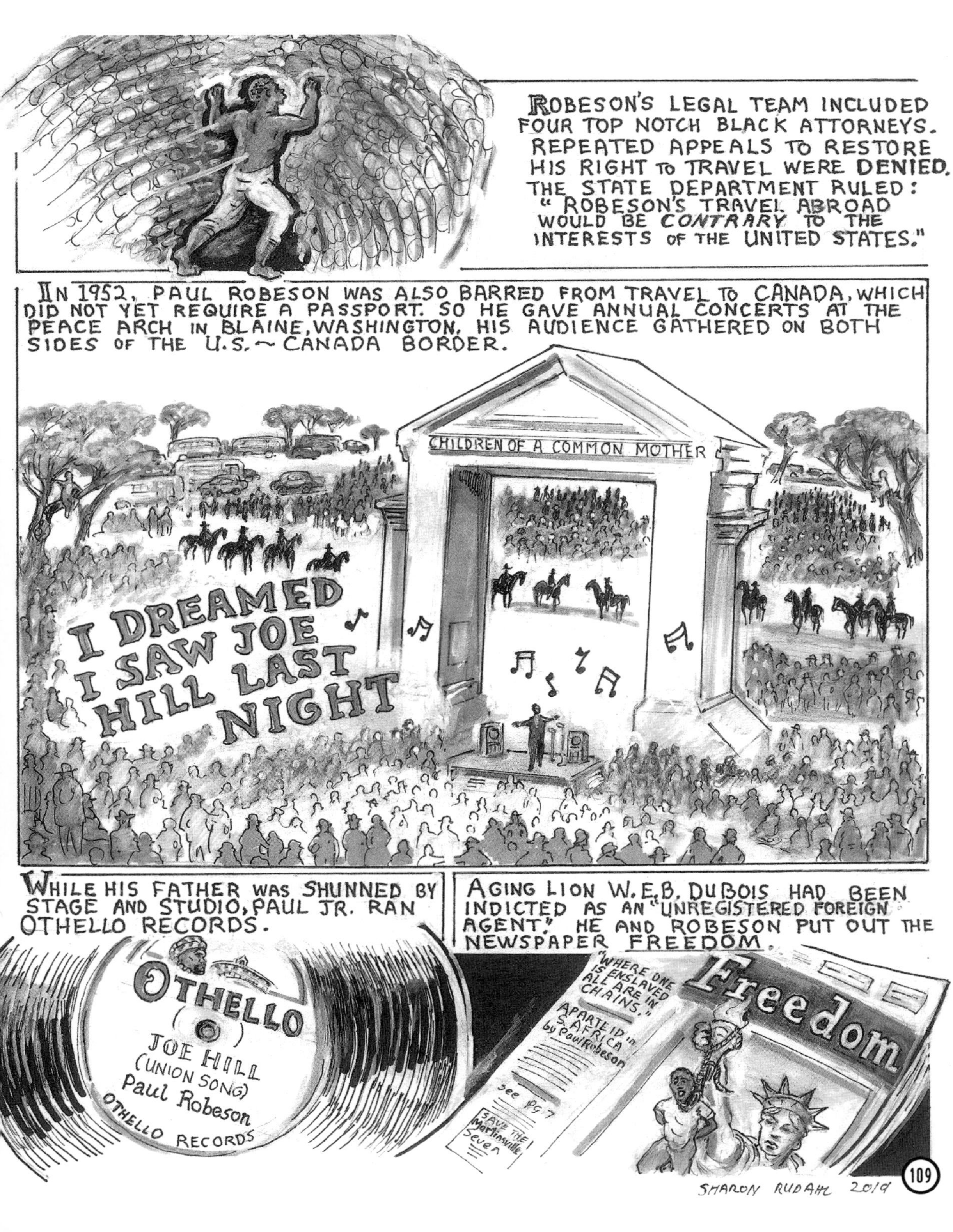

ROBESON'S LEGAL TEAM INCLUDED FOUR TOP NOTCH BLACK ATTORNEYS. REPEATED APPEALS TO RESTORE HIS RIGHT TO TRAVEL WERE DENIED. THE STATE DEPARTMENT RULED: "ROBESON'S TRAVEL ABROAD WOULD BE CONTRARY TO THE INTERESTS OF THE UNITED STATES."
IN 1952, PAUL ROBESON WAS ALSO BARRED FROM TRAVEL TO CANADA, WHICH DID NOT YET REQUIRE A PASSPORT. SO HE GAVE ANNUAL CONCERTS AT THE PEACE ARCH IN BLAINE, WASHINGTON. HIS AUDIENCE GATHERED ON BOTH SIDES OF THE U.S.~CANADA BORDER.
CHILDREN OF A COMMON MOTHER
I DREAMED I SAW JOE HILL LAST NIGHT
WHILE HIS FATHER WAS SHUNNED BY STAGE AND STUDIO, PAUL JR. RAN OTHELLO RECORDS.
AGING LION W.E.B. DUBOIS HAD BEEN INDICTED AS AN "UNREGISTERED FOREIGN AGENT." HE AND ROBESON PUT OUT THE NEWSPAPER FREEDOM.
OTHELLO
JOE HILL
(UNION SONG)
Paul Robeson
OTHELLO RECORDS
Freedom
"WHERE ONE IS ENSLAVED ALL ARE IN CHAINS."
APARTEID IN S.AFRICA by Paul Robeson
see p. 7
SAVE THE Martinsville Seven
SHARON RUDAHL 2019

In the 2nd round of his passport fight, Paul was told to sign an affadavit swearing not to speak his mind while overseas: "Criticism of the treatment of Negroes in the U.S. should not be aired while abroad."

I DO SWEAR

RIPPP!!

SIGNED
DATE

The Robesons never endured dire poverty. Royalties and prudent investments kept them afloat. But after Ma Goode entered a rest home, they sold the Enfield country house and rented rooms in Harlem. Essie reclaimed her rank as champion *thrift-shopper*.

...What *lovely* drapes! Where *did* you find this material?!?

Army surplus parachute silk!!

1953 Essie was called to testify before Joe McCarthy's Senate Committee. She was reportedly "charming" and "ladylike," refusing to answer questions on the basis of the 5th and 15th Amendments.

"I am a second class citizen now, as a Negro. That is the reason I claim this 15th Amendment."

The next year, she was diagnosed with breast cancer. As always, Ess refused to give in to frailty. Her mastectomy went smoothly, and she recovered quickly.

Paul had urinary blockage that required prostate surgery. His recovery was *slow* and *difficult*. He became *depressed, lethargic, moody* — the first foreshocks of a malady more relentless than the U.S. Government, — that would eventually wall him off from the world.

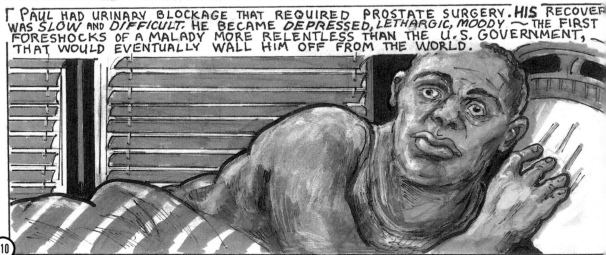

SHARON RUDAHL
2019

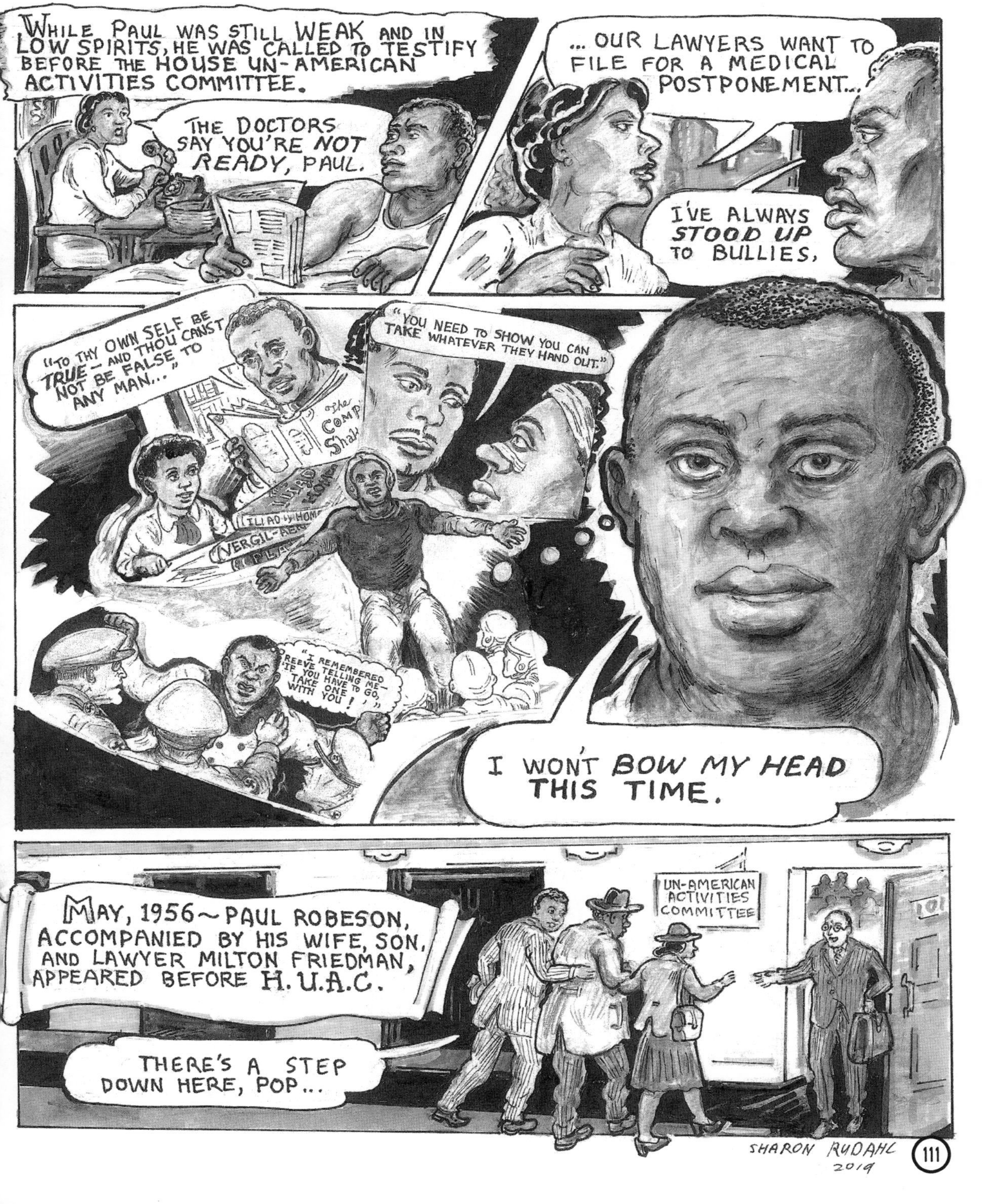

WHILE PAUL WAS STILL WEAK AND IN LOW SPIRITS, HE WAS CALLED TO TESTIFY BEFORE THE HOUSE UN-AMERICAN ACTIVITIES COMMITTEE.
THE DOCTORS SAY YOU'RE NOT READY, PAUL.
... OUR LAWYERS WANT TO FILE FOR A MEDICAL POSTPONEMENT...
I'VE ALWAYS STOOD UP TO BULLIES.
"TO THY OWN SELF BE TRUE — AND THOU CANST NOT BE FALSE TO ANY MAN..."
"YOU NEED TO SHOW YOU CAN TAKE WHATEVER THEY HAND OUT."
"I REMEMBERED REEVE TELLING ME — 'IF YOU HAVE TO GO, TAKE ONE WITH YOU!'"
I WON'T BOW MY HEAD THIS TIME.
MAY, 1956 ~ PAUL ROBESON, ACCOMPANIED BY HIS WIFE, SON, AND LAWYER MILTON FRIEDMAN, APPEARED BEFORE H.U.A.C.
UN-AMERICAN ACTIVITIES COMMITTEE
THERE'S A STEP DOWN HERE, POP...
SHARON RUDAHL 2019

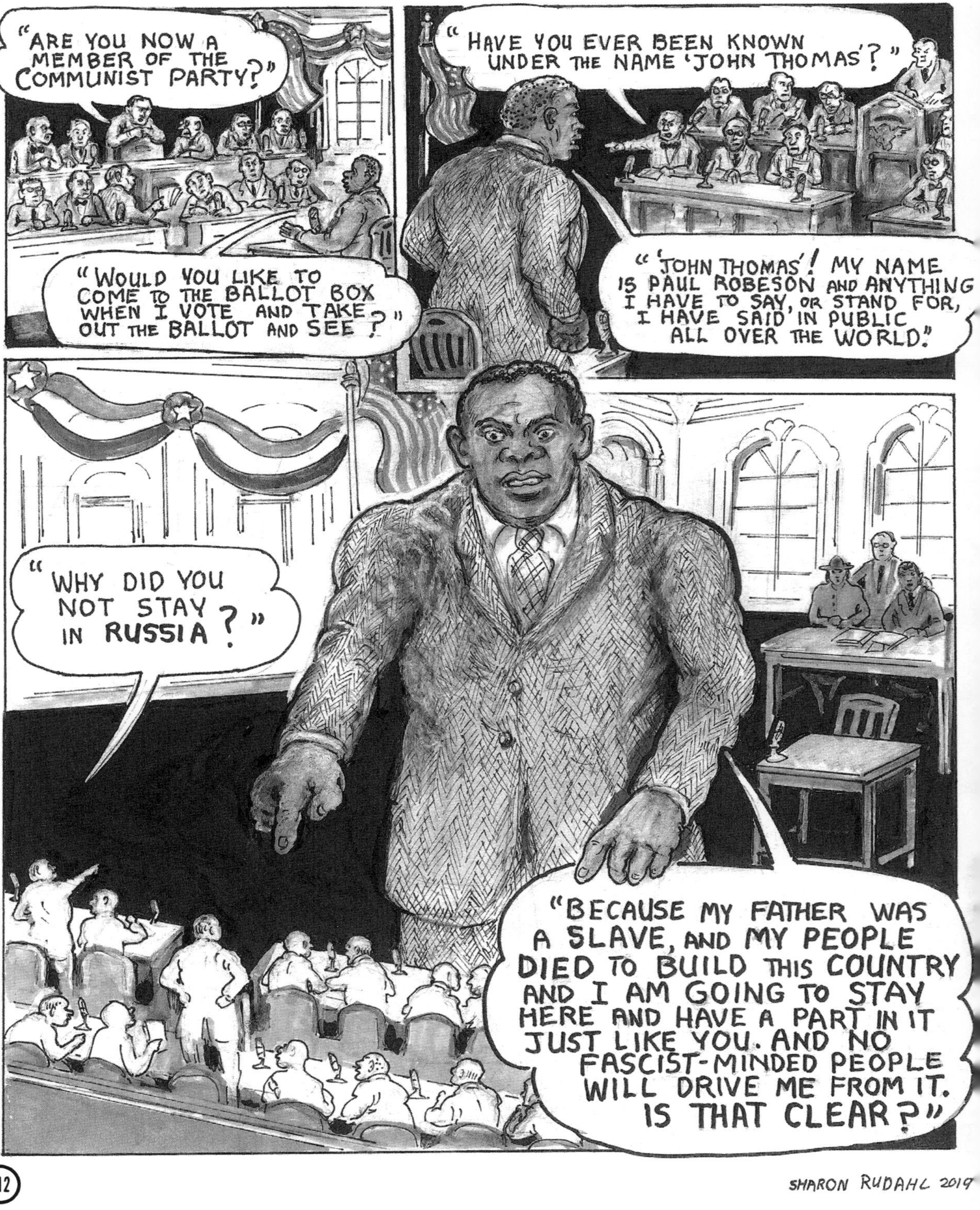
"ARE YOU NOW A MEMBER OF THE COMMUNIST PARTY?"
"WOULD YOU LIKE TO COME TO THE BALLOT BOX WHEN I VOTE AND TAKE OUT THE BALLOT AND SEE?"
"HAVE YOU EVER BEEN KNOWN UNDER THE NAME 'JOHN THOMAS'?"
"'JOHN THOMAS'! MY NAME IS PAUL ROBESON AND ANYTHING I HAVE TO SAY, OR STAND FOR, I HAVE SAID IN PUBLIC ALL OVER THE WORLD."
"WHY DID YOU NOT STAY IN RUSSIA?"
"BECAUSE MY FATHER WAS A SLAVE, AND MY PEOPLE DIED TO BUILD THIS COUNTRY AND I AM GOING TO STAY HERE AND HAVE A PART IN IT JUST LIKE YOU. AND NO FASCIST-MINDED PEOPLE WILL DRIVE ME FROM IT. IS THAT CLEAR?"
SHARON RUDAHL 2019

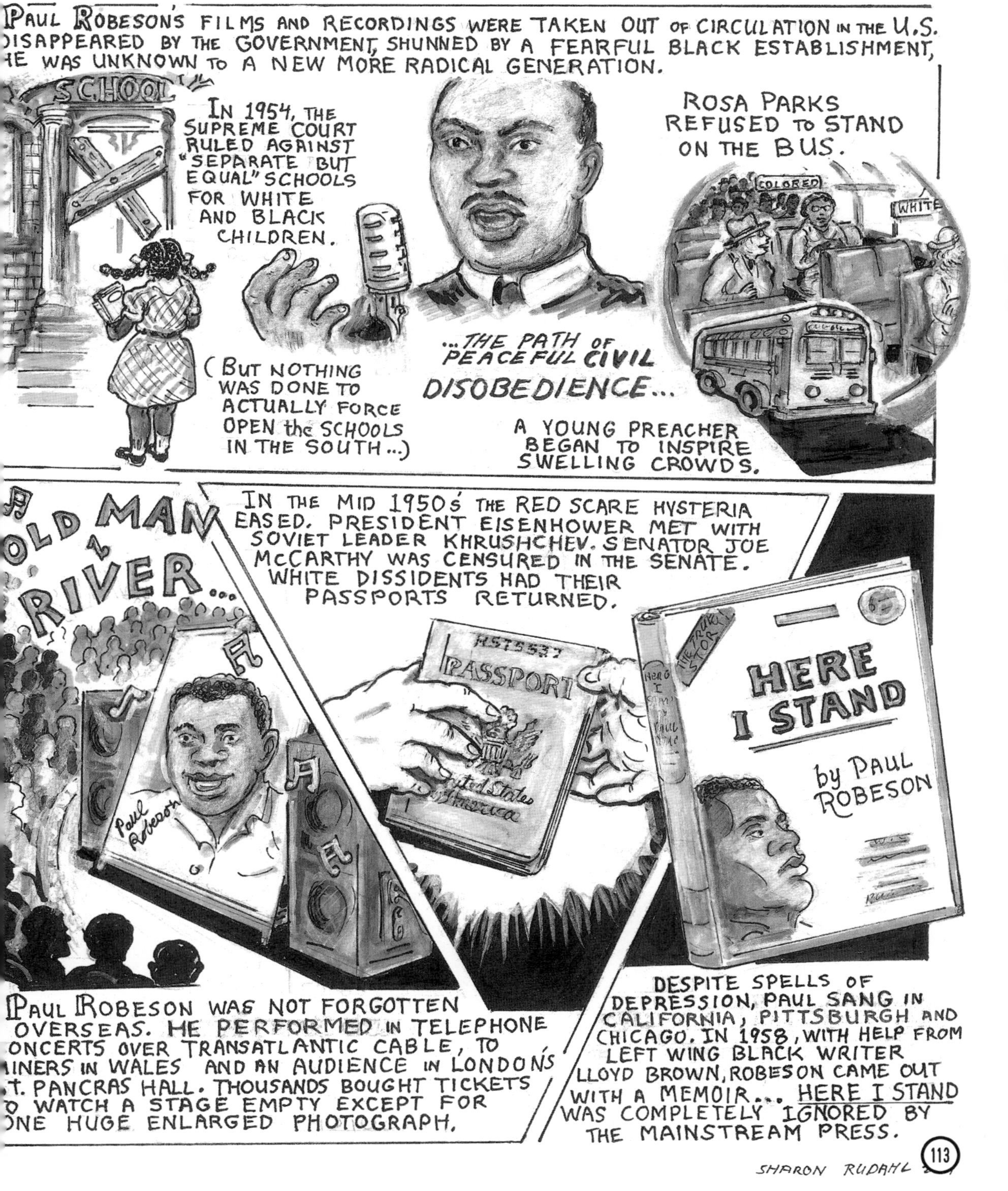

PAUL ROBESON'S FILMS AND RECORDINGS WERE TAKEN OUT OF CIRCULATION IN THE U.S. DISAPPEARED BY THE GOVERNMENT, SHUNNED BY A FEARFUL BLACK ESTABLISHMENT, HE WAS UNKNOWN TO A NEW MORE RADICAL GENERATION.
SCHOOL
IN 1954, THE SUPREME COURT RULED AGAINST "SEPARATE BUT EQUAL" SCHOOLS FOR WHITE AND BLACK CHILDREN.
(BUT NOTHING WAS DONE TO ACTUALLY FORCE OPEN the SCHOOLS IN THE SOUTH...)
...THE PATH OF PEACEFUL CIVIL DISOBEDIENCE...
A YOUNG PREACHER BEGAN TO INSPIRE SWELLING CROWDS.
ROSA PARKS REFUSED TO STAND ON THE BUS.
COLORED
WHITE
OLD MAN RIVER...
Paul Robeson
IN THE MID 1950'S THE RED SCARE HYSTERIA EASED. PRESIDENT EISENHOWER MET WITH SOVIET LEADER KHRUSHCHEV. SENATOR JOE McCARTHY WAS CENSURED IN THE SENATE. WHITE DISSIDENTS HAD THEIR PASSPORTS RETURNED.
PASSPORT
United States of America
HERE I STAND
by PAUL ROBESON
PAUL ROBESON WAS NOT FORGOTTEN OVERSEAS. HE PERFORMED IN TELEPHONE CONCERTS OVER TRANSATLANTIC CABLE, TO MINERS IN WALES AND AN AUDIENCE IN LONDON'S ST. PANCRAS HALL. THOUSANDS BOUGHT TICKETS TO WATCH A STAGE EMPTY EXCEPT FOR ONE HUGE ENLARGED PHOTOGRAPH.
DESPITE SPELLS OF DEPRESSION, PAUL SANG IN CALIFORNIA, PITTSBURGH AND CHICAGO. IN 1958, WITH HELP FROM LEFT WING BLACK WRITER LLOYD BROWN, ROBESON CAME OUT WITH A MEMOIR... HERE I STAND WAS COMPLETELY IGNORED BY THE MAINSTREAM PRESS.
SHARON RUDAHL

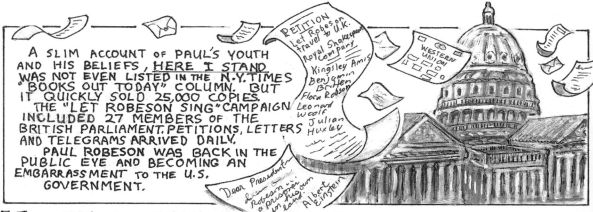

A SLIM ACCOUNT of PAUL'S YOUTH AND HIS BELIEFS, <u>HERE I STAND</u> WAS NOT EVEN LISTED IN THE N.Y. TIMES "BOOKS OUT TODAY" COLUMN. BUT IT QUICKLY SOLD 25,000 COPIES.

THE "LET ROBESON SING" CAMPAIGN INCLUDED 27 MEMBERS OF THE BRITISH PARLIAMENT. PETITIONS, LETTERS AND TELEGRAMS ARRIVED DAILY.

PAUL ROBESON WAS BACK IN THE PUBLIC EYE AND BECOMING AN EMBARRASSMENT TO THE U.S. GOVERNMENT.

PETITION
Let Robeson travel to U.K.
Royal Shakespeare Company
Kingsley Amis
Benjamin Britten
Flora Robson
Leonard Woolf
Julian Huxley

WESTERN UNION

Dear President—Robeson ... a prisoner in his own land — Albert Einstein

JUNE 1958 – JUSTICE WILLIAM O. DOUGLAS RULED FOR THE <u>U.S. SUPREME COURT</u>: "THE RIGHT TO TRAVEL IS ONE OF A CITIZEN'S INALIENABLE RIGHTS." ROBESON'S PASSPORT WAS FINALLY RESTORED.

IN LONDON PAUL AND ESSIE WERE WELCOMED BY JOYOUS FANS. LARRY BROWN ARRIVED BY SHIP TO ACCOMPANY PAUL AT ROYAL ALBERT HALL.

PAUL SANG ON BBC RADIO, AND APPEARED ON BRITISH T.V.

ROBESON BECAME THE FIRST BLACK TO PERFORM IN St. PAUL'S CATHEDRAL.

AFTER JULY IN ENGLAND, PAUL WAS GREETED AS A HERO IN RUSSIA. HE WAS FEATURED ON SOVIET T.V. AND PACKED THE VAST LENIN SPORTS STADIUM.

SHARON RUDAHL 2019

PAUL WAS INVITED TO TASHKENT, UZBEK SSR. THO EAGER TO VISIT THE REGION, HE WAS EXHAUSTED BY THE DESERT HEAT, SUFFERED DIZZY SPELLS AND FELL ILL ON THE TRAIN...

ROBESON SPENT A MONTH RECOVERING IN A POSH REST HOME FOR SOVIET OFFICIALS.

PAUL CAME BACK TO ENGLAND TO STAR AS OTHELLO AT STRATFORD ON AVON. BUT HE WAS NOT THE HARDY TROOPER OF PAST DECADES. RISING YOUNG DIRECTOR TONY RICHARDSON REDUCED PAULS WEEKLY SCHEDULE FROM FOUR PERFORMANCES TO TWO.

SPECIAL LOOSE, LIGHT COSTUMES WERE DESIGNED FOR HIS COMFORT...

RICHARDSON PUT ASIDE AVANT GARDE STYLE HIS OLD ROLE. BUT PAUL ROBESON COULD LINE OF OTHELLO. HE NEEDED A PROMPTER AND LET PAUL RECLAIM NOT RECALL A SINGLE ON STAGE AT ALL TIMES.

"... BUT O, VAIN BOAST— WHO CAN CONTROL HIS FATE?"

"BUT O, VAIN BOAST— WHO CAN CONTROL HIS FATE?"

SHARON RUDAHL 2019

RELATIVELY GOOD DAYS WERE FOLLOWED BY WORSE ONES. BUT PAUL ROBESON SOLDIERED ON, NEVER FORSAKING HIS POLITICAL BELIEFS. HE SANG AT A HUGE BAN THE BOMB RALLY IN TRAFALGAR SQUARE. HIS FINAL CONCERT IN ENGLAND WAS TO RAISE MONEY FOR THE COLONIAL FREEDOM MOVEMENT.

FREE RHODESIA

PAUL GAVE FREE CONCERTS IN HUNGARY AND EAST GERMANY.

"IN A SOCIALIST COUNTRY I CHARGE NOTHING. IN A CAPITALIST COUNTRY I CHARGE AS MUCH AS I CAN."

HE AGREED TO AN ESPECIALLY WELL-PAID TOUR IN AUSTRALIA, WHERE HE SPOKE OUT FOR THE RIGHTS OF THE ABORIGINES.

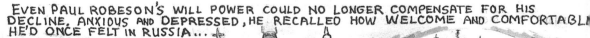

TRAVEL ACROSS AUSTRALIA WAS A GRUELING ORDEAL. BACK IN LONDON ROBESON SPENT HIS DAYS IN BED IN A DARKENED ROOM.

EVEN PAUL ROBESON'S WILL POWER COULD NO LONGER COMPENSATE FOR HIS DECLINE. ANXIOUS AND DEPRESSED, HE RECALLED HOW WELCOME AND COMFORTABLE HE'D ONCE FELT IN RUSSIA...

WITHOUT CONSULTING ESSIE, PAUL IMPULSIVELY BOOKED A FLIGHT TO MOSCOW.

SHARON RUDAHL 2019

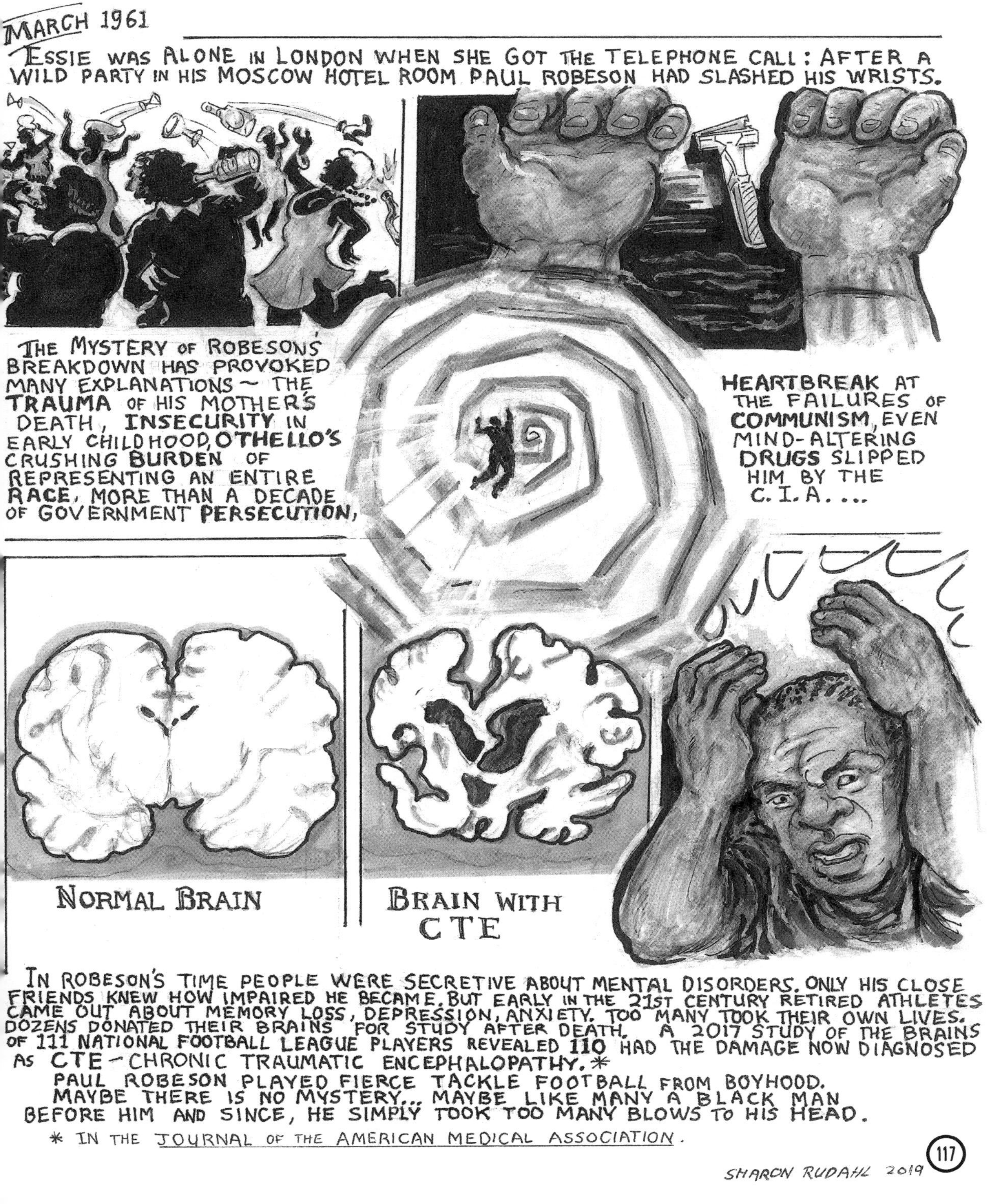

ESSIE WAS ALONE IN LONDON WHEN SHE GOT THE TELEPHONE CALL: AFTER A WILD PARTY IN HIS MOSCOW HOTEL ROOM PAUL ROBESON HAD SLASHED HIS WRISTS.

THE MYSTERY OF ROBESON'S BREAKDOWN HAS PROVOKED MANY EXPLANATIONS ~ THE **TRAUMA** OF HIS MOTHER'S DEATH, **INSECURITY** IN EARLY CHILDHOOD, O'THELLO'S CRUSHING **BURDEN** OF REPRESENTING AN ENTIRE **RACE**, MORE THAN A DECADE OF GOVERNMENT **PERSECUTION**,

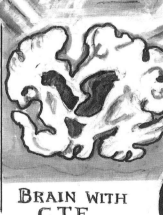

HEARTBREAK AT THE FAILURES OF **COMMUNISM**, EVEN MIND-ALTERING **DRUGS** SLIPPED HIM BY THE C.I.A....

NORMAL BRAIN

BRAIN WITH CTE

IN ROBESON'S TIME PEOPLE WERE SECRETIVE ABOUT MENTAL DISORDERS. ONLY HIS CLOSE FRIENDS KNEW HOW IMPAIRED HE BECAME. BUT EARLY IN THE 21ST CENTURY RETIRED ATHLETES CAME OUT ABOUT MEMORY LOSS, DEPRESSION, ANXIETY. TOO MANY TOOK THEIR OWN LIVES. DOZENS DONATED THEIR BRAINS FOR STUDY AFTER DEATH. A 2017 STUDY OF THE BRAINS OF 111 NATIONAL FOOTBALL LEAGUE PLAYERS REVEALED **110** HAD THE DAMAGE NOW DIAGNOSED AS CTE ~ CHRONIC TRAUMATIC ENCEPHALOPATHY. *

PAUL ROBESON PLAYED FIERCE TACKLE FOOTBALL FROM BOYHOOD. MAYBE THERE IS NO MYSTERY... MAYBE LIKE MANY A BLACK MAN BEFORE HIM AND SINCE, HE SIMPLY TOOK TOO MANY BLOWS TO HIS HEAD.

* IN THE JOURNAL OF THE AMERICAN MEDICAL ASSOCIATION.

SHARON RUDAHL 2019

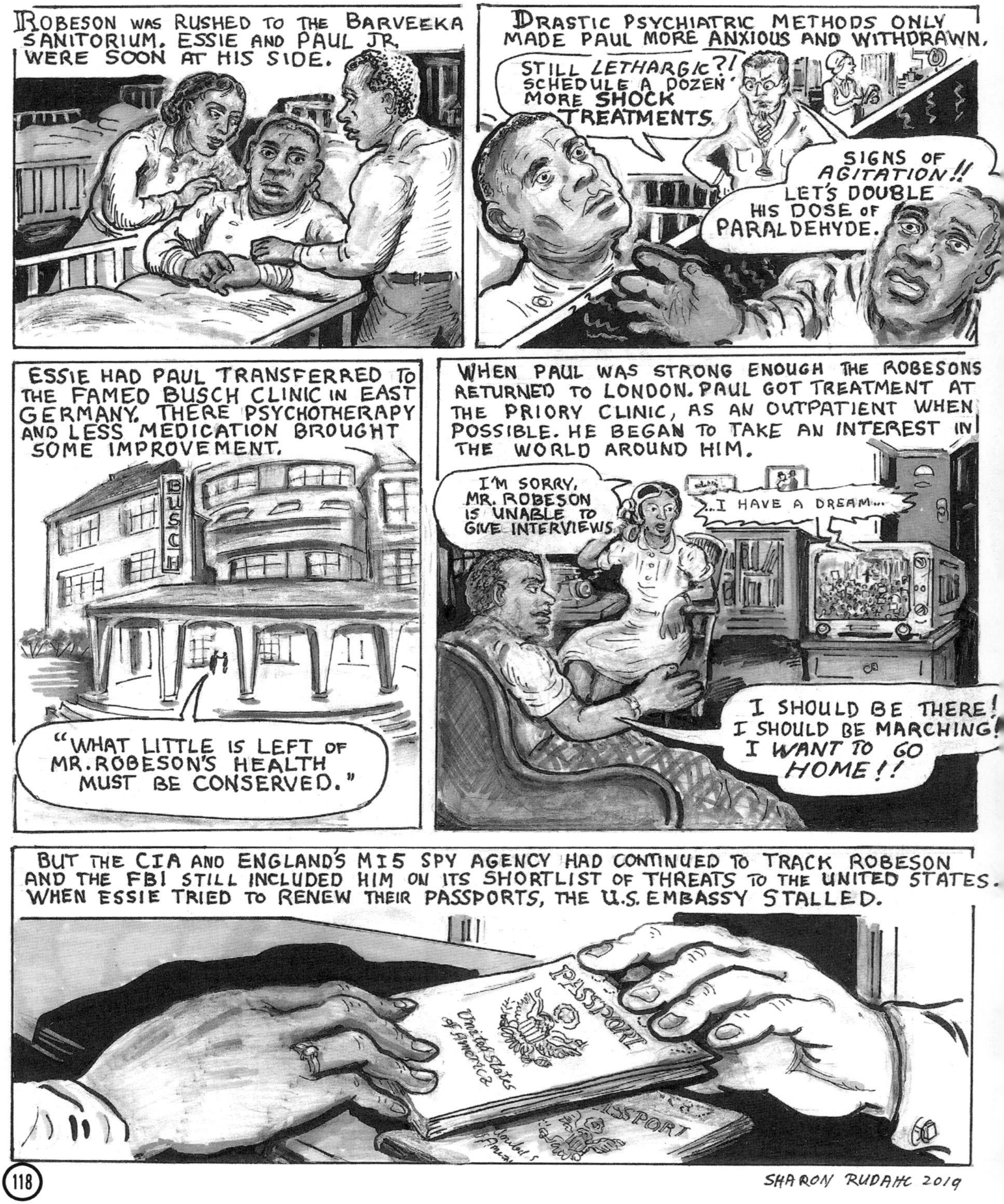

ROBESON WAS RUSHED TO THE BARVEEKA SANITORIUM. ESSIE AND PAUL JR. WERE SOON AT HIS SIDE.
DRASTIC PSYCHIATRIC METHODS ONLY MADE PAUL MORE ANXIOUS AND WITHDRAWN.
STILL LETHARGIC?! SCHEDULE A DOZEN MORE SHOCK TREATMENTS.
SIGNS OF AGITATION!! LET'S DOUBLE HIS DOSE OF PARALDEHYDE.
ESSIE HAD PAUL TRANSFERRED TO THE FAMED BUSCH CLINIC IN EAST GERMANY. THERE PSYCHOTHERAPY AND LESS MEDICATION BROUGHT SOME IMPROVEMENT.
BUSCH
"WHAT LITTLE IS LEFT OF MR. ROBESON'S HEALTH MUST BE CONSERVED."
WHEN PAUL WAS STRONG ENOUGH THE ROBESONS RETURNED TO LONDON. PAUL GOT TREATMENT AT THE PRIORY CLINIC, AS AN OUTPATIENT WHEN POSSIBLE. HE BEGAN TO TAKE AN INTEREST IN THE WORLD AROUND HIM.
I'M SORRY. MR. ROBESON IS UNABLE TO GIVE INTERVIEWS.
...I HAVE A DREAM...
I SHOULD BE THERE! I SHOULD BE MARCHING! I WANT TO GO HOME!!
BUT THE CIA AND ENGLAND'S MI5 SPY AGENCY HAD CONTINUED TO TRACK ROBESON AND THE FBI STILL INCLUDED HIM ON ITS SHORTLIST OF THREATS TO THE UNITED STATES. WHEN ESSIE TRIED TO RENEW THEIR PASSPORTS, THE U.S. EMBASSY STALLED.
PASSPORT
United States of America
SHARON RUDAHL 2019

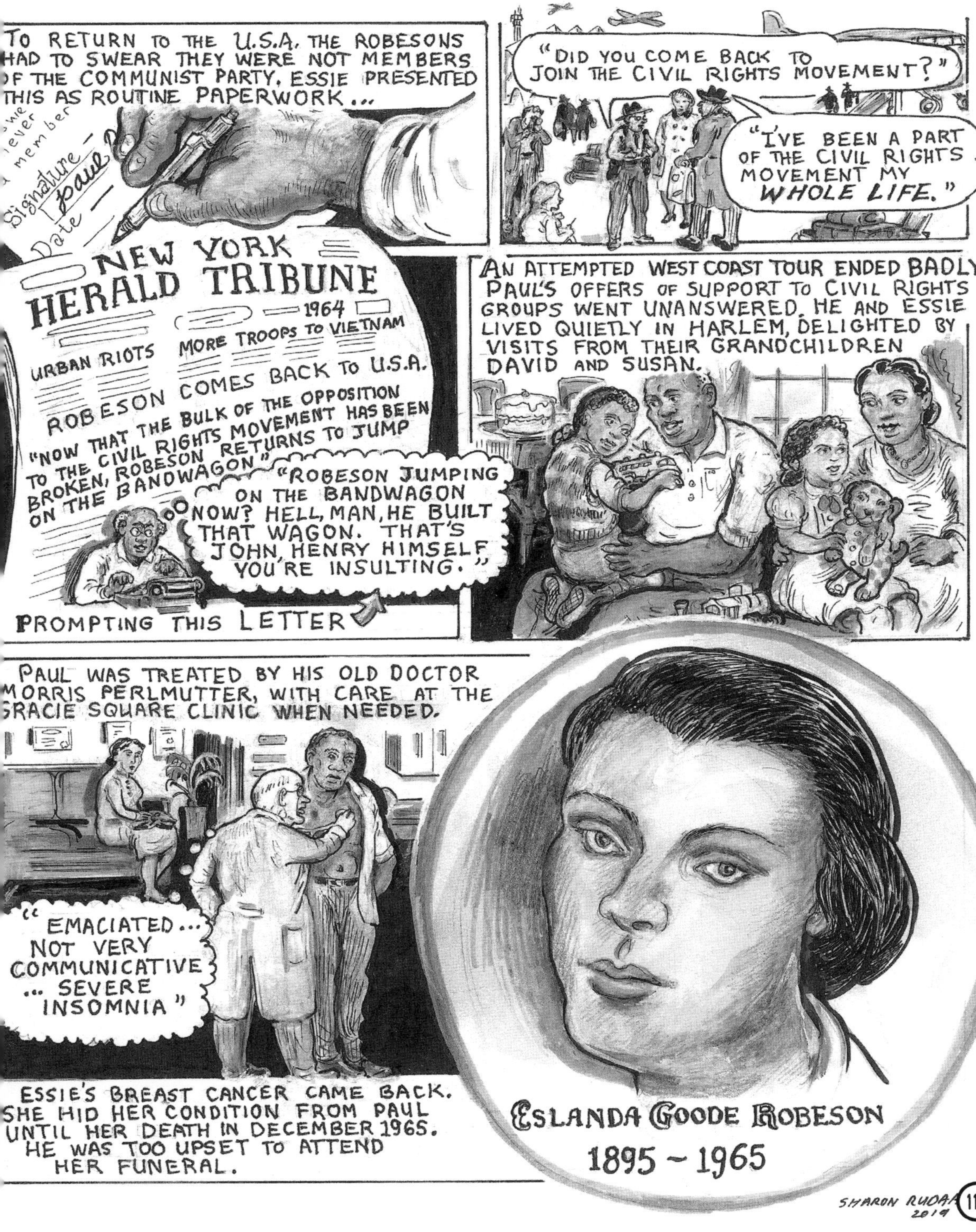
TO RETURN TO THE U.S.A. THE ROBESONS HAD TO SWEAR THEY WERE NOT MEMBERS OF THE COMMUNIST PARTY. ESSIE PRESENTED THIS AS ROUTINE PAPERWORK...
Signature
paul
Date
"DID YOU COME BACK TO JOIN THE CIVIL RIGHTS MOVEMENT?"
"I'VE BEEN A PART OF THE CIVIL RIGHTS MOVEMENT MY WHOLE LIFE."
NEW YORK HERALD TRIBUNE
1964
URBAN RIOTS
MORE TROOPS TO VIETNAM
ROBESON COMES BACK TO U.S.A.
"NOW THAT THE BULK OF THE OPPOSITION TO THE CIVIL RIGHTS MOVEMENT HAS BEEN BROKEN, ROBESON RETURNS TO JUMP ON THE BANDWAGON"
"ROBESON JUMPING ON THE BANDWAGON NOW? HELL, MAN, HE BUILT THAT WAGON. THAT'S JOHN HENRY HIMSELF YOU'RE INSULTING."
PROMPTING THIS LETTER
AN ATTEMPTED WEST COAST TOUR ENDED BADLY. PAUL'S OFFERS OF SUPPORT TO CIVIL RIGHTS GROUPS WENT UNANSWERED. HE AND ESSIE LIVED QUIETLY IN HARLEM, DELIGHTED BY VISITS FROM THEIR GRANDCHILDREN DAVID AND SUSAN.
PAUL WAS TREATED BY HIS OLD DOCTOR MORRIS PERLMUTTER, WITH CARE AT THE GRACIE SQUARE CLINIC WHEN NEEDED.
"EMACIATED... NOT VERY COMMUNICATIVE ... SEVERE INSOMNIA"
ESSIE'S BREAST CANCER CAME BACK. SHE HID HER CONDITION FROM PAUL UNTIL HER DEATH IN DECEMBER 1965. HE WAS TOO UPSET TO ATTEND HER FUNERAL.
ESLANDA GOODE ROBESON
1895 ~ 1965
SHARON RUDAHL 2019

FOR THE LAST DECADE OF HIS LIFE PAUL LIVED WITH HIS WIDOWED SISTER MARIAN IN PHILADELPHIA. SHE HAD ALWAYS ADORED HER BABY BROTHER AND FELT HONORED TO CARE FOR HIM.

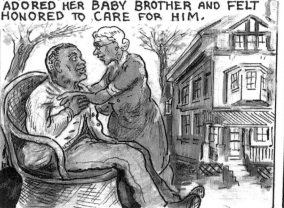

ROBESON DISAPPEARED FROM TEXTBOOKS AND HALLS OF FAME. BUT HIS INFLUENCE ENDURED. SINGERS OF FOLK & WORLD MUSIC BUILT ON HIS DISCOVERIES. ATHLETES AND PERFORMERS OF THE AFRICAN DIASPORA PASSED THROUGH DOORS PAUL HAD OPENED.
  IN 1967 THE PAUL ROBESON CULTURAL CENTER WAS FOUNDED AT RUTGERS UNIVERSITY. IT WAS THE FIRST BLACK CULTURAL CENTER ON A U.S. COLLEGE CAMPUS.

IN 1973 PAUL JR. AND HARRY BELAFONTE ORGANIZED A 75TH BIRTHDAY TRIBUTE TO PAUL AT CARNEGIE HALL. CONGRATULATIONS POURED IN FROM AFRICA, ASIA AND LATIN AMERICA. NOTABLES OF POLITICS, STAGE AND SCREEN ATTENDED, INCLUDING CORETTA SCOTT KING, RAMSEY CLARK, DOLORES HUERTA, SIDNEY POITIER AND PETE SEEGER. BUT ROBESON WAS TOO FRAGILE TO ATTEND. HE WELCOMED HIS GUESTS WITH A TAPED MESSAGE:

"...THOUGH I HAVE NOT BEEN ACTIVE FOR SEVERAL YEARS, I WANT YOU TO KNOW THAT I AM STILL THE SAME PAUL, DEDICATED AS EVER TO THE WORLDWIDE CAUSE OF HUMANITY FOR FREEDOM, PEACE, AND BROTHERHOOD..."

JANUARY 1975 — A WEAKENING HEART DELIVERED PAUL FROM THIS WORLD. HIS FUNERAL WAS HELD AT THE MOTHER ZION A.M.E. CHURCH WHERE HIS BROTHER BEN HAD BEEN PASTOR. THOUSANDS GATHERED IN THE COLD RAIN. CELEBRITIES PAID THEIR RESPECTS, COMRADES IN STRUGGLE, INTIMATE FRIENDS — BUT ALSO ORDINARY WORKING PEOPLE, HARLEM NEIGHBORS WHO HAD NEVER FORGOTTEN PAUL ROBESON.

SHARON RUDAHL
2019

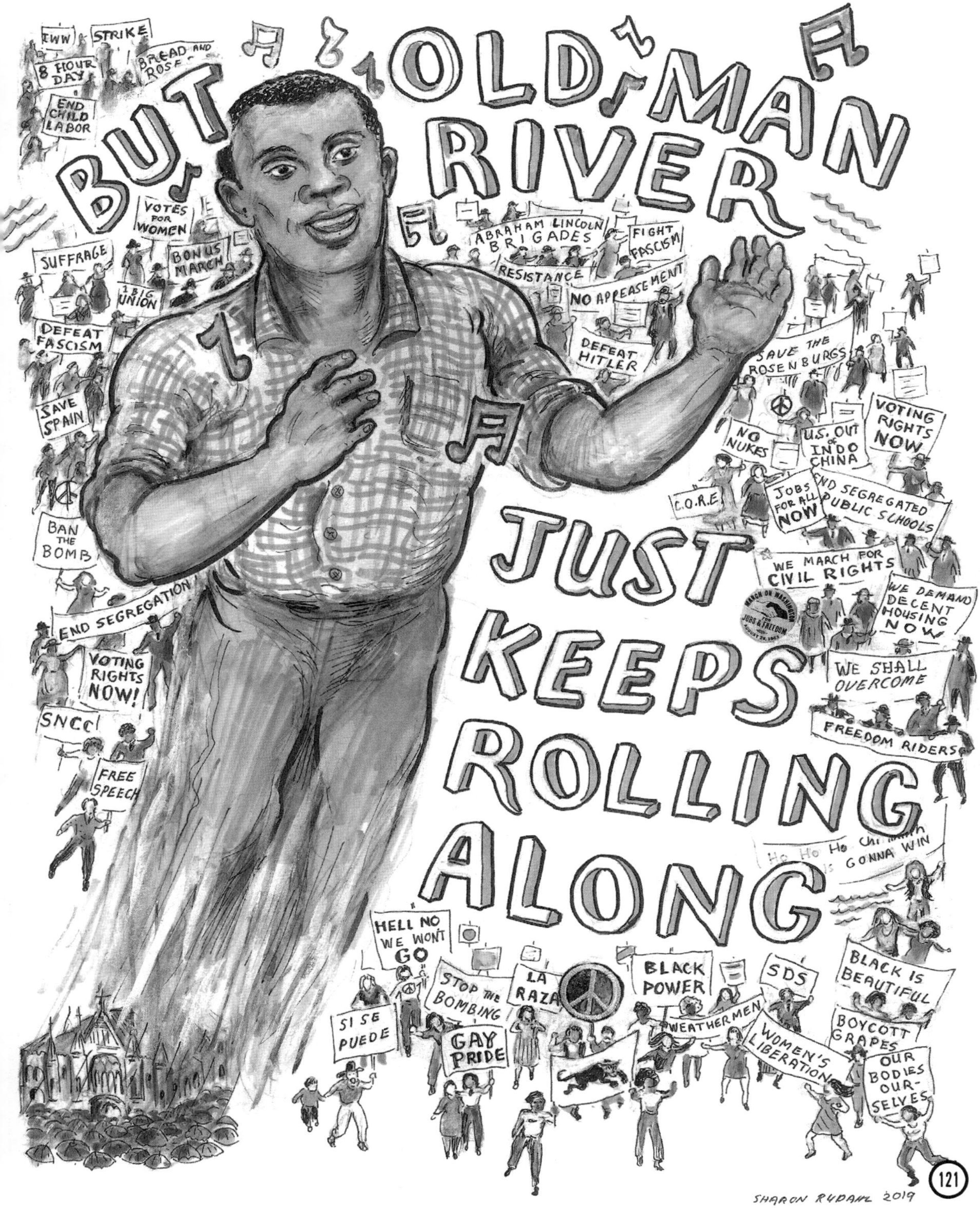
BUT OLD MAN RIVER
JUST KEEPS ROLLING ALONG
IWW
STRIKE
BREAD AND ROSES
8 HOUR DAY
END CHILD LABOR
VOTES FOR WOMEN
SUFFRAGE
BONUS MARCH
1 BIG UNION
ABRAHAM LINCOLN BRIGADES
FIGHT FASCISM
RESISTANCE
NO APPEASEMENT
DEFEAT HITLER
DEFEAT FASCISM
SAVE SPAIN
SAVE THE ROSENBURGS
NO NUKES
U.S. OUT OF INDO CHINA
VOTING RIGHTS NOW
C.O.R.E
JOBS FOR ALL NOW
END SEGREGATED PUBLIC SCHOOLS
BAN THE BOMB
WE MARCH FOR CIVIL RIGHTS
MARCH ON WASHINGTON FOR JOBS & FREEDOM
WE DEMAND DECENT HOUSING NOW
END SEGREGATION
VOTING RIGHTS NOW!
WE SHALL OVERCOME
FREEDOM RIDERS
SNCC
FREE SPEECH
"HELL NO WE WON'T GO"
STOP THE BOMBING
LA RAZA
BLACK POWER
SDS
BLACK IS BEAUTIFUL
SI SE PUEDE
GAY PRIDE
WEATHERMEN
WOMEN'S LIBERATION
BOYCOTT GRAPES
OUR BODIES OURSELVES
SHARON RYDAHL 2019

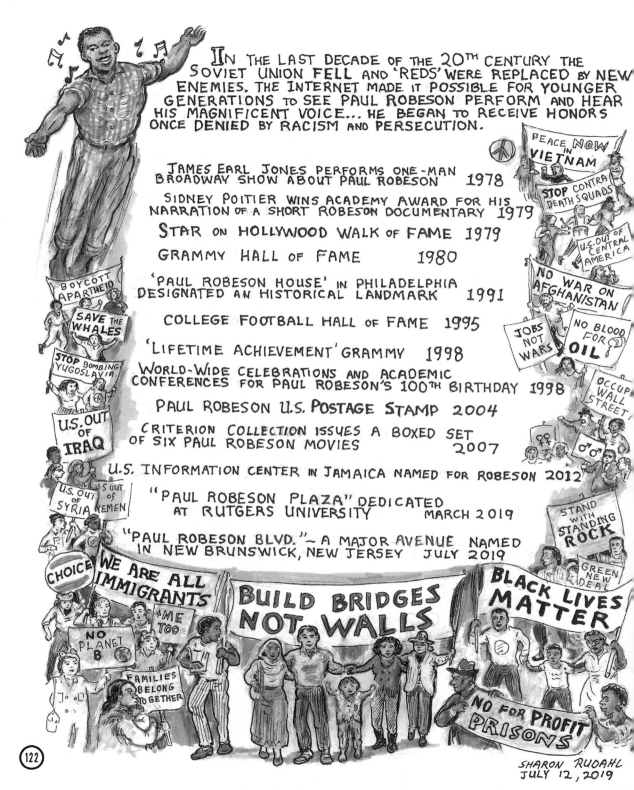

IN THE LAST DECADE OF THE 20TH CENTURY THE SOVIET UNION FELL AND 'REDS' WERE REPLACED BY NEW ENEMIES. THE INTERNET MADE IT POSSIBLE FOR YOUNGER GENERATIONS TO SEE PAUL ROBESON PERFORM AND HEAR HIS MAGNIFICENT VOICE... HE BEGAN TO RECEIVE HONORS ONCE DENIED BY RACISM AND PERSECUTION.

JAMES EARL JONES PERFORMS ONE-MAN BROADWAY SHOW ABOUT PAUL ROBESON 1978

SIDNEY POITIER WINS ACADEMY AWARD FOR HIS NARRATION OF A SHORT ROBESON DOCUMENTARY 1979

STAR ON HOLLYWOOD WALK OF FAME 1979

GRAMMY HALL OF FAME 1980

'PAUL ROBESON HOUSE' IN PHILADELPHIA DESIGNATED AN HISTORICAL LANDMARK 1991

COLLEGE FOOTBALL HALL OF FAME 1995

'LIFETIME ACHIEVEMENT' GRAMMY 1998

WORLD-WIDE CELEBRATIONS AND ACADEMIC CONFERENCES FOR PAUL ROBESON'S 100TH BIRTHDAY 1998

PAUL ROBESON U.S. POSTAGE STAMP 2004

CRITERION COLLECTION ISSUES A BOXED SET OF SIX PAUL ROBESON MOVIES 2007

U.S. INFORMATION CENTER IN JAMAICA NAMED FOR ROBESON 2012

"PAUL ROBESON PLAZA" DEDICATED AT RUTGERS UNIVERSITY MARCH 2019

"PAUL ROBESON BLVD." — A MAJOR AVENUE NAMED IN NEW BRUNSWICK, NEW JERSEY JULY 2019

PEACE NOW IN VIETNAM

STOP CONTRA DEATH SQUADS

U.S. OUT OF CENTRAL AMERICA

NO WAR ON AFGHANISTAN

JOBS NOT WARS

NO BLOOD FOR OIL

OCCUPY WALL STREET!

BOYCOTT APARTHEID

SAVE THE WHALES

STOP BOMBING YUGOSLAVIA

U.S. OUT OF IRAQ

U.S. OUT OF SYRIA

U.S OUT OF YEMEN

STAND WITH STANDING ROCK

GREEN NEW DEAL

CHOICE

WE ARE ALL IMMIGRANTS

ME TOO

NO PLANET B

FAMILIES BELONG TOGETHER

BUILD BRIDGES NOT WALLS

BLACK LIVES MATTER

NO FOR PROFIT PRISONS

SHARON RUDAHL
JULY 12, 2019

PAUL ROBESON: MORE ALIVE THAN EVER

An Afterword by the Editors

To Sharon Kahn Rudahl's marvelous artistic rendering of Paul Robeson's life, we only need add an extended scholarly footnote. Robeson is perhaps now more "present," as we approach the third decade of the twenty-first century, than he has been since his death and possibly since the 1940s. Why should that be? What forces have returned him to the stage, at least the stage of collective memory? In a nation badly divided on multiple lines of race and the assorted issues of "Americanism," these questions are well worth pondering.

Serious scholarly literature about Paul had begun from the time of his passing to a high point of Martin Duberman's prize-winning 1989 volume, *Paul Robeson: A Biography*. The vast detail and considered judgments within its nearly eight hundred pages have made that book definitive in many respects, and it seems likely to remain so. The limitations of Duberman's work have less to do with absent details or specific interpretations than with historical and cultural context. Newer scholarship is bringing other aspects of Robeson's life and work into focus.

Paul Robeson's role in American popular culture has yet to be acknowledged fully, no doubt because many issues within that culture remain uncertain and because the passage of time has excluded many of the devotees who held Robeson dear. There is also another reason: the difficulty of our understanding what became known as the "Popular Front" and its many complicated connections with cultural expressions during the New Deal era and after.

Paul Robeson was a central figure in the broad-based labor, civil rights, and antifascist organizing that took place during the second half of the 1930s and during the war and that helped build the industrial-union movement. He was a key figure in the contemporary explosion of what scholars now call "cultural production." Along with these influences, his less direct but very real role in the booming expansion of the NAACP during wartime and his public concern for refugees fleeing Europe illustrate how deeply the Popular Front reached into the leftward edge of the New Deal coalition.

The crisis precipitated by the Wall Street crash of 1929, followed by the rise of a reform-minded government closely linked to the sweeping social movements of the day, prompted a sort of "discovery of America" and its many cultures. Elite high culture, borrowed from European traditions, was no longer viewed as sufficient to represent democracy in a troubled world. Given the opportunity to change the narrative, artists and writers of every description rose to the occasion.

The Works Progress Administration's murals program, in which hundreds of underemployed artists created visual histories on the walls of post offices and other government buildings, made an unprecedented statement: there was a common "people's history" to be rediscovered. Likewise, government-funded printmaking on democratic themes; Federal Theatre Project troupes in towns and villages performing in a variety of languages; the collecting of local stories and vernacular histories; and the field work of interviews for the oral histories of slavery from its last survivors—these were common coin of the day. Conservatives growled, but the work went ahead until an alliance of Southern Democrats and Republicans in Congress swept most of the programs away.

The dread fear of global fascism supported and emphasized the importance of the emerging people's history. After Pearl Harbor, the wartime drive for national unity encouraged the introduction of antifascist themes, supporting unprecedented challenges to white supremacy and anti-Semitism, in works ranging from Hollywood films and popular theater to radio drama and even comic strips.

African American entertainers, newly liberated from the familiar constraints of being staged as minstrelsy figures for white amusement, were beginning to be allowed to present and personally represent the democratic promise of the country. Paul Robeson thus emerged as one of the key African American performers.

Rightly seen as embodying the multiracial cultural impulses toward a wider democracy, Robeson was understandably despised by racial conservatives, and he inevitably became the target of intelligence-agency surveillance. The striving for racial equality, after all, was considered by someone so high in government as FBI director J. Edgar Hoover to be a communist plot.

These wider developments coincided in time, and overlapped significantly, with the Popular Front. For American communists and socialists as well as many others, the Wall Street crash had seemed to confirm expectations that the capitalist system, long haunted by crises, now could not recover. Yet, of course, it *did* recover, even if barely, in the short run. Within a few years of the crash, President Franklin Delano Roosevelt offered soothing as well as stirring messages to nationwide radio audiences. Reform movements of various kinds prompted his administration, in 1935, to declare a Second New Deal, with sweeping reforms including Social Security and the legal authorization of union organizing.

This was the setting for the American version of the Popular Front against fascism. A phrase apparently coined in Moscow in 1935 by Georgi Dimitrov, a Bulgarian communist leader, it confirmed the seemingly gloomy sense that anticapitalist revolution was no longer on the agenda, even where (as in France) the working class seemed to be bidding for power. The rise of fascism mainly prompted the need for the unity of communists and socialists under the slogan "No enemies on the left." In the United States, where the socialist movement had dwindled and communists were relatively sparse in many parts of the country, this meant unity of the left with liberal Democrats, most of all with the Roosevelt administration itself.

The astounding results surprised no one more, perhaps, than left-wing political leaders. But local activists had already begun to draw important lessons even before the formal declaration of a Popular Front. This was especially crucial in the black community, where resources were more desperately needed by the poor and rising political figures seemed least reluctant to work with communists.

Even in the conservative 1920s, communists and their allies took strong stands against lynching, Jim Crow white supremacy, and institutionalized racism in systems ranging from housing to employment. Furthermore, scholars of leftist activity in Harlem during the 1930s have discovered that neighborhood Reds abandoned extreme rhetoric of near-time revolution for collaborative work with Father Divine, the charismatic black minister who organized assistance for the area's desperately poor residents. Activists had, in other words, gone beyond the political rhetoric of world revolution to take on the required work and engage the necessary political allies to win over a significant neighborhood following. Whereas the alliance with Father Divine was short-lived, they forged a powerful association with the Reverend Adam Clayton Powell Jr., the most influential minister in Harlem, that lasted for more than a generation.

Communists in Chicago, home of the next most important black community in the United States, fought for and won a temporary cessation of evictions for nonpayment of rent, a decision apparently made in the mayor's office. Here, at least in legend, was first heard the black mother's strident appeal to a son, "Johnny, go get a Red!" A neighborhood communist would call together a crowd and make a fuss, sometimes collectively and peacefully moving the furniture back into the apartment as the landlord raged on the sidewalk and pleaded unsuccessfully for police action. In the deep South of Birmingham, Alabama, black sharecroppers and steelworkers felt emboldened by left-wing attention to their organizing and the coverage of their struggles in the *Daily Worker*. Elsewhere, similar stories could be heard.

Soon, newer struggles would gain more popular support, including that of the expanding and empowered liberal community. The industrial-union movement arose, but so did newer social work and housing authorities of big cities, sometimes under heavy leftist influence. As the Popular Front took shape, Robeson would become an inspirational figure for many more whose lives were touched by the activism.

The formal declaration of the Popular Front freed activists to experiment and thus broaden their efforts. This change might be seen most subtly—as has been shown in the scholarship that has emerged—in the ethnic neighborhoods where sympathy for the left had never been absent. Lithuanians, Croats, Ukrainians, and especially Finns and Yiddish-speaking Jews had established themselves in halls that served as headquarters for sickness and death-benefit societies, strike-support centers, and cultural centers to promote ethnic dance and music. Ethnic clubs and foreign-language newspapers had carried over almost smoothly, nearly escaping government repression, from the socialist movement of the 1910s to the communist periphery of the following era. The Popular Front allowed them to come into the open and refashion themselves as hubs of a locally active democracy at the leftward edge of the New Deal. Sons and daughters of the clubs' founders, a crucial cadre in mass-production factories, supplied a generation enthusiastically supportive of Robeson's visits to union and ethnic halls.

These changing moods would be most significant for Paul Robeson as a performer because the Popular Front offered him an admiring audience of middle Americans, an audience that grew ever larger and more eager to hear the message within and behind his songs. People with no background in left or ethnic politics, no union experience or expectations, could hear in his songs what they wished for in a better America.

There were special elements in this appeal for the African American cultural left. If communists and their allies sometimes had difficulty with black nationalists and their street following, the intellectual and cultural elite of Harlem—singers, artists, and poets—rallied to the Popular Front and to Robeson. With hard work and charismatic leadership, Robeson and his devotees meanwhile reached thousands of black political organizers around the nation as well as young people of color in search of a way forward.

A closer, formal affiliation between Robeson and the Communist Party was not on the agenda, as it was deemed unwise for celebrities or union leaders to take such a step. On legal grounds alone, Robeson never disclosed whether he had ever taken out party membership. To do so, he believed, would open him up to unwelcome lines of questioning. Sadly, this attempt at legal self-defense proved no barrier against those who would persecute him when the Red Scare gained steam during the years following Franklin Roosevelt's death. By 1940, the worst, and unforeseen, effects of his close association with the party and of his sympathy for the Soviet Union still lay in the future.

Robeson, then, can best be understood as a key figure within the richest public cultural expressions of the twentieth century. If later developments like the creation of the National Endowment for the Humanities and the National Endowment for the Arts served to legitimate a public scholarship and public culture, the Popular- Front/New Deal era had done the spadework thirty years earlier, embracing cultural expressions within a massive public participation so far still unmatched.

Paul Robeson was not only living proof of racial equality but something still difficult for scholars today to grasp or even define. Within the leftist world of greater New York and cities beyond, he reigned as a supreme symbol of *hope*. A Robeson performance at Carnegie Hall, at a lesser concert venue, or at a union hall created memories sixty years and more later in the now elderly whose parents took them to the show. A YouTube clip from the film *Showboat*, with Robeson singing "Old Man River" against a background of black life in the South, offers a glimpse of the Robeson charisma, as do the audio recordings of his songs. His use of African American spirituals established them as a legitimate, important part of national folklore.

The ideal of a racial egalitarianism was central to the progressive visions of a better society. Americans might not yet be ready to replace the profit system—so the thinking went—but significant numbers had chosen a dramatically improved democratic path out of a deeply racist past. The need for unity against anti-Semitism at home and abroad reinforced a particular Popular Front message and validated a Jewish-American identity in which, for tens of thousands, Robeson was larger than life.

It is nearly impossible to summon up today memories of the liberal movement as it existed in the United States during the Second World War, with its mass anti-fascist rallies held across the country, labor's political action committee, which was crucial to reelecting FDR in 1944, and communists in positions of high if short-lived respectability. Vice President Henry Wallace, for whom Robeson would campaign vigorously in 1948, was until the end of the war said to be the second-most popular political figure in the nation. "Ballad for Americans," the Robeson version, was heard on every radio, running equally (at least until 1946) with Kate Smith's version of "God Bless America."

The good times began to end in 1946 and crashed a few years later. Throngs of Americans in the following decades nevertheless urgently wanted to hear Paul Robeson sing and talk in person but were prevented from doing so. The alliance of progressives—militantly for labor and civil rights and against the Cold War—thinned dramatically during the 1948 presidential campaign with the ferocious and bipartisan attack on Henry Wallace's doomed campaign for president on the Progressive Party ticket. Then it thinned dramatically again during the Korean War.

Robeson and a flock of surviving left-wing institutions had taken upon themselves an additional task or burden: supporting anticolonial movements and the new postcolonial governments of the global South. This effort made them appear more dangerous as the Cold War assumed its long-term dimensions and what President Dwight Eisenhower would call the "military-industrial complex" became a central factor in national life. Powerful American interests would be endangered, it was feared in the State Department, if the global conflict over "freedom" was dramatically set against the absence of racial justice on the domestic front. Paul Robeson himself was singing defiance to that injustice, in the most dramatic terms.

Continuing repression in various forms—ranging from FBI visits to the family door, to a warning to employers to fire any "subversive"—struck hard at even the most dedicated activists. Wider demographic changes completed the physical breakup of familiar left-wing ethnic neighborhoods, including the South Bronx, through the construction of superhighways and welcoming suburbs for the upwardly mobile, while the grim reality of drugs surrounded others, especially those of racial minorities left behind in the crumbling infrastructure.

That the hit-parade success of Pete Seeger and the Weavers during 1950 was swiftly followed by their being banned from major public venues speaks eloquently to the effects of legal and unofficial repressions on the musical corner of American popular culture. The victims did not take the assault lying down, and this tells us a great deal too.

Coping, actually fighting back in the few ways available to them, would be easier for some than others. Screenwriters and film directors, their faces unknown to the public, could with luck work abroad, or sometimes write for films and television under aliases, on the social themes of the day. Some actors could flee successfully to Broadway, and some who were "graylisted" (suspect but not called to testify) could get work on television toward the end of the 1950s. Folksingers under the ban had little such recourse and made do performing at limited venues, such as summer camps with left-wing leanings.

It was an especially strange and bitter irony that television, the new medium, had meanwhile opened up new vistas. Some singers who in the 1940s had been in the same milieu as Robeson, such as Burl Ives and Josh White, confessed their sins to investigating committees, naming former friends and soon reaching new heights of popularity and wealth. That the more conservative African American leaders took every opportunity to distance themselves from Robeson, maliciously insisting that he had never actually possessed an admiring black audience, only made the punishment worse.

In an increasingly desperate effort to keep his political voice in circulation, Robeson published *Freedom*, a newspaper-format magazine, from 1950 to 1955. With editor Louis Burnham and contributors including W.E.B. Du Bois, Lorraine Hansberry, Lloyd Brown, Frank Marshall Davis, and Alice Childress, Robeson offered a guiding light to younger progressive activists in particular. Political harassment and low circulation made the publication's continuation impossible.

Harry Belafonte, Ossie Davis, and Ruby Dee, among other staunch progressives of the 1950s through the 1980s, had been almost too young in the 1940s to be politically active, although they shared an enormous admiration of Robeson and held views similar to his. He counseled them to seize the scarce opportunities available for them in film and television to deliver the message that Robeson himself could no longer deliver. The journal *Freedomways*, launched in 1960 with Esther Cooper Jackson as editor, lifted the work of *Freedom* into the new era, becoming one of the most popular and stylish magazines of the left in the following decades.

Wherever left-wing unions expelled from the CIO managed to hold on, wherever left-wingers continued to gather socially during the 1950s through the 1970s, Robeson records could be found. Friends and supportive periodicals publicized the work of Othello Record Company, established by Paul Robeson Jr. and Lloyd Brown. The *National Guardian*, a weekly founded in the wake of the 1948 Henry Wallace presidential campaign, could almost have been called a "Robeson Paper," so beloved was he to the twenty thousand or so readers. Within greater New York, the Robeson fan base numbered two or three times that size and did not necessarily follow political lines. Beyond New York, beyond even Chicago and the Bay Area, Robeson was a giant, would be a giant for the rest of the lives of his devotees.

Writing in the magazine *Black World* in 1970, C.L.R. James—Robeson's intimate friend and ally during the middle 1930s—sought to explain why Paul had remained in a political circle that included communists and retained a certain reverence for the ideals of the Soviet Union, even when all the revelations of bad behavior past and present had been widely exposed. James, for his part, had become for a time a follower of Leon Trotsky and an intellectual leader of the Trotskyist movement in the UK and then the United States. He nevertheless felt the utmost solidarity with Paul's dilemma as the most fundamental one facing the anticolonial movement.

Liberals and left-wing people of various kinds could express deep sympathy for the mostly peasant peoples rising up against their colonial masters. But only the Soviet Union actually provided material aid and training to the young, radical nationalists. In the face of that reality—from Asia to Africa to Latin America and the Caribbean—even the frequently antirevolutionary behavior of the USSR could be overlooked or at least rationalized. Did the Russians encourage uprising in some places and discourage it elsewhere according to their national interests? Surely. But where would the disillusioned revolutionary go? Such were the dilemmas faced by Robeson when confronting the impoverished and undemocratic realities of life in the Eastern Bloc in particular.

The civil rights movement within the United States had powerful liberal, anti-communist allies, eager to disprove Russian claims of a racist American government or society. But these same anticommunists, for the most part, were also swift to support U.S. actions abroad: the overthrowing of governments at will, the slaughtering of nationalist-minded radicals in Vietnam and elsewhere, support for brutal dictators, and the elevation of American business interests above all else.

Paul Robeson would not be part of the American radical movements of the 1960s. He was waning physically, even more so psychologically, by the time the new crusades reached their apex. We may now theorize that he was likely suffering the mental effects of blows to the head sustained while boxing and playing football early in his life, effects only diagnosed in recent years among former professional football players.

After Robeson's death, a modest revival of interest in his texts emerged, and some media projects took shape. *The Tallest Tree in the Forest*, a 1977 documentary by black filmmaker Gil Noble, foreshadowed a series of public performances of a Robeson monologue in the form of the popular, one-man theatrical performances "about" Mark Twain and others. A controversial James Earl Jones version, written by Philip DeAn Harris, reached many cities during the 1980s. The play continued into the 1990s with other actors taking the part and scholars leading a discussion with the audience after the performance.

Most of the constituencies of the sixties movements belonged to generations younger than Robeson's. Their views of social transformation could not be his. Many young radicals—black, white, Asian, or Latinx—would not have recognized his name. And yet, especially for those who grew up with "Old Left" relatives, the recorded sounds of Paul Robeson's voice remained thrilling memories from their childhoods. For them, and for those discovering him anew, Robeson's example endured and seemed the natural precursor to others who now dared, like Malcolm X and Muhammed Ali, and who paid the price.

Robeson had risked all. He had, in C.L.R. James's words, "committed himself completely" to freeing "the Black people in the United States from the evils of imperialism and capitalism in general . . . [and to] making America a place where all men, Black and white, could live in peace." For that goal, he sacrificed a grand career: "that a man of such magnificent powers and such reputation gave up everything . . . such is the quality which signalizes the truly heroic figure."*

*C.L.R. James, "Paul Robeson, Black Star," in *Spheres of Existence: Selected Writings* (London: Allison and Busby, 1980), 3:261–262.

ACKNOWLEDGEMENTS

Our editor at Rutgers University Press, Peter Mickulas, earns our greatest praise for proposing this project and making it possible, and for working with us closely all the way through. Thanks go to everyone at the press for their collaboration, and to Kyle Post of the Rutgers University Foundation.

The artist adds: I would like to thank my husband, Jack Peters, and my son, Jesse Peters, for online research and essential tech support. Many thanks to my volunteer proofreaders Joel Sachs, Trina Robbins, Becky Wilson, Dr. Anthony Saidy, and Hershl Hartman.

FURTHER READING

Balthaser, Benjamin. *Anti-Imperialist Modernism: Race and Transnational Radical Culture from the Great Depression to the Cold War*. Ann Arbor: University of Michigan Press, 2015.

Boyle, Sheila Tully, and Andrew Bunie, *Paul Robeson: The Years of Promise and Achievement*. Amherst: University of Massachusetts Press, 2001.

Denning, Michael. *The Cultural Front: The Laboring of American Culture in the Twentieth Century*. New York: Verso Books, 1997.

Duberman, Martin. *Paul Robeson: A Biography*. New York: W. W. Norton, 1989.

Goodman, James. *Paul Robeson: A Watched Man*. London: Verso Books, 2013.

Horne, Gerald. *Paul Robeson: The Artist as Revolutionary*. London: Pluto Press, 2016.

James, C.L.R. "Paul Robeson: Black Star." In *Spheres of Existence: Selected Writings*, 3:256–264. London: Allison and Busby, 1980. First appeared in *Black World*, 1970.

Stewart, Jeffrey C., ed. *Paul Robeson: Artist and Citizen*. New Brunswick, NJ: Rutgers University Press and Paul Robeson Cultural Center, 1998.

Swindall, Lindsay A. *Paul Robeson: A Life of Activism and Art*. Rowman and Littlefield, 2013.

ABOUT THE AUTHORS

PAUL BUHLE, retired senior lecturer at Brown University, is the authorized biographer of Pan-African giant C.L.R. James and has written or edited many books on the leftist movement in the United States and the Caribbean. He has, in recent years, devoted himself to nonfiction graphic novels on subjects including Emma Goldman, Abraham Lincoln, Franklin D. Roosevelt, and Eugene V. Debs.

SHARON RUDAHL marched with Martin Luther King as a teenager and began her career as a cartoonist with anti–Vietnam War underground newspapers. She was one of the founders of the 1970s-era feminist anthology *Wimmen's Comix*. Rudahl has contributed to scores of publications and participated in exhibitions in dozens of countries over the last fifty years. She is best known for her graphic biography *Emma Goldman: A Dangerous Woman*.

LAWRENCE WARE is a professor of philosophy and codirector of Oklahoma State University's Center for Africana Studies. He writes widely on race and culture for *The Root*, *Slate*, and the *New York Times*. He has been a commentator on race and politics for *Huffington Post Live*, National Public Radio, and Public Radio International.

Rutgers University Press gratefully acknowledges the support of many friends who contributed funds to make this groundbreaking biography possible.

Special thanks to the Rutgers AAUP-AFT Faculty and Grad Union.

Special thanks to the Union of Rutgers Administrators, Local 1766, American Federation of Teachers, AFL-CIO.

Thanks to the many anonymous donors, as well as those named below, who contributed to our online crowdfunding campaign, sponsored by the Rutgers University Foundation:

AAR African American Review

Karin Ahmed

Rutgers African-American Alumni
    Alliance (RAAA), Inc.

Rima Apple

Patricia Backer

Kazembe Balagun

Jenny Banh

Ross Barkan

Eileen Bertelli

Michael Blakey

Joe Broderick

Richard Brucher

Mike Budd

Henggao Cai

Sean Cronin

Amy Davidow

Richard Deverell

James Dougherty

Selena Ellis

Frank Emspak

Emily Feiner

David Freund

Florence Friedman

Adriana Garriga-López

Jason Gieger

Michael Gochfeld

Octavio Gonzalez

Shane Graham

Jeremy Grainger

Susan Greenbaum

Judith Gueron

Kimberly Guinta

Suzanne Guiod

Alison Hack

Donna Halper

Alex Holzman

Yvonne Howell

Ely Janis

Andrew Jewett

Nathaniel Johnson Jr.

Robin Kelley

Bil King

Lawrence Klein

Marlena Kleit

Micah Kleit

Linda Kligman

Stella Kramer

Debra Lancaster

Richard B. Lee

Jacob Love

Robert Macieski

Elizabeth Maggio

Anastasia Mann

Andrea Rae Markowicz

Elisabeth Maselli

Felicia McGinty

Timothy McManus

Julie Meidlinger

Deborah Mercer

Gerald Meyer

Keith Mitchell

Susan Mitchell

Stan Nadel

Jacob Nieman

BioDun Ogundayo

Jessica Pellien

Alberto Pereda

Mike Phillips

Aminah Pilgrim

Savannah Porcelli

Mark Priest

David Propert

Marcus Rediker

Candida Rifkind

Michael Rockland

David Rosner

Nicholas Sammond

Sally Scott

Ben Shalant

Evie Shockley

Nicole Solano

David Spener

Sabena Stark

Michelle Stephens

Martin Summers

In memory of Constance R. Sutton

Paul Vastola

Michael Vaughn

Klaus von Lampe

Marianne Warhol

William Werick

Qiana Whitted

Seth Wigderson

Carolyn Williams

Jim Williams

Maureen Wilson

Chris Woodward